BURNING
QUESTIONS
ABOUT
ISLAM

BURNING
QUESTIONS
ABOUT
ISLAM

A PANORAMIC STUDY FOR CONCERNED CHRISTIANS

WILBUR LINGLE
with ROBERT DELANCY

TATE PUBLISHING
AND ENTERPRISES, LLC

Published by Tate Publishing & Enterprises, LLC
127 E. Trade Center Terrace | Mustang, Oklahoma 73064 USA
1.888.361.9473 | www.tatepublishing.com

Tate Publishing is committed to excellence in the publishing industry. The company reflects the philosophy established by the founders, based on Psalm 68:11,

"The Lord gave the word and great was the company of those who published it."

Book design copyright © 2016 by Tate Publishing, LLC. All rights reserved.
Cover design by Nino Carlo Suico
Interior design by Manolito Bastasa

Published in the United States of America

ISBN: 978-1-68254-528-7
Religion / Islam / General
16.02.20

CONTENTS

INTRODUCTION

What Sparked My
Interest in Islam

IN 2004, I knew no more about Islam than the average Christian does. I knew that Muhammad was the founder of Islam and that the *Qur'an* was its holy book. I had heard about *jihad* and understood something of its meaning. I knew that most Muslims lived in Asia or Africa, and Christians were expected to pray for them. I had met only a few missionaries to the Muslim world, but I knew that it was a difficult field of ministry. I also had heard that, in many Islamic-ruled countries, when a Muslim converts to Christianity and is baptized, there is a good possibility of that person losing his or her life.

I don't remember ever seeing a *Qur'an* and don't believe that I had ever conversed with a Muslim up to that time. But then something happened that *changed* this situation.

Let me back up a little to start my story. I have been personally involved in witnessing to Jehovah's Witnesses and Mormons for many years. This began in 1975 in Japan, where I was a missionary from 1954 to 1989. Members of those two cults had invaded the area where I had started a church and began to proselytize there. I got involved in order to defend my flock from those false teachers.

God graciously guided me, showing me how to effectively witness to adherents of these two religions and lead them to faith in Christ. And after I left Japan, I continued to do so. Reaching out to those in the cults, and training other Christians to do likewise, became my full-time ministry. I am now the author of three books: (1) *Approaching Jehovah's Witnesses in Love—How to Witness Effectively Without Arguing*, (2) *What the Watchtower Society Doesn't Want You to Know*, and (3) *Approaching Mormons in Love—How to Witness Effectively Without Arguing*. I have also written two booklets: *20 Important Questions for Jehovah's Witnesses* and *25 Important Questions for Mormons*, with Robert Delancy as coauthor. In addition, I have produced a lot of other material designed to help anyone who may be witnessing to these cultists.

I began to get a lot of orders for this material, so I sometimes would visit the post office two or three times a week. Going there so often, I got to know the clerks. One of them, I discovered, was a born-again Christian who really loved the Lord. Over a period of time, we got rather well acquainted, and I visited the church she attended. But then I moved away from that area and saw her no longer.

One Sunday three years later, however, my wife and I visited a church we had never attended before. We didn't know a soul when we entered. But after the service began, a lady came in and sat several seats away from us. I immediately realized that I knew her but couldn't place her. Then the people went around greeting others. She recognized me and came over and identified herself as the lady who worked in the post office. I found out she had moved and was living close by. So we renewed our dormant fellowship.

Then one day, I received a phone call from her. She said that she had a sister in Baltimore who had become a Muslim. Her sister had just sent her a booklet on Islam titled *Understanding Islam and the Muslims*—prepared by the government of Saudi Arabia—in order to proselytize her. She knew I ministered to Jehovah's Witnesses and Mormons and wondered if I knew anything about the Muslim faith. If so, could I give her some help in reaching her sister?

I explained that I really didn't know much about Islam, but if she would send me the booklet, I would read it and see what I could do. She sent me the booklet. I read it, and this started me on my journey to attempt to understand the Muslim religion.

Step 2 was when I heard a speaker who had been a missionary to Pakistan for a number of years and was now reaching out to Muslims in New York City. He gave a seminar on Islam at the church of a friend of ours. We attended the seminar and found it helpful. He invited anyone who wanted to learn more about his ministry in New York City to come along and visit a mosque with him. My wife and I, along with some friends, went. I thought we were just going to watch the daily Muslim prayers.

But that was not so. The imam's (the spiritual leader's) English was poor, so a young Muslim intervened and asked if we had any questions about Islam. But instead of telling us about Islam and its tenets, he began to attack the Christian faith quite aggressively. I don't know where this young man received his information, but the things he was accusing Christianity of were entirely false. He kept assailing Christianity for nearly an hour. I wondered if we would get out of there alive! When we left, he gave me two DVDs that seek to tear down the fundamental Christian beliefs, along with other anti-Christian literature.

Step 3: a while after this, my wife and I were driving on the Pennsylvania turnpike, and I saw a large billboard that read "WHY-ISLAM?" and gave a phone number that I copied. When we got home, I called the number but found that the answerer was someone in Pennsylvania—and I lived in New Jersey. I asked if there wasn't someone closer whom I could contact and was given the name of a Muslim who lived not so far away.

I contacted this man, and that very day, he invited us to come to his house. He was a medical doctor from Pakistan and had been in the States for a number of years. He and his wife were very cordial, but it wasn't very long until I was again being upbraided as a Christian, and once again, I was presented with false charges about Christianity. I had not gone there to argue but to try to understand Islam. We were given a very large volume, written by a Muslim scholar, which was clearly anti-Christian. (We have continued to stay in contact with this couple and have had them at our home for a meal.)

Since I wanted to understand the Muslim religion, I thought it would be a good idea to read the *Qur'an*, so I went to a bookstore and purchased one. I found the *Qur'an* very difficult to read and comprehend because it has no continuing plot or sequence. It is full of repetition. A lot of the incidents and people mentioned therein are taken from the Bible, but the details are greatly changed. It speaks 350 times about hell and 475 times about the "Day of Judgment," but nowhere does it explain how a person can be a hundred percent sure of favorable results on the Day of Judgment.

I quickly realized I couldn't understand the *Qur'an* on my own. Later on, I was told the only true *Qur'an* is in Arabic—and *that* is the only language one can really understand it in. But I don't know Arabic. Also, scholars must explain the *Qur'an*, so you understand Islam by reading what the "scholars" have to say, even though they don't always agree among themselves.

Before long, I was invited to be one of the speakers in a dialogue held at the mosque that this Pakistani doctor attended. There were about forty men in attendance and—seated apart—about the same number of women. The seven speakers had been each allotted ten minutes to address the subject "Does religion promote war or peace?"

A black lady who had turned Buddhist was the first to speak; she thought we all served the same god, so there should be peace. The next speaker was a councilman from that area, followed by a Catholic lady, neither of whom said anything important except that warfare was bad. The fourth speaker was a liberal Presbyterian minister who, without presenting any evidence, concluded that we were all worshiping the same peace-loving God. He was followed by a

Hindu, and since they believe in many gods, it really didn't matter if you added another god.

Then it was my turn. I explained that I had never served in the military so I didn't know anything about fighting actual wars. But I asserted that there was one battle I had fought and won, and that was a spiritual battle over my soul. I then took ten minutes and explained to those Muslims how I came to know Jesus Christ as my personal Savior. The people listened very well.

Last, it was the imam's turn to speak. He didn't stick to his ten minutes but went on and on as to how Muhammad was such a peaceful person and Islam was such a peaceful religion, never mentioning that Muhammad had personally fought in at least twenty-seven battles and his generals in thirty-two more, or that Islam had been spread by the sword.

That day was truly an eye-opening experience for me.

My interest in Islam having been whetted, what did I do next? I quickly obtained a number of books on Islam, some by Christians and others by Muslims, and did a lot of reading. This only confused me more, because I saw a lot of contradictions. Many things about Islam just did not make sense to me. So I phoned another mosque and spoke to the imam, explaining that I had a number of questions about Islam and asked if he would help me. I was invited to come to the mosque after the Friday prayers that day; he promised that he would talk to me at that time.

When I got there, however, I found out he didn't understand much English, so another man acted as an interpreter. But the imam didn't seem too interested in answering my questions, so the interpreter did most of the talking. My purpose in going to the mosque was to obtain clear answers to my questions about Islam, but it turned out that I was again given literature that attacked Christianity. I was also lent three videos that very severely smeared the Christian faith.

I had genuine questions about Islam, but instead of getting answers, I was always told what the Muslims assumed I believed. I was never granted an opportunity to explain what biblical Christianity is all about. I was seeking to find the best way to reach out to Muslims with the message of Christ. I had heard from a number of Christian sources that this might be done by starting in the areas where we have "common ground."

For instance, Muslims believe in only one God, who created the universe; Christians and Jews have the same belief. Muslims also believe in Jesus, though only as a prophet. Both religions believe that man has an eternal soul that will go to heaven or hell after this earthly life. So at first, this approach sounded sensible, but the more I studied Islam, the more I realized that Christians and Muslims do not truly have *any* common ground. Muslims might believe in only one God, but he is certainly not the God of the Bible. The Allah of Islam is a remote, unknowable God. He acts like a taskmaster who sends down laws for his servants to obey, in hope of gaining his favor.

If on the Day of Judgment a Muslim ends up having done more good works than bad, maybe he will be permitted to enter one of the seven Paradises. But of course, if Allah doesn't like you, all your labor is in vain—Allah will gladly send you to hell! The God of the Bible, however, has revealed Himself to us in a personal way through His Son Jesus Christ. God has provided a guaranteed eternal salvation for us through the shed blood of the Messiah. Obviously, the God of the Bible and the Allah of Islam are *not* the same. The two religions are going in opposite directions!

However, while there is a vast difference between the beliefs of Christians and Muslims, there are subjects that can lead to meaningful discussions. They are the following:

1. God is number 1.
2. Rewards are in heaven.
3. We have a spirit or soul.
4. The grave is not the end.
5. There will be a day of judgment.
6. Hell will be a place of punishment.
7. There are conditions for going to Paradise, etc.

Muslims say they believe in the prophets of the Old Testament—like Adam, Noah, Abraham, Moses, David, Jonah, etc.—but their belief as to what these men proclaimed is far different from what the Bible states. Islam declares that these prophets primarily proclaimed God's laws and helped enforce them but that the accounts found in the Bible are unreliable. Also, even though they truly believe that there was a person by the name of Jesus who once lived upon this earth, he is in no way similar to the Jesus of the Bible.

Islam makes a mockery out of Jesus by not acknowledging His eternal Deity as the Son of God and demotes Him to just another prophet in a long list of 124,000 messengers. Muslims do not believe that He died on the cross but claim that someone else died in His place and, of course, that there was no resurrection. They state that the original Bible was given by inspiration of God but that most of the original material has been lost and rewritten in a corrupted form. So as I considered the teachings of Islam and those of the Bible, I realized that there actually is no common ground.

That is why I have been seeking other ways to reach lost Muslims, and this is the main reason I am writing this book.

The fundamental difference between Islam and Christianity is that Islam is based on "works that are to please God and perhaps win his favor" while biblical

Christianity is based on the fact that every one of us was born in sin and had chosen to sin of our own free will, and are thus ungodly, vile sinners before God. Our sins have separated us from God, which makes us spiritually dead before God. Only God can give life to the dead.

The Bible clearly states in Hebrews 9:22, "Without the shedding of blood there is no remission of sin." Thus, without the death of Jesus Christ upon the cross and His resurrection, there can be no forgiveness and acceptance into heaven. But 1 John 1:7 clearly promises, "The blood of Jesus Christ His Son cleanses us from all sin." And Revelation 1:5 also declares, "To Him [Jesus Christ] who loved us and washed us from our sins in *His own blood*."

Since Muslims deny the death and resurrection of Jesus Christ, they do not have any way of going to heaven. However, the Christian is absolutely certain of going to heaven the moment he or she leaves this life. The verse in 2 Corinthians 5:8 reads, "We are confident, yes, well pleased rather to be absent from the body and present with the Lord."

Muslims have put a lot of effort into promoting the felicitous idea that they worship the same God as Christians do in order to gain legitimacy and acceptance in the West. (Sad to say, many people have accepted this false propaganda.) But this tactic is not something that is new, because Muhammad tried the same thing when he started proclaiming his new religion in Mecca. At first, he tried to be friendly with the Christians and Jews. He initially told his followers, as recorded in the *Qur'an*, in Surah (chapter) 29:46, "And argue not with the People of the Book unless it be in a way that is better, save with such of them who are iniquitous; and say, 'We believe in that which has been revealed unto us and revealed unto you; our God and your God is One, and unto Him we surrender.'"

But note the change in what Muhammad taught when he moved to Medina and gained control there. Surah 9:29 urges Muslims to "fight against those from among the People of the Scripture [Book] who do not believe in Allah nor the Last day; who do not forbid what Allah and His messenger have forbidden, and who do not adopt the religion of truth—until they pay the tribute out of hand, utterly subdued." (When Muslims conquered a people-group or nation, they gave the people three choices: (1) become a Muslim, (2) annually pay a very heavy tax, or (3) lose your head.)

In light of what I have just said, and in light of other facts that will be elaborated on in various chapters of this book, some reviewers are sure to call me an Islamophobe and may even jump to the conclusion that I hate Muslims. So let me clearly state my position.

Though I disagree with Islam, I sincerely love Muslims; in fact, I seriously considered giving this book the title

Approaching Muslims in Love—which is what I hope every reader will do. Despite the restrictions imposed on Christian worship in many Muslim-majority countries, I believe Muslims deserve full freedom to peacefully worship in community centers and mosques in the USA and abroad. I recognize that not all American Muslims are radical fundamentalists and that tarring them with that name is wrong. I recognize also that there are various forms of Islam, and those should be carefully distinguished.

All prejudice is unethical, and I deplore the heated statements and actions that some anti- Muslims (and others) have publicly made and taken in recent months. Innocent people are being badly hurt, and my plea is for enlightened tolerance. Whether Christian or Muslim, we are Americans; may we act that way!

In order to try and understand Islam, I have read over a hundred books and booklets, many of them by Muslim authors. In addition, I have read the entire *Qur'an*, large segments of the *Hadith*, and hundreds of pages from Muslim sources found on the Internet. The more I study, the greater my burden becomes to reach out to these religious people with the message of the saving grace of the Lord Jesus Christ. But how is the question. There are many books on Islam that will give you "facts," but I felt there was a need for a book that gives a step-by-step strategy and practical helps for the average layman in reaching out to Muslims.

It seemed that most of the books I read oversimplified the reaching of Muslims.

Here are nine steps in evangelizing Muslims:

1. *Make friends.* That is good advice, but nothing concrete was said about this lengthy process.
2. *Pray.* This is something that is very obvious.
3. *Share with them the Word of God.* This seems to be a good suggestion, but in my reading, I came to realize that most Muslims are convinced that the Bible has been greatly corrupted, changed, that the original has been lost and replaced by a "different Gospel." The typical Muslim has absolutely no respect for the Bible, so using the Bible is not useful until you can get him to realize the Bible has *not* been changed and corrupted, and this can be a very long process.
4. *Ask thought-provoking questions.* This is a very good suggestion, but the book gave me no thought-provoking questions to ask. Consequently, I have given you a long list in this book.
5. *Listen attentively.* Again a good suggestion, but it gave me no details as to how to carry on any meaningful conversation.
6. *Present your beliefs openly, without apology.* This is an excellent suggestion; however, when presenting the Gospel, we have to start with sin, and Muslims do

not believe they are sinners in need of a Savior, so you must deal with a lot of other issues before you can get this far.

7. *Reason, don't argue.* Good.

8. *Never denigrate Muhammad or the* Qur'an. This is very important.

9. *Respect their customs and sensitivities.* This is another good suggestion, but I was not presented with the customs that I needed to be sensitive to.

I realized that in order to reach Muslims effectively, I needed more concrete information, and I knew that could take a long time. Hence, it became my goal to speak with as many Muslims as possible to gain practical information in witnessing so that I might be able to help others. I had spent *years* in actual witnessing to Jehovah's Witnesses and Mormons before I ever wrote my books on reaching out to them. I knew it would take a lot of time to gain the necessary information for reaching Muslims. Most Christians do not have time to read as many books as I have, nor do they have the opportunity to speak to a lot of Muslims.

I felt a special burden to write a book so that any Christian who has a Muslim neighbor, works with one, or comes in contact with one in other ways would have a book that would provide the proper facts and then a step-by-step approach in reaching out to one's Muslim contacts. I have made a lot of mistakes on my journey; I want to help others so that they will *not* make the same mistakes and go through the same long journey that I had to.

It was at this stage that I was fortunate enough to meet a man who had worked directly with Muslims in London for sixteen years. He was able to give me a lot of helpful information that I had not been able to gain through my reading and personal contacts with Muslims. I felt that I was on the right track, and this contact only confirmed what I believed.

I continue to be in contact with Muslims personally and by correspondence. This way, I have been able to test these tactics to make sure they are effective.

I pray that this book will be a help to you and to the Christian community as it gets under the burden of reaching out to the Muslims so that, by God's grace, many of them will come to know our wonderful Lord and Savior, Jesus Christ.

PS: After you have read the book, should you desire more information, refer to my website: lovetoshareministeries. com.

1

---※---

The Five Pillars of Islam

THE BASIC TENETS of Islam are commonly called the Five Pillars, which are the following:

1. Recital of the Creed
2. Ritual Prayer
3. The Giving of Alms
4. Fasting during Ramadan
5. Making the Pilgrimage to Mecca.

Some authorities add a sixth one: jihad, or a holy war. Let us look at these five pillars in some detail.

1. Recital of the Creed

"There is no god worthy of worship except Allah, and Muhammad is His messenger." This declaration of faith is called the *Shahadah*. In order to become a Muslim, all you have to do is publicly make this declaration, preferably in Arabic.

2. Ritual Prayer

Salat is the name for these obligatory prayers. A Muslim is required to pray five times a day—at dawn, noon, midafternoon, dusk, and two hours after sunset. These prayers contain verses from the *Qur'an* and should be said in Arabic, the language of the original *Qur'an*.

In communities where a mosque exists, you might hear the call to prayer, which is known as the *Azaan*. This call is usually made with a loud and penetrating voice by the *muezzin* (the caller), who stands on a high platform such as a minaret for all to hear him. He cries out, "God is most great. I testify that there is no god but Allah. I testify that Muhammad is God's Apostle. Come to prayer, come to security. God is most great."

Today, this is usually done through a loudspeaker. For Islamic prayer, certain preparations are necessary: the Muslim must make sure that his body is clean. To do this, a ritual washing is necessary. Here is how one makes Wud'u and performs the ablution:

a. The hands are washed three times, making sure the water reaches between the fingers and all over the hands. As the water is applied, it supposedly carries away the sins committed by these body parts.

b. A handful of water is brought to the mouth, and it is rinsed thoroughly three times.

c. Water is sniffed up the nose three times to cleanse it. The right hand must be used to bring up the water, and the left hand to expel it.

d. The entire face is washed three times.

e. The arms are washed—up to the elbows—three times, starting with the right arm.

f. The wet hand is used to wipe the top of the head once, from front to back and to the front again.

g. The wet fingers are then used to wipe the inside and outside of your ears once.

h. The feet must be washed up to the ankles three times, starting with the right foot.

i. All this water must be dried off.

j. Then the supplication is made, which states, "I witness that none should be worshipped except Allah, and that Muhammad is His servant and messenger."

The noon service on Friday is the only time when Muslim men are expected to gather together at the mosque. This service includes the weekly sermon, usually about thirty minutes long. If women attend, they do not openly participate. Whenever men and women gather at the mosque, the room is divided down the middle by a curtain, with the men on one side and the women on the other—or the women meet in another room, or upstairs.

The main room of a mosque is carpeted from wall to wall. Upon entering, you must remove your shoes. Everyone sits on the floor; however, there are a few chairs at the back for disabled and older people.

As to the proper posture and positions for prayer, the *Qur'an* has nothing to say. However, the pattern set by Muhammad is followed. The prescribed form must be maintained if the prayer is to be heard, whether the person is praying alone or as part of a group. Also, all the prayers must be said facing Mecca. The prayers contain words of praise and requests for blessings.

Here is the pattern for prayer:

1. The praying Muslim opens his two hands and then touches his earlobes with his thumbs and says, "Allahu Akbar," which means "God is most great."
2. He then goes on to recite the prayers that go with the bowings. Lowering his hands upon his chest and

folding them, with the right hand over the left, he recites the first chapter of the *Qur'an* (the *Fatihah*) and a few other verses.

3. Next, he bows from his hips, with his hands on his knees as he recites, "I extol the perfection of my Lord the great."

4. He returns to an upright position and says, "Allahu Akbar."

5. After this, he gently goes down on his knees and places his hands on the floor while he prostrates himself by placing his nose and forehead on the floor. By taking this position, he shows his full respect and submission to Allah.

6. He then sits back on his heels with his hands on his legs before performing a second prostration with the same words. This completes one's *rak'as*, or bowings. After the last bowing, he recites the *Shahadah* ("There is no god but Allah, and Muhammad is the messenger of Allah.").

7. Then, looking over his right shoulder, he says to the person standing next to him, "Peace be on you and the mercy of God," and then he repeats the same words, looking over his left shoulder. The whole process involves four bowings from the waist and two bowings to the floor.

Having a personal prayer mat is very important. If the worshipper is at home or out where he must pray on the ground, the mat will keep him from getting dirty, which would nullify his prayer.

In the mosque, all the worshippers kneel and prostrate themselves in rows, in complete unity, maintained at each stage. This is done by following the imam (spiritual leader), who leads from the front.

From such practices, it can appear that the Muslim religion has been reduced to postures and rituals. The Muslim follows these faithfully, believing that he is fulfilling the requirements of Allah. However, there is no evidence that Allah ever sanctioned these rituals.

Often, Muslims can be seen carrying a set of ninety-nine beads strung in a circle that are said to represent "the ninety-nine beautiful names of Allah." Muslims use the beads to help them remember those ninety-nine names. Many Muslims believe that if they recite these names they will get special help from Allah. Some have been taught that if a person repeats a certain name one hundred times, he can gain a blessing from the meaning of the name. For instance, if one repeats the name "Merciful" a hundred times after morning prayer, everyone he meets will be friendly to him. If he repeats "Truth," he will be able to find something that he has lost.

3. The Giving of Alms (*Zakat*)

For most purposes, this involves the payment of 2/12 percent of one's income each lunar year. The money is used firstly to support the poor, but some also goes to the collectors and to Qur'anic teachers. It may also be used to help any people who are in trouble because they have become Muslims. And some is used to spread Islam, to build mosques, to start clinics and schools, and even to fight "holy wars."

Additional free-will offerings are known as *Sadaqa*. Almsgiving is believed to bring special rewards and to cleanse a person from sin.

4. The Fast (*Sawm*)

Every year in the month of Ramadan, which is the ninth month of Islam's lunar calendar (moving forward each year), all Muslims fast daily from the first light in the morning until sundown, abstaining from food, drink, inhaled substances (cigarettes), and sexual relations. Some of the stricter Muslims do not swallow their own saliva. But at night, they feast as at no other time of the year. And at the sight of the new moon, the month of Ramadan ends. Muslims then celebrate by feasting, exchanging gifts, buying new clothes, and visiting friends. This celebration at the end of Ramadan is called the Eid.

Although fasting can be beneficial to one's health, Muslims regard it principally as a method of self-purification. However, this month of fasting did not originate with Islam; other religious groups already practiced this type of fasting. At first, Muslims observed the fast between sunset and sunrise, but later, it was changed to the hours between sunrise and sunset. The observance of Ramadan is binding upon all adult Muslims of both sexes, save for the aged, sick, pregnant women, nursing mothers, and travelers. However, when the exempting circumstances of traveling or sickness, etc., have ceased, the one month of fasting must be made up.

5. Making the Pilgrimage (*Hajj*)

Every adult Muslim must make the trip to Mecca, Saudi Arabia, at least once during his or her lifetime—provided he or she is able, with respect to health and finances. The prescribed time for the pilgrimage is one week in the twelfth month, from the seventh to the thirteenth day. The Islamic lunar calendar has twelve months but is eleven days shorter than our calendar, so the pilgrimage is eleven days earlier each year. But pilgrims can also go to Mecca to perform the rituals for a shorter period at other times of the year. This is sometimes called the lesser pilgrimage. The *Hajj* is associated with the life of Muhammad from the seventh century, but the ritual of the pilgrimage to Mecca is considered by Muslims to stretch back thousands of years to the time of Abraham.

It consists of several ceremonies at sacred sites that are meant to symbolize the essential concepts of the Islamic faith, and these are said to commemorate the trials of Abraham and his family. Islamic tradition (not the *Qur'an*) maintains that Abraham took Ishmael and went south to Mecca, and it was Ishmael who was to be offered up— contrary to the Biblical account, which says God asked Abraham to offer up *Isaac* on Mt. Moriah, in *Palestine*. Islam teaches that Abraham and Ishmael restored the *Ka'ba* (place of worship) and placed the Black Stone there—the stone that is claimed to have come down from heaven.

The pilgrims usually arrive at Jeddah, a port city forty-five minutes northwest of Mecca. Before entering Mecca proper, the pilgrim has to be purified by taking a complete bath. This is known as ablution. When this happens, the pilgrim enters into the state of *ihram* (prohibitions), which include the following: (1) foul talk, (2) sexual intercourse, (3) quarrels or disputes, and (4) the cutting of nails and hair.

Men are not allowed to shave and must walk with their feet bare. There is a strict dress code. They remove their worldly clothes and don the humble attire of a pilgrim, which is two seamless white sheets. One is tied around the waist to cover his legs to just below the knees, and the other is wrapped around the top half of his body, leaving the head and left arm and shoulder uncovered. Women need only to be modestly dressed in appropriate attire. They wear a simple white dress and a head covering, but not a veil. Women must avoid any adornment—including jewelry, perfume, and nail polish—as a sign of purification.

Upon arrival in Mecca, the pilgrim enters the Great Mosque (Masjid al-Haram) through one of the 129 gates—starting with the right foot first—and makes seven circuits, known as the *Tawaf*, around the *Ka'ba*, which is in the center of the complex. The *Ka'ba* is a cubical shrine about fifty feet high, having walls about forty feet long, covered in thick black silk, hand embroidered with verses from the Qur'an in golden thread.

The pilgrim starts at the Black Stone (*aja Hajar Aswad*), which is about twelve inches in diameter and is built into the wall at its eastern corner, going counterclockwise around the *Ka'ba*. The pilgrim kisses it each time around if he can get close enough. Since the pilgrims are in the millions, if kissing the stone is not possible because of the crowds, they may simply point toward the stone on each circuit with their right hand as they pass. Men are encouraged to perform the first three circuits at a hurried pace, followed by four times at a more leisurely pace.

Eating is not permitted, but the drinking of water is allowed because of the risk of dehydration. (Also built into the eastern corner is another stone called lucky; this stone is only touched, not kissed.) The distance around the *Ka'ba* itself is very short, but because so many pilgrims are there at one time, the outer rim of the crowd can be as long as a mile around. Of course, those on the outer edge cannot go around it at as quickly as the others up close. The pilgrim then leaves the mosque complex through a different gate than the one by which he entered.

The pilgrims also perform the *Sa'i*. They hurry seven times between two small hills named *Safa* and *Marwah* (now located inside the mosque complex), reenacting Hagar's desperate search for water and food for Ishmael. (This story is found in the Bible in Genesis 21:8–21, but Muhammad greatly altered it.) They also offer prayer, which includes two bowings. The back-and-forth circuit of the pilgrims used to be in the open air but is now entirely enclosed within the mosque and can be completed via air-conditioned tunnels.

On the eighth day of the pilgrimage month, these ceremonies having been completed the previous day at the mosque, the pilgrimage officially begins. After a mosque discourse, the pilgrims set out for Mina, a valley some five miles away. Many walk there, but some take the bus. The lodging place there is known as the Tent City. There are hundreds of thousands of white tents to accommodate the over two million pilgrims. Each tent holds between forty-five and sixty people.

The next day, they travel to the plain of Arafat, which is an open area below the Mount of Mercy thirteen miles from Mecca—where the pilgrims must spend the afternoon within a defined area until after sunset. No specific rituals or prayers are required during the stay at Arafat, although many pilgrims spend time praying and thinking about the course of their lives. A pilgrim's *Hajj* is considered invalid if he does not spend the afternoon on Arafat. This is near a hill from which Muhammad gave his last sermon. This is the ninth day of the pilgrimage and is the climax of the *Hajj*. That evening, the pilgrims move and camp at Muzdalifah, which is a site between Mina and Arafat. Muslims stay overnight and offer various prayers there.

Then the pilgrims return to Mina on the tenth. Until recently, they would throw seven pebbles at three stone pillars that represent the devil. Muslims have been told that Abraham, when he was tempted not to offer his son, was able to expel Satan in this way. The devil challenged Abraham three times, and three times he refused. Each pillar marks the location of one of these refusals. But for safety reasons, in 2004, the pillars were changed to long walls, with catch basins below to catch the stones.

This stoning concludes the pilgrimage proper, and the pilgrim then prepares to withdraw from the state of consecration. He sacrifices a sheep, a goat, or maybe a camel and has his head shaved. The slaughter of an animal can be done either personally or by appointing someone else to do it. He returns to Mecca, where once again he does the *Ka'ba* circuit and bathes in water from the holy well of Zamzam, or at least sprinkles himself with it. Using some biblical facts and changing others, Muslims claim that Hagar, in a desperate desire to find water for Ishmael, ran frantically around until she came to this source of water.

On the eleventh, twelfth, and thirteenth days of the month, the pilgrims enjoy a time of relaxation. Some will take an optional journey by bus to the town of Medina, which includes a visit to the Mosque of the Prophet. Muhammad's tomb is enclosed within that mosque; the tomb of Muhammad's daughter, Fatima, is also found there. After spending a night or more in Medina, the pilgrim returns to Mecca.

Muslims say that the *Hajj* is designed to develop a God consciousness and a sense of spiritual uplifting. It is also believed to be an opportunity to seek forgiveness of sins accumulated throughout life. Muhammad had said that a person who performs *Hajj* properly "will return as a newly born baby [free of all sins]."

The pilgrim is now entitled to be referred to as a *Hajji*. In some countries, *Hajjis* wear a certain color of head covering which indicates they have completed the pilgrimage.

Non-Muslims are not allowed to participate in the *Hajj* or even to enter Mecca.

Before we further investigate the teachings and practices of Islam, we need to take a thorough look at the life of the man who established Islam, the Prophet Muhammad. And then we shall examine the disquieting history of the centuries that followed.

2

Who Was Muhammad?

"MUHAMMAD WAS THE most influential man who ever lived"—so declares Michael H. Hart in his recent book, *The 100: A Ranking of the Most Influential Persons in History*. Even though most non-Muslims are unwilling to accept this evaluation, it is vitally important that we know the basics of his life.

Islam declares that Muhammad was the seal of the prophets, belongs to all times and places, and is the final prophet in a long list of 124,000. Surah 33:40 asserts, "Muhammad is not the father of any man among you, but he is the messenger of Allah and the Seal of the Prophets; and Allah is Aware of all things." Then there is a note under this verse that reads, "When a document is sealed, it is complete, and there can be no further addition. The holy Prophet Muhammad closed the long line of Apostles." Islam also states that while all prophets have preached the same basic message—that of submission to the divine will—nonetheless, Muhammad's message is distinctive in that it was the last and final word of God to humankind, and it was put in perfect written form and has been preserved without error.

Muhammad, whose name in Arabic means "highly praised," was born in the year AD 570, into the powerful Quraish tribe in Mecca, a city in the western part of present-day Saudi Arabia. It was a settlement that grew up along a major caravan route, as also was Medina. Muhammad's father, Abdullah, belonged to the influential Quraish tribe, but he died before the birth of his son.

His mother's name was Amina. It was the custom of the mothers of that tribe to give their infants to be nursed by Bedouins, who dwelt nearby in the deserts of Arabia, so as to secure for their infants the healthy air of the desert. It is said that the grief of her husband's death dried up the fountain of Amina's milk. Thus, for a double reason, Muhammad was entrusted to the care of a Bedouin nurse named Halima until the age of five.

When approaching his fifth year, he appears to have become subject to certain epileptic fits. This scared his foster parent, as such attacks were attributed to the influence of evil spirits and made her resolve to return the child to his mother.

His mother passed on when he was six years old. He was then placed in the care of his grandfather Abdul Muttalib, but the old man shortly died. So Muhammad's paternal uncle, Abu Talib, became his adoptive father, and it was he who raised the boy to manhood.

At the age of twelve, Muhammad was taken on a mercantile journey to Damascus in Syria and to Basra—now in Iraq—for some months. It is highly possible that while in Syria Muhammad was brought into contact with Christianity. Though there were Christians in Arabia also, they were not prominent there. This contact would have given him the opportunity of obtaining some information as to the religious and social customs of Christians.

The Quraish were influential because they controlled the city of Mecca. Mecca was important economically because it served as a convenient resting place for trading caravans. It was important religiously because the *Ka'ba* (or *Ka'aba*), a place of worship, was located there. The *Ka'ba* is a cubical structure about fifty feet high with walls that are about forty feet long, made of brick and covered with black cloth. Of note in the *Ka'ba* is the sacred Black Stone, built into the wall in its eastern corner. This black stone, likely a meteorite, is about twelve inches in diameter, about the size of a football. It played a prominent role in the pagan worship, and this prominence has been carried over by the Muslims. It is kissed by Muslims when they make a pilgrimage to Mecca. Also, built into the eastern corner is another stone called lucky. This stone is only touched, not kissed. At the time of Muhammad, the *Ka'ba* contained 360 pagan idols. Each Arabian tribe had handpicked its own deity, and its members came to Mecca each year to pay homage to its god.

Muslims have been taught that Adam originally built the *Ka'ba*. As the tradition goes, when Adam and Eve were created, they were in Paradise but were expelled from Paradise because of their sin of disobedience. Adam landed on a mountain in Ceylon, and Eve fell to earth at Jiddah on the western coast of Arabia. Another account says that Adam landed in India and Eve in Africa, in the southern part of Ethiopia. Adam had brought with him a "black stone" from Paradise and some seedlings from the foods of Paradise. He continued to plant these seeds on his journey westward.

After a hundred years of wandering, Adam met his wife in Mecca. Receiving instructions and the design from Allah, he constructed a tabernacle on the site of the present *Ka'ba*. Adam put in the "black stone," which he had brought with him from Paradise. (Here the accounts differ, as another source states that the black stone "fell" from heaven when Adam and Eve sinned and not that Adam brought it with him.) It is said that the "black stone" was originally whiter than milk but has since turned black on account of the sins of the pilgrims who have touched it. Also, it is further believed that Mecca stands on a spot directly beneath God's throne in heaven. Tradition further states that the *Ka'ba* was destroyed during the Flood. It lay in ruins for years, but then Abraham and Ishmael rebuilt it. Of course, there is no biblical or historical evidence for such a claim.

As a young man with no fortune of his own, Muhammad had to work for a living. He did various odd jobs, among them tending sheep plus buying and selling goods in Mecca. When he was twenty years old, he was engaged in a war between his own Quraish tribe and another tribe. Scandalously, this conflict occurred within the sacred months and was carried on in sacred territory. Muhammad later said, "In this war, I discharged arrows at the enemy, and I do not regret it."

Eventually, he was employed as an agent by a woman named Khadijah (Khadija), a widow with considerable business interests. On her behalf, Muhammad traveled north with one of the caravans to Syria, which was part of the powerful "Christian" Byzantine Empire. He most likely came in contact with many Christians once more. At this time, powerful outside religious influences were at work in Arabia.

These influences had filtered into the peninsula from Syria and Palestine as well as from "Christian" Abyssinia (Ethiopia) just across the Red Sea from southern Arabia. Some Arabians had been converted to Christianity. Several oases were occupied partly by tribes of Arabian Jews, and there was a colony of Abyssinian Christians who dwelt in Mecca. From these sources, as well as during his trip to Syria, Muhammad undoubtedly heard tales about Jesus and the prophets and about the God worshiped by both Jews and Christians. He would have contrasted this with the gross and degrading idolatry and evil practices then prevailing in Arabia. He thus might have yearned for a purer faith than his ancestors'.

Shortly before the appearance of Muhammad on the scene, there were a few inquirers from among the Arabs who had a strong aversion from idolatry and who accordingly sought to find relief in a better faith. Among the Jews, and possibly from ancient tradition still surviving, it was known in Arabia that Abraham was a worshipper of the one true God. Hence, both at Mecca and Medina, there were men who, seeking after the truth, had abandoned the worship of idols, and these were called *Henefites*. Muhammad was acquainted with six of the men in this movement, and apparently, they had an influence on him. Some of them were actually relatives.

At first, Muhammad was not out to start a new religion but came out again idol worship and the teaching of only one true God. There was quite a similarity in both of their teachings and are thus an influence on each other. Their views about such things as idol worship; the burying alive of infant girls; the unity of God, Paradise, and Hell; and calling God "the Lord most Merciful and Compassionate" were similar. Thus, the source of Muhammad's information about Islam is easily traceable. But sad to say, Muhammad never came to realize that Jesus was the promised Messiah, as revealed to Abraham.

So long as Muhammad entertained the hope of gathering together both Jews and Christians—and also the Arab tribes—by the retention of some of their national practices, there seemed to him the possibility of uniting all Arabia in one grand religion. This is seen in the fact that at first Muhammad said very favorable things about the Jews and the Christians. However, when he found this to be impracticable, then it remained for him either to abandon and eventually destroy the Jews and Christians or else lose the native Arabs as a whole. He chose the latter, and that is why later on the things he said about the Jews and Christians in the *Qur'an* were to destroy them.

When Muhammad was twenty-five years old, Khadijah, his wealthy businesswoman employer who had been married twice before, made a proposal of marriage that he accepted. She was fifteen years his senior.

There are many traditions about Muhammad's personality. He was handsome with a commanding presence, had piercing eyes, a gracious smile, and a flowing beard and used gestures that reinforced each expression when he spoke. He had an extraordinary memory, his wit easy and social, his imagination superb, and his judgment clear and decisive. These natural attributes contributed to his leadership ability and help show why he could have been capable of being the author of the *Qur'an*.

Marriage relieved Muhammad of most of his financial cares and gave him considerable time to himself. It seems that he hated idolatry, degeneracy, and the commercialization of religion in Mecca. It was the custom of those few who were spiritually minded to retreat to a place of solitude once a year to fast and pray. Muhammad observed this practice for several years in a cave on Mount Hira, about three miles from Mecca.

While in this cave, in the year AD 610, at the age of forty, he had his first of many supposed revelations. Here is how he related the story:

> I was lying asleep or in a trance, wrapped in my cloak, when I heard a voice saying, "Read!"
> I answered, "I cannot read."

The voice said again, "Read."

I answered, "I do not know how to read."

Once more, this time with terrible force, the voice said, "Read."

I answered, "What can I read?"

The voice thundered, *"Read in the name of your Lord, the Creator, who created man from a clot of blood! Read! Your Lord is most merciful, for he has taught men by the pen and revealed the mysteries to them."*

I was shown a scroll, which seemed to be of silk with letters of fire written on it. I read the words, though I had never read before, and when I awoke, I remembered them, for they were as though written upon my heart.

Muhammad was clearly frightened by this experience. He was full of doubt as to the source of the revelation and thought perhaps a *jinn* (an invisible angel-like intelligent creature of air and fire) or a demon had possessed him, and maybe this revelation was demonic.

He hurried back to Mecca and expressed these fears to his wife, Khadijah. She, who was a believer in just one God, assured him this revelation was from God. His wife had a cousin Waraqa, to whom she took Muhammad, and they asked him about the strange experience in the cave. At this time, Waraqa was quite blind and close to death. He was a learned man, the first to translate parts of the Old and New Testaments into Arabic. There was a seed of restlessness in Waraqa—who at different times had embraced Judaism and Christianity, only to later return to his ancient primitive faith—and it was perhaps from Waraqa that Muhammad learned some strange and inaccurate traditions of the Talmud that got into the *Qur'an*.

Waraqa assured Muhammad that it was the angel Gabriel who had appeared to him—the same one who, he said, had appeared to Moses. (Even though the *Qur'an* never identifies the one who allegedly gave these revelations to Muhammad, Muslims teach that they were delivered by the angel Gabriel.) This was the beginning of a series of purported revelations that were eventually compiled into Islam's sacred scripture, the *Qur'an*—a word that means "recitations." It seems that Muhammad would go into a trancelike state and sweat profusely when he received these "revelations."

Even though it is unthinkable for most Muslims, some Islamic biographers, not the enemies of Islam, have attempted to attribute Muhammad's "revelations" to recurrent epileptic seizures. A person who is epileptic can be disposed to hallucinations, visions, and dreams and easily be afflicted with a morbid state of body and mind.

Muhammad's wife, Khadijah, along with Waraqa, were his first two converts. They assured him that his visions were

BURNING QUESTIONS ABOUT ISLAM

of divine origin and encouraged him to publicly teach what had been revealed to him. Soon after this, Abu Bakr—who would take over when Muhammad died—also converted. (He seems to at first have believed in the revelations more out of friendship and a desire to please an old friend than because he felt there had been any heavenly manifestation.) Next there was Ali, Abu Bakr's handsome ten-year-old son, who lived in Muhammad's house. (He later married Muhammad's daughter, Fatima, and thus became his son-in-law.) Finally there was Muhammad's slave Zayd, who was so much in love with his master that he refused his freedom when it was offered to him. In the beginning, these were his only followers. Ali and Abu Bakr were both to play an important role in the rise of Islam.

Muhammad, however, did not assume this role of a prophet hastily. For a long time, he received no further messages, and he still suffered fears and self-doubts. He then had a second revelation, ordering him to begin his work—to "rise and warn" the people. Muhammad actually began preaching publicly in Mecca in AD 613, proclaiming a message of judgment, belief in one God only, a resurrection, heaven, and his apostleship.

Conflict began to arise between him and the leaders of his own Quraish tribe in Mecca, who pressured him to keep quiet about his message of strict monotheism. At one point, early in the Meccan period, in order to win the friendship of fellow Quraish, Muhammad praised three of their goddesses—Al-Lat, Al-'Uzza, and Manat. This is found in the *Qur'an* in Surah (chapter) 53:19–21, a passage that has become known as the Satanic verses.

As the number of converts grew, the persecution became more severe. Some of the converts had to leave the city for safety while others went into hiding. There were threats to kill Muhammad. At times, he had to go into hiding to protect himself.

The messages began to come more frequently. These were written down by scribes and distributed to the faithful. Muhammad told the faithful to hold on; the enemy was bound to fail. Did not deliverance come to Abraham? Muhammad's temper, always stern since the visitation in the cave, grew sterner. Increasingly, he demanded complete surrender to the purposes of Allah. More and more his mind turned to the harsh antitheses: for the faithful, peace and abundance; for the enemies of God, hellfire. Everything was to be gained by dying in the faith. He spoke of honor, about merit in the eyes of God, and of the rewards of Paradise, which he painted in brilliant colors.

When the annual holy days came, Muhammad was allowed to go about unharmed. He found himself among a small group of pilgrims who had come from Yathrib, an oasis some 270 miles north of Mecca. He spoke to them about his mission and was a little surprised to find them listening to him attentively. Yathrib had been founded by Jews and was something of a commercial rival to Mecca. The Jewish rabbis in the town were constantly declaring the coming of the Messiah, and these men from Yathrib were inclined to believe that Muhammad was indeed the promised Messiah. However, they were not sure if he would be welcomed in Yathrib, so they requested a year in which to prepare for his reception.

In order to survive, the faith needed a base of operations, preferably a town on one of the trade routes of Arabia where Muhammad in his own person could exercise spiritual and earthly dominion. Such a base might be provided by Yathrib, and more and more, his thoughts were directed to that northern city. He was overjoyed when, a year later, a delegation from Yathrib welcomed him as their expected Messiah. These people made an oath to Muhammad and then went back to make final preparations for his coming.

Those welcomers then began to preach in public the new religion of Muhammad. They were very effective, and many others became converts. So rapidly did this doctrine spread in that city that there was scarcely a house wherein there was not someone who was a follower of Islam. Any idols they had were soon thrown away.

Yathrib was a very rich and fertile city that enjoyed many of the blessings of nature and was likewise a prosperous commercial place. Even though Jews who had been dispersed from Jerusalem after its destruction by the Romans in AD 70 had founded the city, they were only a minority of its population when Muhammad arrived. Though they formed but a small community, still they were far superior to the Arabs in culture, were better equipped with instruments for agriculture, and understood many industries to which the Arabs were totally strangers. So though the Arabs formed the bulk of the population of the city, the Jews were the richest and most powerful. There were also a number of Jewish settlements outside the city.

However, Muhammad was compelled to remain in Mecca where he was disliked. Then news about his disciples in Yathrib got out, and the authorities in Mecca were in a quandary. They disliked Muhammad in their midst, but what if he went to Yathrib and entered in triumph? They realized that he might then extract vengeance. With Yathrib in his power, there was nothing to prevent him from attacking Mecca and trampling down its gods.

During spring and early summer, 150 of his followers went to Yathrib. They went by ones and twos, in secret, going along rarely used pathways so that the authorities in Mecca would not know they were escaping. Finally, Muhammad fled Mecca on September 9, AD 622. This is known as the Hijra (Hegira). Later, this date was designated as the beginning of the Islamic era and the start of the Muslim calendar.

Muhammad was welcomed in Yathrib. (Later, its name was changed to Medina, a shortened form of the name Medinat Nabi Allah, meaning "the city of the Prophet of God.") Those who had come with Muhammad from Mecca were known as *Muhajirun* (refugees from Mecca), and the inhabitants of Yathrib were known as the *Ansar*. Muhammad attempted to build amicability between these two groups. Some of those from Mecca felt superior because they were the original converts and had gone through persecution, but those from Medina felt they deserved a special place because of their welcoming Muhammad to the community.

From this time onward, Muhammad's role changed drastically. While in Mecca, he had been merely the religious leader of a small group, but once settled in Medina, he played a new and more powerful role: spiritual and political authoritarian. In keeping with his new status, the nature of his continuing revelations changed from being purely religious to having greater legislative and social content.

In the first year of his reign at Medina, Muhammad showed himself at his best. He received revelations (seemingly at will, because as different situations came up, he acted like the decisions came from God rather than from himself), issued decrees, signed treaties, but always humbly. He was quietly putting his house in order. Also, much of his time during this first year was occupied in building a mosque. After the mosque was completed, Muhammad made his Negro servant Belal ascend a lofty wall near the mosque early before daybreak and proclaim in a loud voice, "Great is Allah. I bear witness that there is no god but Allah. I bear witness that Muhammad is the prophet of Allah. Come to prayers, come into happiness. Great is Allah."

One of Muhammad's early problems in Medina was with the Jews. Several Jewish clans controlled the richest agricultural lands and had made formal alliances with two of the Arab tribes that dominated the oasis. Muhammad expected the Jews to recognize him as a prophet, thus strengthening his position in Medina. He was indebted to the Jews as his source of information about prophets, revelations, angels, etc.

In an effort to win their support, he adopted some of their religious practices, such as fasting on the Day of Atonement and the custom of praying toward Jerusalem, and he ordered the faithful to be circumcised. But he chose Friday as the Sabbath instead of observing Saturday like the Jews. A few of the Jews became Muslims, but soon, the majority saw that he was not the promised Messiah and concluded they had erred in welcoming him.

The Jews realized that the expected Messiah would rise from the north and had to be of the seed of David and have Jewish blood. Nor would their lawgiver be ignorant of their Hebrew language. They also saw that in the growth of Islam there was a threat to their own political and economic self-interests. Far from accepting Muhammad as a prophet, they rejected his claim and bitterly criticized him, contending that many of his revelations contradicted their Scriptures and were therefore false. Muhammad countered by saying that the Jews had *distorted* their Scriptures and only the *Qur'an* was the true Word of God.

When Muhammad first proclaimed that he was a prophet of God, he tried hard to win the favor of the Jews and Christians; hence, there are places in the *Qur'an* that are very favorable to them. Later, when his attempts failed, he then turned to bitterly attack them, and this is manifest in other parts of the *Qur'an*. (Often, when Muslims are speaking with Christians and trying to win their approval, they will mention the verses favorable to Christians and Jews and completely ignore the harsh statements that Muhammad made later.) He ultimately declared to his community, "Let no two religions be left in the Arabian Peninsula." (To this day, neither Christians nor Jews are allowed to worship publicly in Saudi Arabia. There are no Bibles, no churches, no synagogues. In fact, Jews are not even allowed to visit there.)

Because the Jews rejected Muhammad as a prophet, he now concentrated on building an Islamic community that was primarily of Arabs. There were Arabs who had been members of feuding tribes who gradually submitted to Muhammad, accepting his claim to be the true prophet of Allah. This substitution of faith ties for blood ties made it possible to suppress the old tribal rivalries and gave rise to a revolutionary political unity.

But Muhammad changed abruptly from a benevolent despot—the devoted servant to Allah—into a ruthless conqueror. Perhaps power corrupted him; perhaps he knew the faith would never survive without unsheathing the sword. What is certain is that his character *changed*. Where he had been soft, he became hard. The latter life of Muhammad is seen as a period of war and politics even more than of religion. Hence, his religion became identified with war and politics.

As the Jews became more and more open in their opposition to Muhammad and his relationship with them steadily deteriorated, he knew that something must be done. The Jews inhabited the chief market area in Medina. Even though Muhammad had made a treaty with these Jews when he first came, he attacked their dwellings, ignoring this treaty. Many of the Jews were massacred on the Prophet's orders, and the rest were ordered to vacate their dwellings. Their possessions were confiscated by the Muslims and treated as the spoils of war.

This period in Medina marked the beginning of a new form of activity against the enemies of the faith back in Mecca. Muhammad started leading his followers in raids against Meccan caravans passing through Medinan territory. Some scholars think that the reason for these raids was primarily economic, to help the emigrants acquire food and supplies. In any case, one of these raids led to the first serious armed clash between the Muslims and the Meccans.

Two years after the Muslims had migrated to Medina, Muhammad learned that a richly ladened Meccan caravan was about to pass near Medina. He immediately made plans to attack it. But word of this reached the caravan, whose leader promptly changed its route and rushed a messenger back to Mecca, asking for reinforcements. The caravan subsequently escaped, and the Muslims then ran into the reinforcements at Badr, a caravan stop southwest of Medina.

Muhammad had about three hundred men, the largest force he had ever assembled, but the Meccans had close to a thousand. Obviously, the Muslims could not turn back without loss of face while for the Meccans, it was an opportunity to teach Muhammad and his followers to leave Mecca and its trade alone. Muhammad directed his followers from a nearby shelter. Surprisingly, the prophet's small band inflicted a crushing defeat on the proud Quraish, who had not expected such fierce opposition.

This was a memorable battle because on this occasion, Muhammad for the first time drew his sword in assertion of his claim as the commissioned Apostle of the Most High God. He claimed it was *Allah* who gave them the victory, thus giving divine sanction to using the sword ruthlessly. After the battle, he remained three days at Badr, most of which he spent in butchering the prisoners. First of all, Muhammad personally put to death two prisoners whom he hated, along with a woman by the name of Asma who had composed some verses against Muhammad. She was put to death in cold blood while she was asleep with her baby by her side. Anyone who did not embrace the new faith or did not free himself by payment of a heavy ransom was cruelly put to death.

This startling Muslim victory had far-reaching effects. Arabs everywhere looked upon it as a miracle, a sign of God's favor upon the Prophet's cause, thus strengthening Muhammad's claim that he was the Apostle of God. In addition, the Muslim warriors shared in the booty from the raids, and word soon spread that the cause of God could bring rewards on earth as well as in heaven. Very conveniently, Muhammad received a revelation from Allah that one-fifth of the spoils were to be devoted to God and the Prophet. This plunder and booty would be put in the public treasury to be spent by Muhammad according to his good pleasure.

The new religion showed that it was to be founded upon human passions, upon pride of domination, upon fanaticism, just as much as upon simplification of truth and belief about God.

Nearby tribes now began to join Islam and to fight under its banner. If victorious, they got booty. If killed in battle, martyrdom was considered the highest prize, the quickest and surest means of entering Paradise, where the Prophet had promised them they would enjoy sensual delights far superior to any known on earth.

(Here is the Islamic concept of heaven: It is a place where a Muslim man will be reclining, eating meat and delicious fruits, drinking exquisite wines, and engaging in sex with beautiful women, and with eternally young beautiful boys or young men. There is no mention of women's rewards. It is interesting to note that many of the things that are forbidden to Muslims here on earth are allowed to them in abundance in Paradise. Some of these delights are drinking wine, practicing homosexuality, and engaging in sex every day with dozens of virgins, for whom Allah will automatically restore their virginity.)

The Meccans, however, did not accept their defeat at Badr lightly. The following year, a force of three thousand attacked the Muslims at Medina, inflicting on them a minor defeat. Muhammad himself was wounded in the action.

Two years later, in AD 627, the Meccans—determined to wipe out Muhammad—mounted a full-scale assault on Medina with ten thousand troops mustered from among their allies, including a powerful front line of six hundred horsemen with which they hoped to overwhelm the

Muslims. Muhammad, allegedly on the advice of a Persian convert experienced in fortification, had dug a deep dry moat in front of the exposed portion of the city—a novel tactic in desert warfare. The innovation so confused the attackers that it rendered their cavalry useless and halted their charge.

So, changing tactics, the Meccans camped outside Medina, meanwhile negotiating with a Jewish clan inside the oasis to attack the Muslims from within. The negotiations broke down, however, and the weather turned cold. After forty days the Meccans, now demoralized and short of supplies, returned home.

Muhammad, who had learned about the Jews' negotiations with the Meccans, marched against a Jewish settlement in April of 627 and dealt harshly with these Jews. He sanctioned and personally presided over the beheading of six to nine hundred men. (It is interesting to note that when Muhammad offered them a chance to become Muslims, only four of them saved their lives by accepting Islam.) The wives and daughters were sold for sex slaves and the boys for labor. He then allowed his followers to settle on their fertile land.

Among the captives was Safiyah, the widow of the Jewish leader Rihanah who had been killed. One of Muhammad's followers wanted her for himself, but Muhammad, struck by her beauty, threw his mantle over her and took her into his harem that very night. Is it any wonder that from that day to this, unbridled hatred characterizes the feeling Jews and Muslims have for one another!

It was during this expedition that Muhammad instituted *Mut'ah*, an abominable temporary marriage, which allowed the members of his army to satisfy their carnal desires while away from their wives. They could marry other women for a couple of hours, a day, a week, etc. This practice is still allowed today among the Shi'ites.

At one of the Jewish villages, Muhammad allowed the people to depart with all that they could carry, but they had to leave their houses and lands to the Muslims.

Muhammad had attacked another Jewish settlement, Bani Quraiza. For twenty-five days, the fortress was besieged. The starved defenders began to seek peace at any cost. Muhammad offered to allow them to surrender on condition that the Aus, their supposed allies, should decide their fate. The Jews were hoping the verdict would simply be exile, though all the property they could not carry with them would fall into the hands of Muhammad. But the men were condemned to death, their property to be divided by the victors, their women and children to be slaves.

The terrible judgment was carried out in complete detail. Muhammad himself superintended the massacre. The Muslims dug trenches in the marketplace. The next morning, the seven hundred Jewish men, with their hands tied behind their backs, were taken out in groups of five or six at a time and forced to sit on the edge of the trench. There they were beheaded, and their bodies tumbled into the trench. Where was the "merciful God" that Muhammad continually spoke about? The women and children were then sold into slavery—except one, the beautiful Jewess Rayhanah, who was kept by Muhammad as a slave concubine even though he had just beheaded her husband. She absolutely refused to marry him or change her faith, but there was no escape from the sensuality of the Prophet of Islam.

Muhammad was setting up entirely new rules. He totally disregarded the long-standing alliance between the Jewish and Arab tribes—an alliance considered virtually sacred under the Bedouin code. By this drastic act of wiping out this Jewish settlement, Muhammad was not only showing the Jews—and any future enemies of Islam—that opposition would no longer be tolerated but also showing his fellow Arabs that their previous tribal loyalties were at an end. The only loyalty now recognized was that given to Islam itself—and, of course, Muhammad was the head!

In 628, Muhammad set out on a pilgrimage to Mecca with 1,400 of his followers. The Meccans, hearing about this force, sent out two hundred horsemen to stop it. Fighting threatened, but the two sides agreed upon a treaty that provided for a ten-year truce, and for the Muslims to return to Medina on the condition that they could come back to Mecca on a pilgrimage the following year. Both sides saved face, but Muhammad had won a victory by establishing himself as the equal to the Quraish, as a result of having entered into a treaty with them. Also, by going on the pilgrimage—an old pagan custom—he had shown Arabs that Islam was a religion with an Arabian character.

The following year, Muhammad led two thousand Muslims on the promised pilgrimage to the *Ka'ba*. But subsequent clashes between Muslims and Meccans ended the truce in AD 630; Muhammad marched on Mecca to settle the issue with a force of ten thousand men. Mecca, weakened by the loss of many of its leading men in the battle against Muhammad and consequent dissensions over the leadership of the city, fell with little more than a token show of resistance. Muhammad entered the *Ka'ba* in triumph, exclaiming, "Truth has come and falsehood has vanished." Later, a tradition was established forbidding anyone but Muslims to enter the city, which holds true to this very day. The purified *Ka'ba* in Mecca was now the spiritual center of Islam, just as Medina was its political capital.

With the surrender of Mecca, the first act of Muhammad and his forces was to cleanse the *Ka'ba* of its 360 gods and goddesses, idols and fetishes. However, the Black Stone that was worshiped by the Quraish tribe was allowed to remain. Muhammad did not abolish the stone but kissed it as had been done before, when the people worshiped this stone. Not only did he kiss it but also he ordered his followers to kiss it, much to their surprise and some objection.

War and the use of force were incorporated as a doctrine of faith. Muhammad personally fought in twenty-seven battles. We are all familiar with the word *jihad*. A part of the *Hadith* (the acts and saying of Muhammad) describes the conduct of Muhammad during his wars. As the leader of the new Islamic community, Muhammad led his followers into battle against those who refused to submit to his leadership or acknowledge his prophethood.

The Arabs converted to Islam not because of spiritual revival or religious persuasion but because of their fear of Muhammad's army. The new religion, which began by merely seeking to introduce monotheism to the Arabs, developed into a means of military conquest. Muhammad was able to take control of Arabia because of intertribal strife, the lack of foreign domination, and the cultural backwardness of the people.

Within a year of Mecca's submission to Muhammad, he was able to forcibly unify a good many of the tribes of the Arabian Peninsula under the religion of Islam. The Arabian rulers and tribes that had not yet submitted to his authority now thought it wise not to oppose him and began to journey to Medina to accept his religion and pay him homage. Four of the neighboring provinces sent to the Prophet half of their produce before he came and took away all they had and then submitted themselves to Muhammad's Islamic religion.

To those tribes that did not come, Muhammad sent Khalid, the fearful jihad warrior and his men, with instructions to tell the tribes to accept Islam within three days or else they would be attacked and, of course, the men would be killed. After one tribal leader accepted these terms, Khalid notified Muhammad that they had done so. Muhammad then said, "If I had not received word that they accepted Islam and now I had no need to fight, I would have thrown their heads beneath your feet."

At first, Muhammad let the Jews and Christians remain in this "newly Muslim land," but they had to regularly pay a poll tax—for every adult, male or female, free or slave, one full dinar. However, they were not allowed to baptize their children. Muhammad reminded the leaders of the Jews and Christians that their lives depended on their paying this tax. Next, he sent orders to his governors that the churches and synagogues should be demolished everywhere and that mosques should be erected on their sites.

Ultimately, Muhammad determined that Jews and Christians would no longer be allowed in Arabia at all. He said, "I will expel the Jews and Christians from the Arabian Peninsula." To this day, this is still enforced. The Kingdom of Saudi Arabia labors zealously that Muhammad's wishes in this regard shall be scrupulously honored.

Muhammad gave some other unbelievers four months to leave Arabia, but before this order was carried out, he gave them one more chance to convert to Islam. These unbelievers were pagan Arabs, not Jews and Christians—hence, there is no mention of the poll tax option being offered to them, like to the Jews and Christians who, at first, were given the choice of conversion, subjugation, or war. For the pagans, the choice was conversion or war. If these pagan Arabs did not leave within the "four-month guarantee of safety," the Muslims were to kill them.

As the various chieftains and princes came and submitted to Islam, they were confirmed in their rights and their old titles were retained. Muhammad sent back with each of them an official whose business was to collect the alms from the believers and the tribute from the unbelievers. Another official, who was to instruct the new converts in the religion of Islam, conducted religious services and taught them the *Qur'an*.

Muhammad now had a vision of conquering the world. After subduing the Arabian Peninsula, Muhammad began to send messages to all the neighboring princes and kings, suggesting the advantages of submission to the faith of the One God. One of these messages went to Cyrus, the Byzantine governor of Egypt, who didn't want any trouble on his eastern border and therefore returned a civil reply with some presents, including two beautiful slave girls.

Muhammad gave one to his court poet and kept the other, Mary the Copt, for himself. She was the most attractive of his concubines and the only one who gave him a son, but the child died sixteen months later.

Let us take a look at Muhammad's personal life. Muhammad remained monogamous until Khadijah died in AD 620 at the age of sixty-five. But in the ten years following her death, he married at least eleven other women and took two (maybe more) others as concubines. It is important to note that the *Qur'an* sets a limit of four wives in Surah 4:3. However, Muhammad claimed that he had received a "revelation" from Allah making a special exception for him but not for anyone else. Surah 33:50 declares, "O Prophet! We have made lawful unto you your wives whom you have paid their dowries, and those whom your right hand possesses of those whom Allah has given as spoils of war…: a privilege for you only, not for the (*rest of*) believers."

Muhammad goes on with this claim in Surah 33:51, which adds, "You may defer (*the turn of*) whoever you desire of them and you may lodge with whom you please, and whomsoever you desire of those whom you have set aside (*temporarily*), it is no sin for you (*to receive her again*)." But it seems that later Allah thought Muhammad had exceeded in this permission to take as many wives as possible, because Allah had to put the brakes on Muhammad's love for beautiful women. Surah 33:52 states, "It is not allowed to you [Muhammad] to take other women henceforth, nor that you should change them for other wives even though their beauty pleased you." From all the accounts I have read, Muhammad had a real weakness for women, and especially the beautiful ones.

Many of his wives were widows from the military campaigns, and two were daughters of his enemies. One— Aisha, who became his favorite wife—was betrothed to him at the age of six, and he consummated the marriage when she was nine years old and he was fifty-three. (This is a fact based on Muslim writings and not something made up by the enemies of Islam.) Three other of his wives were only seventeen, eighteen, and twenty when he married them. In addition, he had sexual relations with slave girls whom he owned.

One of Muhammad's cousins died, leaving his widow, Zainab. The Prophet subsequently gave her in marriage to Zaid Ibn Harisah, his freed slave and adopted son. But upon visiting Zaid's house in his absence, he cast his eyes on Zainab, who was ill clad, and was so smitten with her beauty that he exclaimed, "Praise belongeth unto Allah, who turneth the hearts of men even as He will." On the return of Zaid, his wife reported that she had made an impression on Muhammad, and so Zaid offered to divorce her in preference to his friend and benefactor. However, the relations of Arabs to their adopted children were so strict that nothing short of a divine revelation could settle the matter. So Muhammad (in the name of Allah and His apostle) produced the Qur'anic verses 33:36–38 in order to sanction his sinful desire.

But having that many wives and concubines had its problems. Muhammad, as just mentioned above, said a man could have four wives if he could afford them but was to treat them all *equally*. With all the booty that Muhammad got from his many raids and battles and the taxes he levied on people he subjected, he could afford the wives, but he didn't treat them equally. His harem became too numerous to be easily governed. The young Aisha was one of his favorite wives, but it seems that Mary the Copt became his favorite, and this caused quite a bit of jealousy.

To try to keep peace among his jealous wives, he hit upon the idea of casting lots among them to decide which one was to accompany him on a particular expedition. But the spirit of jealousy and rivalry grew very strong among the wives. Finally, there was a revolt. Hafsah was the head of the discontented. Muhammad resolved to leave his harem and threatened to divorce *all* of them, and even produced a "revelation" allowing him to do so. But eventually, they all submitted to Muhammad.

Unlike Jesus, Muhammad never healed anyone or performed any other kind of miracle, except the receiving of the supposedly divine revelations, which ultimately became the *Qur'an*. It is very obvious that his many revelations did not come from God, and the *Qur'an* is not a book that has come down from heaven, for Muhammad was able to get a revelation anytime he was in a situation that needed divine sanction to support his wishes, desires, and decisions.

I would like to mention here the famous "Night Journey," mentioned once in the *Qur'an* and elaborated on in the *Hadith*. Surah 17:1 merely says, "Glory to Him who did take His servant for a journey by night from the Sacred Mosque to the Farthest Mosque, whose precincts We did bless, in order that We might show him some of Our signs: for He is the one who hears and sees (*all things*)." The Prophet supposedly was awakened by Gabriel, who then mounted him on a Buraq (a half-mule, half-donkey with wings on its thighs). They went swiftly to the Temple Mount in Jerusalem and from there to heaven itself, Gabriel leading.

Upon entering the first heaven, Muhammad encounters Adam, who welcomes and praises him. At the gates of the second heaven, both John the Baptist and Jesus greet him. In the third heaven, Joseph greets him. Moses, in the sixth heaven, weeps and says, "I weep because after me there has been sent as a prophet this young man, whose followers will enter Paradise in greater numbers than my followers." And in the seventh heaven, he meets Abraham, who tests him by offering him cups of milk and wine. There he also receives a startling command: that the Muslims must pray "fifty times a day."

On his journey back to earth, Moses meets Muhammad and advises him, "Your followers cannot bear fifty prayers a day. I know—I have tested people before you. Go back to your Lord and ask Him for a reduction to lessen your followers' burdens." So Muhammad keeps traversing between the Lord and Moses until the number of daily prayers for the Muslims is reduced to only *five*. Whew!

Muhammad, at first, claimed that this experience was a bodily journey, but later, he retreated from this claim. His youngest wife, Aisha, explained, "The apostle's body remained where it was, but God removed his spirit by night."

On June 8, AD 632, only two and a half years after his conquest of Mecca, Muhammad died unexpectedly at the age of sixty-three.

Muhammad is described as being like a rocky desert with red pinnacles: he changed with the changing colors of the sky. His mind, filled with brilliant contradictions, moved helplessly from pole to pole, between asceticism and world conquest. He despised the world as "play, and idle talk, and pageantry," and at the same time, he was so much a creature of the world that his love for t, and the people in it (especially beautiful women) is manifest by his actions. He possessed none of the angelic qualities that we see in Jesus.

Muhammad died without having designated any successor (*khalifa*). As "the last and greatest of the prophets," he could not, of course, be replaced. But the community he had founded was a *theocracy*, making no distinction between church and state, and someone clearly must succeed him— to enforce the law, to lead in war, and to guide in peace: a caliph. And so we proceed to the next chapter.

3

The History of Islam after
the Death of Muhammad

AS YOU READ this study on the expansion of Islam, you need to remember that when Muslim armies conquered other countries, they gave the people only three choices: (1) Convert: become a Muslim; (2) Continue in the Christian or Jewish religion but become a *dhimmi*, an ignominious second-class citizen having restricted rights and being subject to oppressive taxation (*jizya* in Arabic) in perpetuity; and (3) Lose your life.

The *Qur'an* states in Surah 9:29, "Fight against those from among the People of the Scripture [Jews and Christians] who do not believe in Allah nor the Last Day; who do not forbid what Allah and His messenger have forbidden, and who do not adopt the religion of truth—until they pay the tribute out of hand, utterly subdued." Here is what was involved in the Jews and Christians being "utterly subdued."

They were known as infidels and had to promise that they would not renovate a church, synagogue, or monastery nor rebuild ones that were destroyed. They were not allowed to erect crosses on the outside of their churches or place them anywhere that Muslims could see them; nor could they ring church bells or raise their voices during prayer or while reciting the Torah or the Bible; nor could they make a public display during their funerals or feast days.

They had to feed for three days any Muslim who passed their home (including those engaged in war), they could not greet Muslims with the traditional Muslim greeting "Peace be with you" (*as-Salamu 'alaykum*), they had to stand up when a Muslim wished to sit in one's spot, they could not occupy the middle of the road when a Muslim was passing. They could not imitate Muslims in dress—like caps, turbans, sandals, etc.—or in their speech; nor could they have similar nicknames or the same names as Muslims. They had to wear a wide cloth girdle over all their garments, which had to be visible at all times.

They could not ride horses (mules were okay, on wooden saddles, but they had to ride them sidesaddle). They could not own a sword or arm themselves with any kind of weapon. They were not allowed to sell wine or liquor. They must shave their hair in front so as to make them easily identifiable. They could not incite anyone against the Muslims or strike a Muslim. They were not allowed to prevent any of their followers from embracing Islam but were strictly forbidden, on pain of death, from proselytizing any Muslim. If they violated any of these conditions, they no longer had any protection, which meant they could be killed (probably be beheaded) or sold into slavery at the discretion of the Muslim leader.

These laws largely governed relations between Muslims and non-Muslims in Islamic states for centuries until Western pressure—brought to bear on the weakened Ottoman Empire in the mid-nineteenth century—led to the emancipation of the *dhimmis*. But even though these regulations were relaxed or ignored for various periods of time, they still remain on the books, ready to be enforced again by any ruler having the desire to do so. There are present-day Muslims who are strongly urging that such practices be reinstituted, and if Islam ever became a dominant world religion, they would be enforced once again.

The First Four Caliphs: 632–661

Caliph is the term applied to the leaders who succeeded Muhammad. These men were vested with absolute authority in all matters of state, both civil and religious.

Abu Bakr (632–634)

After the death of Muhammad, it was immediately necessary to choose a successor to him. A contention arose between the people of Mecca and Medina as to the man who was to succeed Muhammad, since he died without leaving male issue. Ali, who was a cousin to Muhammad and was married to his daughter Fatima, laid claim to be the lawful successor of Muhammad on both grounds. The dispute was settled through the influence of Umar (Omar)—who later became the second caliph—in favor of Abu Bakr, who was one of the first converts to Islam and a most intimate confidant to Muhammad. He was also the father of Aisha, the favorite wife of Muhammad and the premier of his harem. She did not like Ali, and used her influence in favor of her father. So Abu Bakr was chosen, and most of the other "companions of the Prophet" agreed in selecting him. He reduced to submission all those who had contested his authority.

He believed that all true Muslims must fight till all people were of the true religion. He felt that to engage in a holy war was the most blessed of religious duties and conferred on those who engaged in it special merit, and side by side with it lay the bright prospects of spoil and females slaves, conquest, and glory. No wonder an immense army of greedy and fanatic Muslims gathered around his banner. He already knew how to carry out offensive warfare (*jihad*) because of his association with Muhammad prior to becoming his successor.

He achieved three main goals:

1. Though he ruled for only two years, he secured the Arabian Peninsula from chaotic revolt and firmly fixed its lasting Islamic heritage.

2. Under him, the first written version of the *Qur'an* was produced. Prior to this, it was mainly oral, preserved in the minds of Muhammad's followers, though some parts had been written on bones, perishable palm leaves, stones, etc., and kept in an unorganized manner. He gave orders to Muhammad's secretary Zayd ibn Thabit to collect as much material as possible, and the work of compiling the *Qur'an* continued slowly during the following years. To Zayd's carelessness and incompetence can be attributed the curious state of the *Qur'an*. Some of the revelations clearly received in Mecca are inserted haphazardly among revelations received in Medina.

3. His conquest fulfilled Muhammad's command: "No two religions are to exist in the Arabian Peninsula." Upon Muhammad's death, many tribes tried to desert the Muslim alliance, refusing to pay their *zakat* (taxes) and fulfill other Islamic duties. This rebellion

led to what is called the Battles of Riddah (apostasy). An apostate, to a Muslim, is anyone who renounces Islam. Abu Bakr, in obedience to Muhammad's command, took up the sword and killed those who were leaving Islam. The others soon got the message, which stopped a large exit from Islam. From that day till now, all non-Islamic places of worship and their symbols have been forbidden in the country of Saudi Arabia. Still today, in Muslim-dominated countries that are ruled by *shari'a* (Muslim law), the renouncing of Islam for another religion is a crime warranting capital punishment. This is not just a threat, for conversion to another religion usually means certain death. But in spite of the fact that many wanted to leave, there were others who joined the movement, inspired by the hope of booty. They announced their conversion only because they felt the need to identify themselves with the winning side.

Umar (634–644)

He took the title Commander of the Faithful, which was adopted also by the succeeding caliphs. He was made of sterner stuff. There was no aristocratic blood in him, but he behaved like an aristocrat. Calm, unyielding, demanding and receiving instant obedience, he sometimes gave way to ferocious bursts of anger. He was a revolutionary dictator, a man of inflexible will who rode roughshod over the wishes of his people, introduced harsh punishments, and placed the whole nation on a war footing.

With their Arabian base secure, Umar—whom Abu Bakr had designated as his successor—extended the Muslim Empire through the conquest of Syria (634), Mesopotamia (636), Egypt (639), and Persia (642). Jerusalem also submitted to Muslim control. Umar was assassinated while in his vigor when a Christian slave from Persia, who was enraged at being required to pay tribute, stabbed him just as he was starting to pray in the mosque at dawn.

Uthman (644–656)

Though an "early believer," he became a selfish ruler, concerned only with his own kin. He was an aristocrat, known in his youth for his love of elegant clothing, and was a member of the wealthy and powerful Umayyad clan. At its beginning, his reign was peaceful, but later, it was disrupted by many forces that he could not control, among them the Arabs' own fierce resistance to centralized rule. The immediate cause of his undoing, however, was his appointment of many of his relatives and friends to office. His greatest achievement was the standardization of the *Qur'an*. (In just a very short period of time, a number of different versions and variations of the *Qur'an* had evolved.) After his version was completed (in 30 AH, Muslim dating), he had all the other *Qur'ans* destroyed. His is the version used by Muslims today.

Discontent came to a head in Egypt when he replaced its capable governor with his own cousin. This caused much dissension. A handful of rebels eluded the guards posted at his gate and, climbing a back wall, gained entry to his house. Uthman was reading the *Qur'an* when the murderers broke in and "spilled his blood over the book he had served." In this case, a caliph was murdered by his fellow Muslims.

Ali (656–661)

The new caliph elected by the elders to replace Uthman was Ali. He was the son of Muhammad's uncle Abu Talib, who raised Muhammad, and was the husband of Muhammad's daughter Fatima, who bore him two sons, Hasan and Husayn. Ali had been among the very first Meccans to accept Muhammad's revelations. He was admired for his ability as a soldier. Many Shi'ite Muslims to this day believe that he should have been the first of the caliphs rather than the fourth because of his family ties with Muhammad.

From the beginning of his caliphate, Ali was faced with fervent opposition. Among his many enemies were two men who had unsuccessfully sought the caliphate and

Aisha, the influential widow of Muhammad. Ali was able to overcome this opposition. He decided to change his headquarters from Mecca, in central-west Saudi Arabia, to Kufa, in what today is southern Iraq, close to the head of the Persian Gulf—more central to his extensive empire than Mecca was.

One problem was solved, but soon, a more serious crisis developed in Syria. Upon becoming caliph, Ali had made enemies by replacing some of Uthman's relatives who held office; one of these was Mu'awiya, the powerful governor of Syria and a member of the Umayyad family, an influential Meccan clan. But Mu'awiya refused to step aside, and challenged Ali as caliph. There were some battles fought between these two, and so the matter was brought up for arbitration.

It was decided that both should step aside and a new caliph be named. Ali, however, would not accept this. After some more battles, in 661, Ali was assassinated by some of his enemies as he was entering the mosque—they plunged a dagger into him, killing him instantly. Since the assassination of Ali, Islam has been divided between Ali's followers, the Shi'ites (about 15 percent of the Muslims), and traditional Muslims—the Sunnis—who are the majority.

While Sunnis believe that Muhammad's friend and adviser Abu Bakr was the legitimate successor, Shi'ites believe that Ali, the Prophet's first cousin and son-in-law, was the rightful heir. They also believe that Muhammad's legitimate lineage ended with the "occultation"—disappearance—of Muhammad al-Mahdi around AD 874. This Twelfth Imam (however, some Shi'ites hold to five, seven, or twenty-one imams) is believed to have been hidden by God and is destined to return before the Last Judgment.

The Umayyad Caliphate: 661–750

It should be noted that the first century of Islam found Muslims possessors of a vast empire, including Persia, Mesopotamia, Syria, Egypt, and North Africa. The Muslims there lived a life of luxury, with concubines and slaves, such as was unknown by their ancestors. This new affluent lifestyle was supported by taxation of the conquered lands and booty from ongoing military campaigns.

After the assassination of Ali, Mu'awiya became caliph and established his capital at Damascus, Syria, because this is the land he knew best. However, Ali's dismayed followers then pledged their loyalty to his eldest son, Hasan, so there were now two caliphs. But after a few months, Hasan, who was weak and politically unambitious, surrendered his claim to the caliphate in return for an immense subsidy from Mu'awiya—who, at last, was generally recognized as caliph. After his resignation, Hasan was murdered.

However, in 680, when Mu'awiya died, the Shi'ites tried to make Ali's younger son, Husayn, the new caliph.

Accompanied by his family and a small group of supporters, Husayn set out from Medina for his father's former capital at Kufa, where he expected to be eagerly received as the new caliph. But on the way, he was stopped by troops of Mu'awiya's son Yazid, who had already succeeded to the caliphate (though he was an arrant drunkard),and who ordered Husayn to return; but his followers persuaded him to refuse.

Yazid's soldiers seized him and held him captive for ten days; then Umayyad troops killed him on October 10, AD 680, and sent his head to Yazid in Damascus. This slaying of the Prophet's grandson shocked all Islam and made still more enemies for the Umayyads. The death— or "martyrdom" of Husayn, as the Shi'ites view it—has had a significant effect on the Shi'ites down to this day. They fervently believe that Ali was the true successor to Muhammad. The Shi'ites also consider Ali and his successors infallible teachers who were endowed with "the divine gift of impeccability."

Even to this day, each year, the Shi'ites commemorate the martyrdom of Husayn, whose shrine is in Karbala, Iraq. They have processions in which some cut their bodies with knives and swords and otherwise inflict suffering upon themselves. (You've likely seen pictures of this on TV.)

When this internal strife subsided, Islam gained a larger vision: conquest of the known world. By 732, the goal seemed within reach. Their expansion swallowed up Tunisia in North Africa (670), Kabul in modern Afghanistan (670), the Mediterranean island of Rhodes (672), the region around besieged Constantinople (677), Algeria (700), Spain (711), the Chinese-Turkestan border region (715), and Morocco (722).

By the end of the first century from its origin, Islam stretched all the way from the western border of China to the southern border of France. North Africa, once largely Christian, was completely dominated by its adherents. The seemingly unstoppable expansion of the Muslim empire was finally terminated at Tours, in central France, in 732 by Charles Martel and his brave soldiers, who saved Europe. The importance of this crucial victory cannot be exaggerated. If France had lost and been occupied, then Italy, the center of western Christianity, would have been the next easy prey.

Islam's wealth and conquests grew virtually unhindered. In 691, the Dome of the Rock mosque was built in Jerusalem on the Jewish Temple Mount to demonstrate the superiority of Islam over Judaism.

But all was not peaceful. The tribal wars that Muhammad had long tried to abolish among the Bedouin tribes once more erupted. But now, instead of fighting in small groups, they merged into two large factions, one Bedouin group claiming ancestry from northern Arabia and the other from its south.

While the Umayyads were occupied with these difficulties, there appeared a new revolutionary force that, in the end, overthrew them. This was the Abbasid party, headed by a ruthless Muslim named Abbas, a descendant of an uncle of Muhammad. The center of the Abbasid movement was in Persia, where there was much ill feeling against the Umayyads. The Persians considered themselves heirs to a higher culture than those proud Arab conquerors who treated them as inferiors. But Abbas won the support not only of the Persians; many Arab Muslims also, who had grievances against the Umayyads, joined his cause.

In June 747, the Abbasids revolted and subsequently overthrew the Umayyad governor in Persia and took power. They then moved west, defeating the Umayyad armies that opposed them. In 749, Abbas was acclaimed caliph by his followers, although the Umayyads still held Syria. The following year, his troops met those of Marwan II, the Umayyad caliph, and defeated him. The deposed Marwan II fled to Egypt but was caught there and killed, and his head was sent to the new caliph as a present. Abbas, the new ruler of Islam, began wiping out the rest of the Umayyads. He made Hashimiya, which was near Kufa in southern Iraq, his capital.

And this bloody history continues on and on.

Before I go further into the expansion and the history of Islam, I would like to present some informative general facts about the Muslim rulers (caliphs), which show that most of them were more interested in living in luxury and power than in simply promoting the religion of Islam. They left the study of Islamic theology mostly to the scholars. (This is not a charge made by non-Muslims. Arab chroniclers delight in describing the private lives of their rulers, and so we know the number of their mistresses, their behavior during drinking parties, and what went on in their private sitting rooms.)

One caliph was drunk every day.

Still another one, Abd al-Malik, enjoyed beheading people and having the heads brought to him for display. On his deathbed, he is reported to have told his son Walid, "When I am dead, put on your leopard skin, gird yourself with your sword, and cut off the head of everyone who gets in your way"!

Walid's successor was his younger brother Sulayman, whose chief interest was in luxury and the gratification of one's sensual appetites. He had a passion for soft silks, which he wore on all occasions, and demanded that he be buried in them.

Of all the many caliphs, it is said that there was only a small group of four who could be ranked as "righteous."

Some came to power with obvious talents but were immediately corrupted by power.

Some of the caliphs were just children.

One was even an atheist.

On the positive side, poets were highly respected, having access to the courts—and some were very influential.

One of the Spanish caliphs had a whole new city built on three terraces, with gardens at the bottom and the houses of the court in the middle. His palace had four hundred rooms and apartments, standing high above all the other buildings. The throne room's roof and walls were of marble and gold.

However, for the most part, the rulers were incompetent and incapable of understanding the roles they were required to play as religious leaders, but they clearly understood the art of war—not only against non-Muslim nations but also among themselves. At one time, three rival dynasties of caliphs existed simultaneously: the Abbasids in Baghdad (750–1258), the Umayyads at Cordoba in Spain (756–1031), and the Fatimids in Egypt (969–1171).

The Abbasid Caliphate (750–1258): The Golden Age of Islam

The Abbasid dynasty lasted for five hundred years years. Abbas was succeeded by his brother Mansur in 754. He founded a new capital, Baghdad, which was just a little north of the previous capital, in 762. This proved to be an ideal capital as it lay on the west bank of the Tigris River.

The Umayyads were accessible to the people, but the Abbasids ruled more like monarchs and surrounded themselves with many officials who needed to be bribed before a hearing could be arranged. They included some of the most tyrannical leaders the world has known.

Baghdad flourished in wealth and scientific learning and was a gateway for commerce and culture. Inventions made there include the clock pendulum and algebra. Baghdad had an unmatched library that housed the writings of Aristotle and Plato. Literature was enhanced as Muslims learned the art of papermaking from the Chinese.

In medicine, Muslims were the first to use anesthesia in surgery, the first to discover that epidemics spread through contact and by air, and the first to develop an ambulatory hospital (carried around on a camel's back). However, this prosperity was short-lived, and the unity of the Islamic empire began to crumble as Persia, Spain, Morocco, Tunisia, and Egypt all broke away from the Abbasids.

In 833, Mu'tasim became caliph and had himself guarded by Turkish slaves because he did not trust the Persian ones. In 836, he moved his capital to Samarra, slightly north of Baghdad. But in 892, it was abandoned, and Baghdad once again became the capital. In 1219, the

Mongol forces of Genghis Khan invaded Islamic territory from Central Asia, and by 1221, they reached Persia. Six years later, Genghis died, but the Mongol hordes under his grandson Hulagu swept onward, destroying everything in their path. In 1258, they laid siege to Baghdad and took it almost without a fight, ending the Abbasid rule.

As mentioned earlier, a number of regions broke from Abbasid rule and became independent Islamic states. Morocco became independent in 788, and in 799, Tunisia followed suit. In 910 the Fatimids, Shi'ites, seized a portion of North Africa and reigned as caliphs. The Fatimids conquered Egypt in 969 and built Cairo, making it their capital. It soon became the center of Islamic thought. The oldest Islamic theological seminary, the University of Al Azhar, with its Splendid Mosque, was founded in 969, the same year Cairo was built; Cairo remains the intellectual center of Islam today.

Islam after 1258

It was not the sword but Islam itself that ultimately defeated the Mongols. Many of the Mongol warriors converted to Islam, and in 1295, Ghazan Khan, the Mongol ruler of Persia, himself became a Muslim.

In 1453, the Ottoman Turks took Constantinople from the Byzantines and renamed it Istanbul. For a while, the Ottoman Empire stretched northward from Baghdad to the borders of Hungary and Poland, southward to the tip of the Arabian Peninsula, and westward to Morocco. Jerusalem, Mecca, Cairo, Tunis, Athens, and Belgrade were all under Turkish control.

The ancient "silk routes" to China all passed through Ottoman territory, adding to the region's strategic importance. However, in 1497, the Portuguese explorer Vasco da Gama sailed south, around Africa's Cape of Good Hope, and on to India. This opened up a new trade route to the East, bypassing the Islamic centers of population.

In 1529, and again in 1683, the Muslim Turks besieged and attempted to capture Vienna, but both times, their forces were repulsed. The latter calamitous defeat marked a turning point in the fortunes of the Ottoman Empire.

All this time, the Ottomans were notorious for their cruelty. A comparatively recent example is the genocide committed from 1877 to 1922 against a segment of their population, the Armenians, who were Christians.

All this contributed to the steady decline of the Ottoman stranglehold on the Middle East.

At the other end of the Mediterranean, the Moorish Empire in Spain was also evaporating. In 1492, Granada finally fell. Ferdinand and Isabella then burned the Muslim libraries and expelled both Muslims and Jews.

During the following three centuries, great advancements were being made in science, education, and economics in much of Europe. The monarchs of Great Britain, Spain, Holland, Portugal, and France were steadily expanding their navies. They built many ships for the rough Atlantic Ocean while the Ottomans were building only a few ships, and for the calmer Mediterranean Sea. So the European nations were able to ignore Turkey, and they began to establish colonies in a number of the Muslim regions. From here on, it was decline for all the Islamic nations.

However, by 1583, Islam had reached eastward to the Philippines, Malaysia, and Indonesia.

Islam had slowly died. Even though the *muezzins* still cried from the minarets that Muhammad was the Prophet of the One God, Islam had lost its savor. There was no vigor, no religious feeling, only the interminable and empty recitation of the *Qur'an*. The great thinkers of the past were no longer read; their books were gathering dust in the libraries. The Ottoman rulers had failed to fertilize the Arab genius of their citizens. The sun had gone down, and there seemed no hope of a dawn.

Islam and its followers seemed incapable of dealing with the problems of the modern age. Their roots were locked in the events of the seventh century on the Arabian Peninsula. The vast forces in the service of the Western powers baffled them.

Napoleon occupied Egypt in 1798.

The British occupied Egypt, and the French took Tunisia, in 1881.

In 1908, young Turks revolted and created parliamentary rule in Turkey.

The years 1914–1918—these were the pivotal years. The Ottoman rulers made a fatal miscalculation by throwing in their lot with the German Empire under Kaiser Wilhelm.

Modern Times: From 1918 to the Present

After World War I, the Ottoman Empire was broken up. In Europe, six independent nations were formed in the Balkans, and the Asian portion of the realm was parceled out as either European protectorates or "spheres of influence." Since the end of World War II, however, most Muslim societies (of which there are forty-nine) have evolved into independent nations or portions thereof.

A small number of these Muslim countries—such as Turkey, Pakistan, and Indonesia—presently have regimes that can claim some features of democracy. (Even this is in flux.) But the majority of the new governments are overwhelmingly nondemocratic: monarchies, one-party systems, military regimes, personal dictatorships, or some combintation of these—usually resting on a limited family, clan, or tribal base. A few are highly dependent on foreign support, like Egypt and Pakistan. And most are repressive, corrupt, divorced from the needs and aspirations of their people. In many of them, strict Islam is becoming stronger.

The real turning point for Islam came in the mid-1970s with the oil embargo and in 1979, when the Iranian revolution occurred. Muslim rulers gleefully discovered that they had real power over the world as they began to come into great wealth; they could bring the rest of the world to its knees because of their large oil resources. However, this wealth was not passed on to the average citizen. For instance, the wealth in Saudi Arabia was largely divided between the king and his sons; some was spent on private airplanes for the Saudi princes. Millions of dollars more were spent on building ornate palaces, fitted with modern air-conditioning. But the social fabric of the state has remained unchanged; the wandering tribesmen are only mildly richer than they were before. Much of this excess wealth, especially from Saudi Arabia, has been used also for the spread of Islam all over the world, which includes jihad.

The desire of the Muslims to get rid of the State of Israel has become a broadly unifying aim of the Islamic nations. Down through the history of Islam, Muslims have had problems living peaceably with their non-Muslim neighbors. but never so glaringly as now, with the "Zionist" entity "encroaching" on them.

The twentieth century saw the creation of many new Islamic "revivalist" movements. Groups such as the Muslim

Brotherhood in Egypt and Jamaat-e-Islami in Pakistan advocate a totalistic and theocratic alternative to secular political ideologies. Sometimes called Islamist, they see Western cultural values as a threat, and hence, they promote Islam as a comprehensive solution to every public and private question of importance. In countries like Iran and Afghanistan (under the Taliban), revolutionary movements replaced secular regimes with Islamist regimes, while transnational groups like Osama bin Laden's al-Qaeda engage in terrorism to further their goals.

Islam has, from the very beginning, been a religion of the sword and has glorified military virtues. It originated among "warring Bedouin nomadic tribes," and this violent origin is stamped in the foundation of Islam. Muhammad himself is remembered as a hard fighter and a skillful military commander. Thus, one of the major problems of the countries where the Muslims are in the majority and are governed under Islamic law is that the *Qur'an* and the *Hadith* have locked the citizens into the seventh-century Arabian-desert style of thinking and governing.

The Nation of Islam

Before I close this chapter, I want to mention something about "the Nation of Islam" (NOI), sometimes wrongly referred to as "the Black Muslims." This movement began here in America among the African Americans. A sense of oppression is deeply woven into the fabric of many blacks here in America, a circumstance that goes all the way back to the time of slavery. It is alleged by the NOI that many of the slaves were Muslims before being shipped from Africa, and that though a few maintained their Islamic beliefs and rituals, most were "corrupted" here by their Christian masters. And so African Islam withered here in America. (Even though Portuguese Christians captured Muslims and sold them as slaves, the Muslims themselves also sold their fellow Muslims into slavery.)

At the turn of the twentieth century, when Muslims were just beginning to migrate to the United States, they discovered a receptive audience among many of these former American slaves and their descendants. A number of the Negroes came to see Islam as their original and true religion. The Islamic faith became a means of expressing an independent black identity in a mainly white society. Their beliefs were not purely Islamic but seem to be drawn from both the *Qur'an* and the Bible. (Today, some of them prefer to call themselves "reverts" to Islam, rather than converts.)

Previously, there had been several small movements of this sort, but the Nation of Islam is a sect founded on July 4, 1930, in the black slums of Detroit, Michigan, by a man called Wallace Fard ("religious duty") Muhammad (1877–1934), of which very little is known. The NOI took the self-proclaimed goal of revitalizing the spiritual, mental, social, and economic condition of the black men and women of America. "Master" Fard claimed to be the Messiah of Christianity and the Mahdi of Islam (a coming world leader in Islamic eschatology). Many of his followers believed that he was Allah in person! His goal was to establish a new world order of peace and righteousness on the foundation of truth and justice, to put down tyrants, and to change the world into a heaven on earth.

The way he intended to do this was to restore and to resurrect the lost-and-found people whom he asserted were the "original members of the Tribe of Shabazz from the Lost Nation of Asia." He maintained that these lost people of African descent had been captured, exploited, and dehumanized to serve as slaves in America for over three centuries. He taught that the blacks were systematically denied knowledge of their past history, language, culture, and religion and, as a result, had lost control of their lives.

Fard's mission was to teach those downtrodden and defenseless black people a thorough knowledge of God and of themselves, thereby putting them on the path to self-independence with "a superior culture and higher civilization" than they had previously experienced. To do so, he mixed Islamic principles with predictions of an apocalyptic resurgence of the black race. He even asserted that black people's experience of slavery was the fulfillment of the Bible prophecy given to Abram in Genesis 15:13.

Of course, Fard never mentioned that Muhammad owned black slaves and that Islam has maintained slavery up to this present time. Or that Muslims treated their slaves differently—they castrated the men, who were not allowed to marry and have families; and Muslim slave owners were permitted to have sex with the women.

Elijah Muhammad (1897–1975)—born as Robert Poole, the son of Georgia slaves—who had only a fourth-grade education, came under the influence of Wallace Fard Muhammad. When Fard disappeared mysteriously in 1934, Elijah Muhammad assumed leadership of the group, first in Detroit and then in Chicago. Elijah, who was physically frail but a compelling figure, portrayed Fard as an incarnation of Allah and himself as Allah's chosen Messenger. Of course, this claim was in stark opposition to the entire theological foundation of orthodox Islam: that God has never taken on human form (denying that Jesus is the Son of God) and that the original Muhammad was the *last* of the messengers of God.

Elijah Muhammad wore neatly tailored suits, bow ties, and a Turkish-style fez (a brimless cone-shaped flat-crowned hat) decorated with stars and crescent moons. He connected with hundreds of thousand of poor and working-class urban blacks by attributing their woes to white racism and prescribing self-reliance as the best response.

As for the beliefs and theology of the Nation of Islam, it declared that there is no true God but Allah but (as just mentioned) that Allah had come to earth in the person of Wallace Fard Muhammad. Elijah claimed he revealed a great truth, wisdom that would free this old world of Satan's dominion. The NOI further taught that the earth and moon were once alike, that the earth is over seventy-six trillion years old, and that its entire landmass is properly called Asia. It also taught that not only is the black man the original man but also that the black race created the heavens and the earth—and themselves! From the primal black man have come all brown, yellow, red, and white people. By using a special method of birth control, the black race was able to produce the white race.

And here is another strange one: Elijah said that Moses used dynamite with a fuse to kill three hundred of his followers. (But dynamite was not invented until 1860.) He maintained also that the mountains were created by bombs dropped from a spaceship circling the earth. He further asserted that the mouths of black Christian preachers are controlled by devils and hence are a great hindrance to the truth. And he strongly denied that Jesus was the Son of God.

The NOI had a do-it-yourself philosophy that resulted in their owning and operating hundreds of businesses nationwide, including food-industry services, bakeries, restaurants, and a large amount of farmland in Georgia. This gave jobs to thousands of people.

To their credit, the Nation of Islam worked to clean up drug addicts, reform prostitutes, and keep black youths out of gangs. It helped many newly released ex-convicts make a new start and stay out of jail.

Muhammad Ali, the boxer, was a member of the NOI for a while but then left and became a Sunni Muslim.

Elijah Muhammad's most talented and influential aide was the well-known fiery Malcolm X. He preached that black people are genetically superior to white people but have been dominated by a system of white supremacy. However, tension between Elijah Muhammad and Malcolm X developed. In 1964, Malcolm X left the NOI and founded Muslim Mosque Inc. Elijah called him a traitor, who should be killed. In 1965, at the age of thirty-nine, Malcolm X was assassinated by three black men, possibly Elijah Muhammad's followers.

In 1975, the Nation of Islam was shaken by news that Elijah Muhammad had died at the age of seventy-seven. His son, Wallace D. Muhammad (later Warith Deen Muhammad), took over after his father's death. He was very unassuming and vastly different from his father. He exhorted African American Muslims to reject racial separatism and learn the *Qur'an*. He preached a far less inflammatory version of Islam. He aligned the organization with the international Islamic community, moving toward Sunni Islamic practices. He ultimately disbanded the Nation of Islam and started a new movement that he initially called the World Community of Islam in the West. Later, it was called the American Society of Muslims. He stepped down as its leader in 2003.

Back in 1977, a group of Black Muslims, led by Louis Farrakhan, split off from the organization, disillusioned by the new leader's integrationist ideals and lack of allegiance to his father's brand of Islam. Farrakhan revived the old Nation of Islam, kept its base in Chicago, and sought to follow in the footsteps of Elijah Muhammad.

He described the white people as potential humans who haven't evolved yet. He seemed to be able, however, to appeal to more than just the blacks. This aroused the attention of the media and helped him cultivate a reputation in the 1980s and 1990s as *the* spokesman for African American Muslims and also spiritual heir to Malcolm X. Most people remember him for the Million-Man March held in Washington, DC, on October 16, 1995.

But in the late 1990s, the NOI began to embrace some traditional Islamic practices, so in 2000, Farrakhan and Wallace D. Muhammad publicly declared an end to the rivalry between their groups. Because of illness and his eliminating the cultish quirks of the Nation of Islam, Farrakhan's standing as a religious guide began to fade. His group has greatly shrunk in influence and size.

Even though the Nation of Islam was a mixture of some Christian (not biblical) and Islamic teachings, several of the Islamic nations helped this organization financially and did not put a lot of pressure on it to become more Islamic. Some who were in this movement in America were given scholarships by Saudi Arabia to study Islam in Egypt and other countries. This caused them to come under the influence of orthodox Islam. Then in the 1970s and 1980s, more and more Muslims immigrated to the USA, and Muslim students poured into American universities. Mosques began to spring up all over America. Pressure was put on the deviant American Muslims, and they have gradually amalgamated into the mainstream of Islam.

Demographics

Approximately 85 percent of Muslims are Sunni and 15 percent are Shi'a, with a small minority belonging to other sects.

The World's Main Religions by Number

Buddhist	500,000,000
Chinese folk religions	437,000,000
Christian (all groups)	2,300,000,000
Roman Catholic	1,200,000,000
Hindu	1,000,000,000
Jews	15,000,000
Muslim	1,500,000,000

Top 20 Countries with the Largest Muslim Population (2012)

1.	Indonesia	209,120,000	87.2%
2.	India	176,190,000	14.4
3.	Pakistan	167,410,000	96.4
4.	Bangladesh	133,540,000	89.9
5.	Nigeria	77,300,000	48.8
6.	Egypt	76,990,000	94.9
7.	Iran	73,570,000	99.0+
8.	Turkey	71,330,000	98.0
9.	Algeria	34,730,000	97.9
10.	Morocco	31,940,000	99.0+
11.	Iraq	31,340,000	99.0

12.	Afghanistan	31,330,000	99.0+
13.	Sudan	30,490,000	90.7
14.	Ethiopia	28,680,000	34.6
15.	Uzbekistan	26,550,000	96.7
16.	Saudi Arabia	25,520,000	93.0
17.	China	24,690,000	1.8
18.	Yemen	23,830,000	99.0+
19.	Syria	18,930,000	92.8
20.	Malaysia	18,100,000	63.7

4

What Is the Qur'an?

MOST MUSLIMS HOLD the *Qur'an* to be the eternal, uncreated, infallible, and unalterable Word of God, inscribed on a preserved tablet in heaven and mediated by inspiration through the angel Gabriel to Muhammad. It is "a faithful record of the exact words revealed to him." (However, the *Qur'an* itself never identifies the agent through whom Allah revealed His will to the Prophet. Muslims only *speculate* when they say it was the angel Gabriel.)

As written, recited, or preserved in the hearts of believers, the *Qur'an* is finite and temporal. Viewed this way, the *Qur'an* has two natures and, in this sense, is analogous to the Christian two-nature concept of Jesus Christ. For Muslims, the eternal Word of God became "enbooked"; for Christians, the eternal Word of God has become "enfleshed."

Unlike the Bible, the *Qur'an* is not designed to reveal God per se but rather to set forth His commands for His creatures. Islam maintains that the *Qur'an* is the final revelation from God, declaring that it "perfects and fulfills all previous divine revelations."

Each claimed revelation given by Allah to Muhammad was first dictated to his companions, who would then memorize it, and in due time, the utterances were combined with others and then written down by scribes. The *Qur'an* is divided into 114 chapters known as *surahs*. These are not arranged in any sensible order, either as to content or as to when they were received but are placed simply according to the length of the chapter. Except for the initial chapter, "The Opening," the longest chapter (286 verses) is found at the beginning and the shortest at the end (6 verses). There is no continuity of plot or history within; it is often repetitious and is very difficult to read.

A large portion of the *Qur'an* was taken from the Bible. Probably the largest amount of borrowed material found in the *Qur'an* was taken from the Old Testament Talmud, the Law. As stated before, there were many Jewish people living in the area from which Muhammad could have learned these things. There were Jews in Mecca. After leaving, Muhammad went to the town of Medina, which was founded by the Jews. There were three large Jewish settlements living in the area of Medina. In the Qur'an, there are recorded conversations that Muhammad had with Jewish leaders. The *Qur'an* mentions creation, Abraham, Joseph, Moses in Egypt in detail, and the giving of the Law; many of the details have been changed, but the source is recognizable.

Among the Jewish people, beside the Torah, they had built up a lot of mythological writings known as the Midrash, which means "hidden truths, not found on the surface." At first, this was passed on by oral tradition. However, it was in script form by Muhammad's time, and he took advantage of it. Strangely, a lot of this unbiblical material is found in the *Qur'an*! Much of this has been changed slightly, but some is taken word for word, and it is easily recognizable as to where it came from.

Muhammad knew about David and the Psalms and mentioned a few of the prophets.

Since Muhammad had traveled to countries where there were Christians and there were Christians in the area of Mecca—along with the fact that his first wife, Khadijah, was a Nestorian Christian—there was ample opportunity for him to learn about Christianity. He was rather familiar with the Gospels, speaking a lot about Jesus and His miracles. Muhammad never accepted Him as the Son of God.

Once again, many of the facts from the Bible found in the *Qur'an* have been changed and twisted. There were a number of false Christian cults in the area and, thus, much false teaching and traditions about Christ and Christianity that had been passed around. Strangely enough, a lot of material found in these false traditions and writings found their way into the *Qur'an* but, as usual, were slightly changed, but the source is recognized. The false teaching that Jesus spoke in the cradle, that Jesus made birds out of clay, etc., found in the *Qur'an* are found in the false traditions.

He doesn't seem to have been familiar with the Epistles, but take note that he was familiar with the book of Revelation, because there are many facts found in this book that are included in Islam.

There is also a lot of material included in the *Qur'an* found in the other religious groups in existence at that time like the Sabeans, Zoroastrianism, and Hinduism. The Muslims practice of praying five times a day—at first toward Jerusalem—fasting, the pilgrimage, etc., were all taken from other religions. However, some of the pagan practices by the Arabs in the area were carried on into Islam, like kissing the Black Stone in the Ka'ba. There doesn't seem to be any religious teachings that are really new and found only in Islam and the *Quran*. (All these stated facts are documented in detail in the book *The Origins of the Koran: Classic Essays on Islam's Holy Book* edited by Ibn Warraq, in 1998 and published by Prometheus Books, Amherst, New York.)

Muslims, however, claim that the *Qur'an* is the final revealed Word of God, so it is the prime source of every

Muslim's faith and practice. Christianity teaches that "in the beginning was the Word…and the Word became flesh [Jesus Christ]," but for Islam, "in the beginning was the Word and the Word became a Book"!

The *Qur'an* was not designed for the average person to understand but has to be interpreted by a group of "scholars." Muslims teach that the *Qur'an* can only be understood properly in its original Arabic language and that a translation into any other language is insufficient to portray the true meaning.

The *Qur'an* is held in the greatest esteem and reverence among Muslims as their holy Scripture. Every surah in the *Qur'an* is prefaced by the words "In the name of Allah, the Compassionate, the Merciful." Because it is a sacred book, Muslims will never underline a word or write in a *Qur'an*, or set another object upon it. They dare not touch it without first being washed and purified. They read it with the greatest care and respect, never holding it below their waist. They swear by it and consult it on all occasions. They carry it with them to war, write sentences of it on their banners, suspend verses from it from their necks as a charm, and always place it on the highest shelf or in some place of honor in their house. It is said that the devil runs away from the house in which a portion of the *Qur'an* is found. The absolute confidence in the miraculousness of the *Qur'an* has remained unshaken among Muslims to this day.

I was given a book on *The Noble Qur'an* by a Muslim, which I think provides a clear and honest evaluation of the book. The following is the gist of what it states.

Uniqueness of the *Qur'an*

It is unlike conventional books in that it does not contain information, ideas, and arguments about specific themes arranged in a particular literary order. A stranger to the *Qur'an* is baffled at the beginning because he does not find the enunciation of its themes, its division into chapters and sections, a separate treatment of varied topics, or separate instructions for different aspects of life arranged in serial order. Conversely, there is an obscurity because it does not conform to the conception of a "book." Subjects are repeated in different ways, and one topic follows another without any apparent connection.

Intermittently, a new topic emerges in the middle of another, following no obvious structure. The speaker, the receiver, and the direction of the address may change without any prior notice. There are no signs of chapters or divisions, and historical events are presented unlike those in ordinary history books. The *Qur'an* follows its own method of solving cultural, political, social, and economic problems.

All the subjects are blended together. The unwary reader begins to imagine that the *Qur'an* is a book without any order or interconnection between its verses and the continuity of its subjects. He feels that the book handles miscellaneous topics in an incoherent manner. This is because the reader has approached the *Qur'an* with common literary notions; he is puzzled by its style and presentation. Consequently, the ordinary reader is unable to benefit fully from the treasures contained in the *Qur'an*, though occasionally he may succeed in discovering a few gems here and there.

After reading the *Qur'an*, I would fully agree with this Muslim's evaluation of it. The following paragraphs are equally revealing.

Central Theme

The subject of the book is man: it discusses those aspects of a person's life that lead either to real success or failure.

The central theme is the exposition of the reality and the invitation toward the Right Way based upon it.

The aim and object of the book is to invite man to the Right Way and to present clearly the guidance that man has lost because of his negligence, perversion, and wickedness. (In other words, man is basically good but has gone astray and needs help in going back to this "goodness." This supposition is contrary to the theme of the Bible, for *it* teaches that each person is born with a fallen, sinful nature;

willfully sins; is a slave to sin; and can be freed only by the power of the Lord Jesus Christ—because of the blood that He shed upon the cross.) As the aim of the *Qur'an* is to guide man and not to teach the study of nature, history, philosophy, or any science or art, it does not concern itself with these subjects. Its purpose is to warn mankind of the consequences of a wrong attitude.

Background

One cannot adequately understand many of the topics discussed in the *Qur'an* unless one is acquainted with the background conditions at the time of its revelation. One needs to know the social and historical antecedents that help to explain each topic. Accordingly, the *Qur'an* is a jumble of topics that reveal the intrinsic nature of the Islamic movement at different stages of its development. (How true!)

Meccan Chapters

Muhammad started his ministry in the town of Mecca, so early portions of the *Qur'an* relate to the situation there and give brief answers to the common inquiries that had misled those people into adopting the wrong ways of life. The people of Mecca were invited to abide by basic principles of morality and to accept the attitude that by itself would lead to the success and welfare of all humanity. The material written in Mecca hence pertained to its own history, traditions, monuments, beliefs, morality, and evil ways.

Medinan Chapters

After thirteen years of minor success in Mecca, Muhammad was forced out of that town and went to Medina. There, the movement entered its second stage, under totally changed conditions. He and his small community (the *ummah*) now succeeded in establishing the Islamic State.

While in Mecca, Muhammad was attempting to gain the acceptance of the local Christians and Jews for his movement, so his revelations were amicable and positive toward them. But once he went to Medina, Muhammad came into conflict with the Jews and Christians because of his Islamic State, so a different attitude pervades the Medinan chapters when they speak of the Jews and Christians.

Now that Muhammad had political power in Medina, with an army behind him, he was in a position to extend his message of reform to the non-Muslim world—and if this could not be accomplished peacefully, then Muhammad would use force.

During this Medinan period, the revelations of Muhammad began to change. When he faced a new situation, he would receive a revelation for that specific problem. Thus, some of the proclamations were fiery rhetoric, the language of a warrior. Other verses were in the form of royal edicts from the Lawgiver. Some verses adopted the method of a teacher, trainer, and reformer, espousing the principles and methods for organizing a community, building a state, and constructing a civilization to conduct the different affairs of life. The discourses gave the people instructions for their guidance, warned them of their weaknesses, and then exhorted them to sacrifice with their lives and properties in the way of Allah. Muhammad taught the people the lessons he felt they needed in defeat and victory, adversity and prosperity, and war and peace. The Medinan style is much different from that of the Meccan period.

Style

The different portions of the *Qur'an* are written according to the requirements of the various phases of the movement. The various portions of the *Qur'an* were not intended to be published in the form of pamphlets at the time of their being presented but were to be delivered as addresses. Thus, it is very obvious that the *Qur'an* is not in the style of a written work. Muhammad appealed to the people's emotions and feelings. (This explains why the same things are often repeated over and over.) Everywhere, there is confusion: inconsistencies, improvisations, passages where the meaning seems to be deliberately obscured, and others where the sentences are left in midair. There are interminable passages of full dialogue in which God relates His own speech and then tiresome replies. Scraps of myth and legend are introduced but then abandoned before their relevance has become clear.

Order

The *Qur'an*, with the exception of the first chapter, is mostly arranged in order of the length of the chapters, The longest chapter is chapter 2, then each succeeding chapter is shorter, and the shortest one is at the very end. It is not alleged that Muhammad recited the *Qur'an* in the above-mentioned order, but the arrangement was made when it was written down.

Compilation

When Muhammad received these revelations, they were sometimes recorded on leaves of date palm, bark of trees, bones, etc. These were then placed into a bag. Many of his hearers, however, had committed portions the *Qur'an* to memory. It was never complied in book form during the lifetime of the Prophet. So the original *Qur'an* was largely in the mind of Muhammad and some of his followers.

WILBUR LINGLE WITH ROBERT DELANCY

After his death, Muslims fought quite a number of wars, and many of the Muslim men who had memorized the *Qur'an* were being killed, especially after the battle of Yamamah in AD 633. It was obvious that to depend exclusively upon those who had learned the *Qur'an* by heart was not wise, so it was decided to put it in writing.

Abu Bakr, who became the leader after the death of Muhammad, was persuaded to take this task upon himself. Zayd, one of the Prophet's most trusted secretaries, was appointed by Abu Bakr to aid him in this task. Arrangements were made to collect and gather together all the pieces of the *Qur'an* that were in the possession of his companions, both written and memorized. The resultant authenticated copy of the *Qur'an* was kept in the house of Hafsa, Umar's daughter and one of the wives of the Prophet. (Note carefully this last sentence.)

But at this point, the story of the *Qur'an* takes some strange twists and turns. The third caliph, Uthman, who took over just twelve years after the death of Muhammad in AH 22 (AD 644), in due time had yet *another* "authenticated" copy made and gave orders that all the copies of the *Qur'an* in the provincial libraries should be publicly burned. As Islam spread, so the story goes, it had come into contact with Arabs speaking different dialects, and so copyists were making alterations of the text.

However, when Uthman was making his revision, he took possession of one of the original copies of the *Qur'an* that had been entrusted for safekeeping to *Hafsa*, one of Muhammad's widows—and this copy also was burned! There was no possible way that this original copy in the custody of such a loyal follower of Muhammad could have been altered! Is it not obvious that the *Qur'an* compiled right after the death of Muhammad was the most authentic? So why was it destroyed, along with the supposedly altered copies? Why was the first edition not made the "official" one? If Uthman was not tampering with the text, there was absolutely no reason for him to destroy the original text! In fact, Abdallah ibn-Masud, Muhammad's secretary, announced publicly that this canonical version of the *Qur'an*, as revised by Uthman, was a monstrous falsification.

Shi'ites claim that Muhammad had taught that the continuing leadership should fall to someone in the family, but these passages, it seems, were removed from the *Qur'an* by Uthman in order to continue the practice of leadership choice by consensus, as had occurred after the death of the Prophet. Shi'ites allege that Ali, who was a cousin of Muhammad and was married to his daughter Fatima, was wrongly overlooked. (This is one of the major reasons for the schism between the Shi'ites and Sunnis.)

However, a Sunni Muslim made the following statement, which I think is very revealing: "There is clear and irrefutable proof that the *Qur'an*, which is in use today, is the very same *Qur'an* which was presented to the world by Muhammad. A skeptic may entertain a doubt about its being a revelation from Allah, but none can have any doubt whatsoever regarding its authenticity, purity, and immunity from any and every kind of addition, omission, or alteration."

This is indeed a puzzling statement. Where is the proof? The original *Qur'an* existed only in the mind of Muhammad. Thus, there is no original *Qur'an*, since Muhammad is dead. Since it is claimed that Muhammad could not read or write, then he obviously had to dictate the contents to someone. As stated above, even when his words were written down, it was on different materials—some perishable—and these were not kept in an organized form. How are we to know that everything Muhammad had memorized (or formulated as he went along, when he faced new situations) was written down, and how do we know that it was recorded accurately? Also, if no confusion existed in the early days, then why was the so-called authenticated copy that Abu Bakr originally compiled destroyed by Uthman just a few years later?

Another Muslim sent me a long article on the formation of the *Qur'an*. That article concludes that all we can be sure of is that the copy of the *Qur'an* made by Uthman is still being used today, but we have no assurance that everything Muhammad taught, and his followers memorized, was completely recorded along with the various parts that were written down.

But here an even more important question. Even if the present *Qur'an* is a perfect word-for-word copy of the original as given by Muhammad, this does not prove the original was given by God! All it shows is that today's *Qur'an* is a carbon copy of whatever Muhammad said. The *truth* of what he taught is not proven.

Muslims claim that Islam is the true religion because it has "the only perfectly copied" Holy Book. However, it is not a matter of someone having the original, but was the original God's Word? Though Muslims may claim that the angel Gabriel gave these revelations to Muhammad, the *Qur'an* never identifies its source—contrary to what the Bible repeatedly does. So while the *Qur'an* claims to be the Word of God, this does not prove that it *is* the Word of God.

Furthermore, the original inscribed *Qur'an* did not contain consonantal dots or vowel points, which makes it unclear how some portions should be read and interpreted. Muslims admit that there are variations in the readings and interpretations. So even if we do have a copy of the *Qur'an* that dates from close to the death of Muhammad, there is confusion as to what certain parts really mean.

Also, it is claimed by most Muslims that the *Qur'an* can only be understood in Arabic and all translations of it have their limitations.

Universality

The *Qur'an* claims to provide guidance for the whole of mankind, but when one reads it, he finds that it is primarily addressed to the Arabs who lived at the time of its coming forth, though at times it also addresses other peoples in general. The book mainly discusses those things that appealed to the taste of the Arabs and that were linked to their environment, history, or customs. As for the practical aspects of the Islamic way of life, the *Qur'an* only defines the limits and bounds for the components without giving detailed rules and regulations.

The actual work of building the Islamic way of life in accordance with the instructions contained in the *Qur'an* was entrusted to Muhammad, who set forth the pattern of life for individuals, society, and the Islamic State. The *Qur'an* contains rules relating to social life, commerce and economics, marriage and inheritance, and penal laws. It does not contain any specific prophecies like the Bible does or records of historical events.

Another question that troubles the minds concerning the *Qur'an* is the divergence in the interpretations of the

Qur'an. People say that, on the one hand, the *Qur'an* very severely condemns those who create differences about the book of Allah to cause division in their religion. On the other hand, so many different interpretations of its injunctions have been made that there is hardly to be found any command with an agreed-upon interpretation. And it is not the people of the later periods alone who differed with one another; even the great scholars of the early periods, including the companions of Muhammad and their followers, did not all agree in every detail regarding its commands and prohibitions.

Do all these people then deserve the condemnation pronounced in the *Qur'an* for making different interpretations? If this is not so, then what kind of differences of opinion have been condemned in the *Qur'an*? The problem is very big and extensive. Suffice to say here that the *Qur'an* is not against healthy divergence of opinion in the interpretation of its injunctions.

Conclusion

Muslims claim that the poetic style of the *Qur'an* in Arabic is very beautiful and cannot be matched. Since I do not know Arabic, I cannot comment on that aspect of it, but I have come to some conclusions after reading it in English:

1. You really do not read the *Qur'an*, you just wade through it.
2. There is no consistent theme or themes, and it does not have a discernable plot.
3. It jumps from one subject to another without any connection.
4. There is a lot of repetition.
5. There are many accounts taken from the Bible, but these are often greatly changed.
6. It is very confusing because while claiming there is only one God, it uses the plural word *we* hundreds of times when speaking about Allah. (Muslims claim that this is like a king speaking and including either his court or all his subjects in the *we*. But to me this is not very convincing.)
7. There are a number of contradictions in the *Qur'an*.
8. The *Qur'an* was not written for the average person to understand. It must be interpreted by the "scholars."
9. The *Qur'an* is about the size of the average New Testament, containing about four hundred pages. However, if all the repetitive segments were removed, along with much that is not essential, the book could be condensed to about fifty pages.

The *Qur'an* can be fitly describes in this way: It is a toilsome reading. A wearisome confused jumble; crude, endless iteration; long-windedness; entanglement with insupportable arguments.

Nothing but a sense of duty could carry any European through the *Qur'an*.

There are over seventy different English translations of the *Qur'an* available today, and forty can be obtained free on the web. These range from the very literal to the more easily readable. I presently possess five versions:

1. The translation by Marmaduke Pickthall, an English convert to Islam, was published in 1909; it is quite conservative.
2. *The Qur'an*, translated by M. H. Shakir is readily obtainable at your local bookstore. Stylistically, it is the most idiomatic English translation. It is also slanted to make Islam palatable for the Western reader.
3. *The Qur'an*, translated by Professor (Dr.) Syed Vickar Ahamed, which is a simplified version for young people.
4. *The Holy Qur'an*, which was translated in 1934 by Abdullah Yusuf Ali. This is considered a standard version, so it is preferred by many Islamic scholars.
5. *The Glorious Qur'an with English Translation and Commentary*. It was translated by four Turkish Muslims

and published by Why-Islam in 1992. There are many parenthetical comments in the text itself and frequent additional comments following many verses. Unless I note otherwise, all my quotes are taken from this version.

5

---※---

What Is the Hadith?

IN ADDITION TO the *Qur'an*, Islam also has the *Hadith*, which contains the purported sayings of Muhammad. These sayings were not collected until two hundred years or more after the death of Muhammad. None of them were written down during his lifetime, but they were all passed on by word of mouth. It is maintained that in order for a saying to be recorded in the *Hadith* the initial hearer had to know Muhammad personally, and this witness was reliably heard by a second person, who was later heard by someone else—and so it was passed on down the line. Hence, the verification of a tradition depends not upon its substance but primarily on the chain of attestation!

The question is not so much "Could the Prophet have said this? Is it reasonable and in character?" but rather "Who said that he said such and such? Was that reporter an eyewitness? Was he honest? And who tells us *now* that someone heard or saw the Prophet say or do it? Is the chain of attesters unbroken?" In other words, did each communicator personally know the man preceding him in the sequence, going back to the first source (at least two hundred years)? So the exactness of the process is more important than the substance.

No Muslim claims that the *Hadith* is inspired, but it ranks second to the *Qur'an* and plays a very important part in Islam. It is said that one cannot really understand the *Qur'an* without the explanations found in the *Hadith*, because it helps to explain and clarify the *Qur'an* and presents it in a more practical form. Muslims say that their knowledge of Islam would be incomplete and shaky if they did not study and follow the *Hadith*. Nor can an outsider truly understand Islam if he ignores the *Hadith*. It is a much-larger volume than the *Qur'an*, which contains only about four hundred pages.

The word *hadith* means "tradition." There are a number of different collections of *hadiths*. The *Hadith*, which was compiled by Bukhari fills nine volumes, and other compilations are possibly larger yet. The individual traditions within them can be categorized as follows:

1. Sahih, *or "authentic."* Contains unbroken chains of narrations from people who were known to be exceptionally moral and truthful. Of these, the collections by Bukhari and Muslims seem to be the most reliable. If both of these compilers mention something, then it is considered "authentic."

2. Hasan, *or "sound."* There may be some gaps in the chain of narrations, but the reporters were known to be exceptionally moral and truthful individuals.

3. Da'eff, *or "weak/fabricated."* The narrators were known to be untruthful and immoral, or there is no chain of narration. Some of these statements also go clearly against the most basic principles of Islam.

Bukhari lived from AH 194 to AH 256—that is, about two hundred years after the death of Muhammad. He traveled extensively in the Muslim world, collecting the many apparent sayings of the Prophet. It is purported that over five hundred thousand sayings of Muhammad were then circulating among his followers. It is said that Buhkari collected three hundred thousand of these and personally memorized two hundred thousand, most of which he later discarded as unreliable. He undertook the mammoth task of sifting through these many sayings, trying to determine whether they were authentic, sound, or likely fabricated. He chose approximately 7,275 "with repetition" (that came from multiple sources) and about 2,230 "without repetition"—all of which he concluded were beyond doubt and thus authentic. The total: 9,505.

A man named Muslim also lived during that second century after Muhammad. He too traveled widely, collecting the purported sayings of Muhammad. In the end, he selected approximately four thousand *ahadith*, which he felt were authentic.

All these *ahadith* (the *a* makes it plural) are supposedly accurate, despite the gap of over two hundred years. There are collections by others that were assembled even hundreds of years later than this.

I was corresponding with a particular Muslim, and the issue we were discussing was that of the seventy-two virgins promised to those who die while engaged in jihad. I pointed out that Muhammad taught that there would be far more women in hell than men, yet both the *Qur'an* and the *Hadith* narrated by Muslim (see *hadith* 188) promise all men two or more wives in Paradise. How could both teachings be true? There could not be even one wife for each man in Paradise!

So I asked this Muslim to explain to me how there could be enough virgins to give seventy-two of them to each man killed in holy war. Here is what he wrote: "The tradition about 72 virgins falls under category #3. It is not considered an authentic *hadith*." I wrote back and said that this was hard to comprehend. The fact the some honest Muslims would even collect sayings that were "weak and possibly fabricated" and put them in a book was amazing to me. I explained that just about anyone who has heard even a little concerning Islam has heard about the seventy-two virgins promised to those who die in jihad. Thus, it is Muslims who are responsible for continuing a very great misunderstanding among both Muslims and non-Muslims. Since the early Muslim caliphs possessed great power, why didn't they stop this untruth from being spread all over the world?

I never received a reply to this query.

Having noted the means by which they were collected, let us now get a taste of these *hadiths*. I have copied out some of them in order to give you examples of the weird teachings found among the alleged sayings of Muhammad. Each of these has a long string of attesters attached, which I will omit. (All these quotes from the *Hadith* are taken from the book *Pearls & Corals* by Al-Lu'lu'wal-Marjàn, Arabic-English, "A Collection of Agreed upon *Ahadith* from Al-Bukhari & Muslim," volumes 1 and 2. Compiled by Fuwad Abdul-Baqi. Translated by Dr. Muhammad Muhsin Khan. Published by Dar-us-Salam Publications, Riyadh, Saudi Arabia, 1995.)

The Prophet was asked, "What is the best deed?" He replied, "To believe in Allah and His Messenger." The Questioner then asked, "What is the next (in goodness)?" He replied, "To participate in *jihad* in Allah's Cause."

"If any one of you improves (follows strictly) his Islamic religion then his good deeds will be rewarded ten times to seven hundred times for each good deed and a bad deed will be recorded as it is."

"By Allah in Whose Hands my soul is, surely the son of Mary—Jesus—will shortly descend amongst you people (Muslims) and will judge mankind justly by the Law of the *Qur'an* (as a just ruler) and will break the cross and kill the pigs and abolish the *Jizya* (a tax taken from the non-Muslims, who are under the protection of the Muslim government. This tax will not be accepted by Jesus, and all mankind will be required to embrace Islam with no other alternative). Then there will be abundance of money and nobody will accept charitable gifts."

Muhammad asked Abu Huraira, "How will you be when the son of Mary, Jesus, descends amongst you, for he will judge people by the Law of the *Qur'an* and not by the Law of the Gospel?"

Aisha [the child-wife of Muhammad] said, "And whoever tells you that the Prophet (Muhammad) knows what is going to happen tomorrow, is a liar."

"Then it will be said to the Christians [on the Day of Judgment], 'What did you used to worship?' They will reply, 'We used to worship Messiah, the son of Allah.' It will be said, 'You are liars, for Allah has neither a wife nor a son. What do you want (now)?' They will say, 'We want You to provide us with water.' It will be said to them, 'Drink,' and they will fall down in Hell (instead)."

"When the people of Paradise will enter Paradise and the people of Hell will go to Hell, Allah will order those who have had faith equal to the weight of a grain of mustard seed to be taken out from Hell. So they will be taken out, but (by then) they will be blackened (charred). Then they will be put in the river of *Haya* (life) and they will revive like a grain that grows near the bank of a flood channel. Don't you see that it comes out yellow and twisted?"

"Allah will gather all the people on the Day of Resurrection and they will say, 'Let us request someone to intercede for us with our Lord so that He may relieve us from this place of ours.' Then they

WILBUR LINGLE WITH ROBERT DELANCY

will go to Adam and say, 'You are the one whom Allah created with His Own Hands, and breathed in you the soul and ordered the angels to prostrate to you; so please intercede for us with our Lord.' Adam will reply, 'I am not fit for this undertaking,' and will remember his sin, and will say, 'Go to Noah.' [Noah gives the same reply to them, and so they are sent to Abraham and then to Moses, but all of these prophets refuse to intercede.] Moses will say, 'Go to Jesus.' They will go to him and he will say, 'I am not fit for this undertaking,' and will send them to Muhammad. They go to Muhammad who says, 'I will intercede, but Allah has fixed a limit for me (i.e., certain types of people for whom I may intercede), and I will take them out of (Hell) Fire and let them enter Paradise.'"

But also recorded is another statement by Muhammad, one that is exactly the *opposite* of what was quoted above:

Muhammad got up and said, "O Quraish people! Save yourselves (from the Hell-fire) as I cannot save you from Allah's punishment...Ask me anything from my wealth, but I cannot save you from Allah's punishment."

However, Muhammad boastfully declared, "I have been given five things which were not given to any amongst the prophets before me. These are:

1. Allah made me victorious in fighting my enemies.
2. The earth has been made for me (and my followers), a place for offering prayer and a thing to purify. Therefore any one of my followers can offer prayer wherever he is, at the time of prayer.
3. The booty [from battles he fought] has been made (lawful) for me (and was not made so for anyone else).
4. Every prophet used to be sent to his nation only, but I have been sent to all mankind.
5. I have been given the right of intercession (on the Day of Resurrection)."

Whoever does not recite the first surah of the *Qur'an* in his prayer, his prayer is invalid.

If anyone of you rouses from sleep and performs the ablution [the proper washing of face, hands, arms and feet before set times of prayer], he should wash his nose by putting water in it and then blowing it out thrice, because Satan has stayed in the upper part of his nose all the night.

If a person raises his head in formal prayers before the leader does, Allah may transform his head into that of a donkey, or his figure into that of a donkey.

> When Muslims pray together in the mosque, they stand in straight rows. Why? The Prophet supposedly said, "Straighten your rows or Allah will alter your faces." (A comment is given on this *hadith*, which says, "Allah may change your faces to that of an animal [e.g., a donkey, etc.] or make them like the backs of the neck, etc.")

Muhammad said the following:

> Women should not raise their heads (from prostration when praying) till the men sit down straight (after bowing while praying).
>
> It is a grievous sin to pass in front of another person who is praying.
>
> Say your prayer neither loudly nor in a low voice.
>
> It is forbidden to eat (uncooked) garlic or onion or leek or anything similar of offense before one goes to the mosque to pray.

Sometimes, when Muhammad was leading in prayer, there were times of silence. Someone once asked him,

"What do you say in these time of silence?" His reply was, "I ask Allah to set me apart from my sins (faults) as the east and west are set apart from each other, and cleanse me from sins as a white garment is cleaned of dirt. O Allah! Wash off my sins with water, snow and hail."

Muslims are supposed to pray five times a day: (1) early morning, (2) midday, (3) afternoon, (4) after sunset, and (5) at night.

Muhammad said the following:

> Whoever misses the afternoon prayer (intentionally), then it is as if he lost his family and property.
>
> Whoever offers the two cool prayers (afternoon and morning) will enter Paradise.
>
> The reward of a prayer in congregation is twenty-five times superior in degree to that of a prayer offered by a person alone.
>
> If one performs ablution and does it perfectly, and then proceeds to the mosque with the sole intention of offering prayer, for each step which he takes toward the mosque Allah upgrades him a degree in reward and crosses out (forgives) one sin, till he enters the mosque. When he enters the mosque, he is considered in prayer as long as he is waiting for the prayer, and the angels will keep on asking Allah's forgiveness for him.

The child bride of Muhammad, Aisha, is reported to have said, "When the last moment of the life of Allah's Messenger came, he started putting a woolen blanket on his face; and when he felt hot and short of breath, he took it off his face and said, 'May Allah curse the Jews and Christians, for they build places of worship at the graves of their prophets.'"

Muhammad said the following:

> Whoever has built a mosque with the intent of seeking Allah's Pleasure, Allah will build for him a similar place in Paradise.
>
> No one will enter Paradise except a person who is a Muslim.

When Muhammad prayed, he would often say, "O Allah, I seek refuge with You from my sins and from being in debt." Somebody said to him, "Why do you so frequently seek refuge with Allah from being in debt?" He replied, "A person in debt tells lies whenever he speaks, and breaks promises whenever he makes (them)."

Muhammad also said the following:

> We (Muslims) are the last (to come), but we will be the foremost on the Day of Resurrection, though the former nations were given the Book (i.e.,

Scripture) before us and we were given the Holy Book after them. This (i.e., Friday) is the day about which they differed. So the next day (i.e., Saturday) was prescribed for the Jews and the day after it (i.e., Sunday) for the Christians.

The taking of a bath on Friday is compulsory for every Muslim who has attained the age of puberty, and (also) the cleaning of his teeth and the using of perfume, if it is available.

The deceased is tortured in his grave for the wailing done over him.

Allah increases the punishment of a disbeliever because of the weeping (crying aloud) of his relatives.

Women are prohibited from following funeral processions, but not strictly.

A man asked Muhammad, "My mother died suddenly, and I thought that if she had lived she would have given alms. So if I give alms now on her behalf, will she get the reward?" He answered in the affirmative.

Muhammad added the following:

> Whoever died and he ought to have observed the fast (the missed days of Ramadan), then his guardians must observe the fast on his behalf.

Fast three days a month, as the reward of good deeds is multiplied ten times and that will be equal to one year of observing the fast.

A woman should not travel for more than three days except with a *Dhu-Mahram* (i.e., a male with whom she cannot marry at all, e.g., her brother, father, grandfather, or her own husband). [In another *hadith* it states "one day and night" instead of "three."]

None plots against the people of Medina but that he will be dissolved (destroyed) like the salt is dissolved in water.

One Muslim serving in Muhammad's army came to him and asked, "We have no women (wives) with us. Should we castrate ourselves?" He forbade his people to do that, and thenceforth, he allowed them to marry a woman (temporarily) by giving her even a garment. [This is known as *Mut'ah*. A man is allowed to take a woman contractually for a couple hours, a day, a week, etc. Muslims say it was allowed for a limited period of time, then prohibited, then again was allowed and prohibited later; but the Shi'ites still practice it today.]

In the days of Muhammad, a father could give his virgin daughter in marriage even if she was not fully grown up. Most people, even those who know just a little about Islam, have heard about Aisha, the girl who was betrothed to Muhammad at the age of six, and the marriage was consummated at the age of nine. Here are the facts *in her own words*:

> My marriage (wedding) contract with Muhammad was written when I was a girl of six (years). We went to Madina (where Muhammad lived) and stayed at the home of Khazraj. Then I got ill and my hair fell down. Later on, my hair grew (again) and my mother came to me while I was playing in a swing with some of my girlfriends. She called me, and I went to her, not knowing what she wanted to do to me. She caught me by the hand and made me stand at the door of the house. I was breathless then, and when my breathing became normal she took some water and rubbed my face and head. There in the house I saw some women, who said, "Best wishes and Allah's Blessing and good luck." Then she entrusted me to them and they prepared me (for the marriage). Unexpectedly, Muhammad came to me in the forenoon and my mother handed me over to him. At that time I was a girl of nine years of age.

In another place Aisha said, "I used to play with dolls in the presence of the Prophet, and my girlfriends also used to play with me. When Muhammad would enter (my dwelling place), they would hide themselves, but he would call them to join and play with me." [The playing with dolls and similar images is forbidden, but it was allowed for Aisha at that time because she was a little girl, not having yet reached the age of puberty.]

Muhammad said the following:

> If a woman spends the night deserting her husband's bed (does not sleep with him), then the angels send their curses on her till she comes back (to her husband).
>
> Whoever keeps a (pet) dog which is neither a watchdog nor a hunting dog, will get a daily deduction of two *Qirat* (rewards) from his good deeds.
>
> Allah made me wealthy through conquests.
>
> If ever I take an oath to do something, and later on I find that it is more beneficial to do something different, I will do the thing which is better and give expiation from my oath.
>
> Allah curses a thief who steals an egg and gets his hand cut off, or steals a rope and gets his hand cut off.
>
> The penalty for whoever confesses illegal sexual intercourse is "Take him away and stone him to death."

It is forbidden to ask too many questions in disputed religious matters.

Whosoever believes in Allah and the Last Day should entertain his guest generously by giving him his reward.

It was asked, "What is his reward, O Allah's Messenger?" He said, "To be entertained generously for a day and a night with high quality of food; and the guest has the right to be entertained for three days (with ordinary food)."

Here are other things Muhammad said;

It is allowed to attack suddenly, without a warning, the disbelievers who have already been invited to accept Islam.

Deceit in war is permissible.

It is allowed to cut or burn the trees of disbelievers.

War-booty has been made lawful for this (Muslim) nation specially.

Whoever obeys me, he obeys Allah; and whoever disobeys me, he disobeys Allah.

It is forbidden to take the *Qur'an* to the land of disbelievers when it is feared that it might fall into their hands.

Allah assigns for a person who participates in *jihad* (holy battles) in Allah's cause and nothing causes him to do so except belief in Allah and His Messengers, that he will be recompensed by Allah either with a reward or booty (if he survives), or will be admitted to Paradise (if he is killed in the battle as a martyr).

A man came to Muhammad and said, "Guide me to such a deed equal to *jihad*."

He replied, "I do not find such a deed."

On the day of the battle of Uhud, a man came to Muhammad and said, "Can you tell me where I will be if I should get martyred?"

He replied, "In Paradise."

The man threw away some dates he was carrying in his hand and fought till he was martyred.

Muhammad said the following:

Never return to your family from a journey at night. You should return either in the morning or in the afternoon.

When night falls (or it is evening), keep your children close to you, for the devils spread out at that time. But when an hour of the night elapses, you can let them free. Close the doors and mention the Name of Allah, for Satan does not open a closed door.

There is healing in black cumin for all diseases except death.

If there is an evil omen in anything, then it is in a woman, a horse and a house.

A woman came to Muhammad and asked, "How is the Divine Inspiration revealed to you?"

He replied, "Sometimes it is (revealed) like the ringing of a bell. This form of Inspiration is the hardest of all, and then this state passes off after I have grasped what is inspired. Sometimes the angel comes in the form of a man and talks to me and I grasp whatever he says."

Aisha, his child bride, added, "Verily, I saw the Prophet being inspired (Divinely) and noticed the sweat dripping from his forehead on a very cold day (as the Inspiration was over)."

Muhammad said the following:

> Show respect to Allah's Messenger and give up asking too many questions—especially those for which there is no need, and those which burden one, and those which have not happened.
>
> The best among you [Muslims] are those living in my century (generation), then those coming after

them, and then those coming after them. There will be some [Muslim] people after you who will be dishonest and will not be trustworthy, will give witness (evidence) without being asked to give witness, and will take vows but will not fulfill their vows, and fatness will appear among them.

He who makes peace between people by inventing good information or saying good things is not a liar.

(The matter of the creation of) a human being is put together in the womb of the mother in forty days, and then he becomes a clot of thick blood for a similar period and then a piece of fish for a similar period. Then Allah sends an angel who is ordered to write four things. He is ordered to write down his deeds, his livelihood, his (date of) death, and whether he will be blessed or wretched (in the Hereafter). Then the soul is breathed into him. So a man among you may do (good) deeds till there is only a cubit between him and Paradise, and then what has been written for him decides his behavior, and he starts doing (evil) deeds characteristic of the people of the (Hell) Fire. And similarly a man among you may do (evil) deeds till there is only a cubit between him and the (Hell) Fire, and then what has been written for him decides his behavior, and he starts doing deeds characteristic of the people of Paradise. [In other words, one's whole life history is determined for a person while that person is still in his mother's womb.]

There is none among you nor any person created but has a place assigned [while in the womb] for him in Paradise or in Hell, and it is also determined for him whether he will be among the blessed or wretched. Good deeds are made easy for the blessed, and bad deeds are made easy for the wretched.

A man came to Muhammad and asked, "Can the people of Paradise be known [differentiated] from the people of the Fire?"

He replied, "Yes."

The man said, "Why do people [try to] do [good] deeds?"

He said, "Everyone will do the deeds for which he has been created to do, or he will do those deeds which will be made easy for him to do."

Muhammad said the following:

Adam and Moses argued with each other. Moses said to Adam, "O Adam! You are our father who disappointed us and turned us out of Paradise." Then Adam said to him, "O Moses! Allah favored you with His talk [talked to you directly] and He wrote [the Torah] for you with His Own Hand. Do you blame me for action which Allah had preordained for me forty years before my creation?" So Adam confuted Moses.

In the *Qur'an* there are verses that are entirely clear and others not entirely clear…but none knows its hidden meanings save Allah.

Recite [and study] the *Qur'an* as long as you agree about its interpretation, but when you have any difference of opinion [as regards its interpretation and meaning], then you should stop reciting it [for the time being].

Near the establishment of the Hour [Last Days] there will be days during which [religious] knowledge will be taken away and general ignorance will spread, and there will be much killing.

Allah has ninety-nine names [i.e., one hundred less one], and whoever counts them [believes in their meanings and acts accordingly] will enter Paradise.

If a person says one-hundred times in one day, "None has the right to be worshipped but Allah, the Alone, Who has no partners, to Him belongs Dominion and to Him belong all the Praise, and He has Power over all things," that person will get the reward of manumitting [releasing] ten slaves, and one-hundred good deeds will be written in his account and one-hundred bad deeds will be wiped off or erased from his account; and on that day he will be protected from morning till evening from Satan, and nobody will be superior to him except someone who has done more than that which he has done.

Cleanse my heart with the water of snow and hail, and cleanse my heart from all sins, as a white garment is cleansed from filth; and let there be a far-away distance between me and my sins as You made the east and west far away from each other.

[If Muhammad had consulted the Bible and believed it as written, he would have received an answer to this prayer. Isaiah 1:18 declares, "Come now, and let us reason together, says the Lord: though your sins are like scarlet, they shall be as white as snow; though they are red like crimson, they shall become like wool." Also, Psalm 103:12 says, "As far as the east is from the west, so far does he remove our transgressions from us." The verse in 1 John 1:7 states, "The blood of Jesus his Son cleanses us from all sin." The verse in 1 John 1:9 promises, "If we confess our sins, he is faithful and just to forgive us our sins and to cleanse us from all unrighteousness." Revelation 1:5 adds, "To him

[Jesus Christ] who loves us and has freed us from our sins by his blood."]

When you hear the crowing of a cock, ask for Allah's blessings, for [its crowing indicates that] it has seen an angel. And when you hear the braying of a donkey, seek refuge with Allah from Satan for [its braying indicates] that it has seen Satan.

During the lifetime of the Prophet, the moon was split into two parts, and on that day, the Prophet said, "Bear witness [to this]."

I stood at the gate of Paradise and saw that the majority of the people who entered it were the poor, while the wealthy were stopped at the gate [for the accounts, etc.]. But the people destined for Fire were ordered to be taken to the Fire. Then I stood at the gate of the Fire and saw that the majority of those who entered it were women.

The deeds of anyone of you will not save you from the [Hell] Fire.

The people asked Muhammad, "Even you [will not be saved by your deeds], O Allah's Messenger?"

Muhammad said, "No, even I [will not be saved] unless and until Allah protects me with His Grace and His Mercy."

Muhammad mentioned the following:

There is a tree in Paradise (which is huge); a rider can travel in its shade for one-hundred years without crossing it.

The first group of people who will enter Paradise will be glittering like the moon on a full-moon night, and those who will follow them will glitter like the most brilliant star in the sky. They will not urinate, pass stool, spit, or have any nasal secretions. Their combs will be of gold, and their sweat will smell like musk. Aloewood will be used in their censers. Their wives will be *houris*. All of them will look alike, as if they are one person, in the image of their father Adam, sixty cubits [ninety feet] tall.

Allah created Adam, and his height was sixty cubits...People have been decreasing in stature since Adam's creation.

A tent (in Paradise) is like a hollow pearl which is thirty miles in height, and in every corner of the tent a believer will have a family that cannot be seen by the others.

The width between the two shoulders of a disbeliever [in Hell] will be equal to the distance covered by a fast rider in three days.

Once, the Prophet went out after sunset and heard a (dreadful) voice, and he said, "The Jews are being punished in their graves."

When a Muslim is put in his grave and his companions depart, even (while) he hears their footsteps two angels come to him and make him sit up and ask, "What did you use to say about this man [i.e., Muhammad]?"

Then the faithful believer will say, "I testify that he is Allah's slave and His Messenger."

Then they will say to him, "Look at your place in the Hell-fire. Allah, instead of it, has changed for you a place in Paradise. So he will see both his places."

Jews will fight with you, and you will be given victory over them, for a stone will say, "O Muslim! There is a Jew behind me; kill him!"

Yawning is from Satan, and if anyone of you yawns, he should check his yawning as much as possible, for if anyone of you (during the act of yawning) should say, "Ha," Satan will laugh at him.

The *Sunna*

The vast majority of Muslims refer to themselves as Sunni—Muslims who follow the *sunna* (path) of Muhammad as recorded in the *Hadith*. A Muslim writer gives this advice: "Know that the key to happiness is to follow the *Sunna*.

One should imitate the Messenger of God in all his comings and goings, his movement and rest, in his way of eating, his attitude, his sleep, and his talk."

Because of this, even the smallest idiosyncrasies of the Prophet have become significant. A few examples are the following:

- You must sit while putting on your trousers, stand when winding a turban.
- You must begin with the right foot when putting on your shoes and must eat with your right hand.
- When cutting your nails, you must begin with the forefinger of the right hand and finish with its thumb.
- When trimming the toenails, you must begin with the little toe of the right foot and finish with the little toe of the left.

The ideal of imitating Muhammad has provided Muslims from Morocco to Indonesia with a uniformity of action. Wherever one may be, one knows how to behave when entering a house, which formulas of greeting to employ, what to avoid in good company, how to eat, and how to travel. For centuries, Muslim children have been brought up in these ways.

6

Major Beliefs of Islam: God, Determinism, Islamic Law, Folk Islam, Jihad

THE TERM *ISLAM* means submission to the will of God. The person who submits is called a Muslim—a submitted one. This submission involves both beliefs (*iman*) and practices (*deen*).

God

The central doctrine of Islam is that God is one and no partner is to be associated with Him. In Surah 112, which is called the essence of the *Qur'an*, God is defined this way: "Say: 'He is Allah, the One! Allah, the eternally besought of all! He begat none. Nor was He begotten. And there is none comparable to Him!'" To confess this surah, an Islamic tradition affirms, is to shed one's sins as a man might strip a tree in autumn of its leaves.

The doctrine of the Trinity is offensive to Muslims because it accords with the belief that God has a Son who, in essence, is equal with the Father. In traditional Islamic theology, God is beyond all comprehension. He remains above, withdrawn, transcendent, and cannot be known personally. Muslims are not expected to visualize God but to worship and adore Him as a protector. The substance of what God reveals is His "will" rather than His "nature," and so the purpose of revelation is obedience rather than obtaining perfect knowledge. Response and submission are the sole necessities.

But how can a person worship someone about whom he can know nothing? The relationship of Allah to men is best described in terms of master and slave. God is the sovereign monarch who requires man to submit to Him as an obedient slave. Thus, the crux of Islam is law. You just hear what the *Qur'an* has to say and obey it. It is not to be understood.

Islam lacks the Christian view of God as a Heavenly Father who desires a personal relationship with the children whom He loves. This is abhorrent to a Muslim. The

Islamic concept is that Allah is far away and unknowable, which leads to the belief that there needs to be an intermediary—either a prophet or another recognized leader of an organization—between God and man.

This is the only way that humans can gain even a little knowledge about God. He does not communicate or reveal Himself directly to lesser humans in order to make Himself known. Since God is so distant, Muslims feel that Allah today can be approached only through a belief in Muhammad's words. There is a saying, "God himself would not exist without the assistance of the revelations given to Muhammad."

As mentioned in an earlier chapter, Islam declares that Allah has "ninety-nine beautiful names." These ninety-nine names are scattered throughout the *Qur'an* with no formal identification as such. Wikipedia gives a listing of these divine attributes and tells where they are to be found.

Islamic tradition relates that Muhammad said, "Verily, there are ninety-nine names of God and whoever recites them shall enter heaven." Muslims believe that many of their outward religious acts will give them merit and cancel out sins. But their relying on these ninety-nine names sadly deprives them of the thrill of saying "God loves me." These names are not really capable of expressing His true essence but speak largely of "the sovereign free will of God." (*Love* is mentioned in the *Qur'an*, but it is not emphasized.) In a real sense, a Muslim's awareness of God is merely the awareness of the unknown. These revelations communicate God's law; they do not reveal God. He is inaccessible to their knowledge.

Determinism or Predestination

Allah determines everything! For instance, if you say to a Muslim that you will see him tomorrow afternoon at one, he will reply, "*Inshallah* [God willing]." The *Qur'an* clearly states that Allah decrees both good and evil.

Surah 9:51 states, "Say: 'Nothing will befall us except what Allah has ordained. He is our Guardian. In Him let the believers put their trust.'"

Surah 7:178–179 teaches, "He whom Allah leads, he indeed is led aright, while he whom Allah sends astray— they indeed are losers. Already have We urged to hell many of the *jinn* and humankind."

And here is the real shocker! Surah 32:13 declares, "And if We had so willed, We could have given every soul its guidance, but the word from Me concerning evil-doers took effect: that I will fill hell with the *jinn* and mankind together."

Islamic Law

Islamic law, known as *Shari'a* (literally "the path leading to the watering place"), is all-embracing. Islamic law is formed by traditional Islamic scholarship. In Islam, *Shari'a* is the expression of the divine will of Allah and constitutes a system of duties that are incumbent upon a Muslim by virtue of his religious belief.

There is no division between religion and the state. Islamic law controls every part of the life of a Muslim from the cradle to the grave, whether it is concerned with oneself or with the whole of society. It covers the rites of worship, one's social activities, his economic transactions, and his political life in countries that have a majority of Muslims. (Even in countries having only a small percentage of Muslims, they often have won the right to judge their own affairs by *Shari'a*. France, with an 8 percent Muslim population, is a classic example of this. The Muslims usually live clustered in certain areas, which makes this feasible. As of this writing, there are a number of other countries, including England and Canada, that are considering letting local Muslims be ruled by *Shari'a*.)

Shari'a divides one's activities into five categories:

1. Those that are *obligatory*, such as praying five times a day, fasting during Ramadan;

WILBUR LINGLE WITH ROBERT DELANCY

2. Those that are *recommended*—giving money to the poor;
3. Acts toward which the Divine law is *indifferent*—the kind of vegetables one eats or the exercises one performs;
4. Acts that are *reprehensible* or *abominable*—divorce (in spite of the fact that a divorce is very easy to obtain); and
5. Those things that are *forbidden*

   a. Murder (but there are three situations where murder is permitted and *un*punishable: in the time of war, the killing of a Muslim who leaves Islam and converts to another religion, and the killing of infidels, which includes Jews and Christians)
   b. adultery (yet even today, some groups in Islam permit temporary marriages—for a couple of hours, a night, a weekend, etc.—which is a convenient way to have an affair and is not classified as adultery)
   c. Theft
   d. Certain dietary prohibitions such as the eating of pork and its derivatives and the drinking of alcoholic beverages

The observance of these five categories alone does not produce an extravagance of saintliness. There are a great number of actions in the third category—indifference—that grant Muslims and their society a wide range of freedom. There are actions not commended but tolerated, not prohibited though disapproved.

A Muslim can fail to practice the injunctions of *Shari'a* and still remain a Muslim, though not a practicing or upright one. But if he or she no longer considers *Shari'a* to be valid, then that person practically ceases to be a Muslim.

However, *Shari'a* is not the complete heart and soul of Islam. It is like the circumference of a circle, each point of which represents someone who stands on that circumference. But a Muslim can move within this circle toward the center of Islamic ideology.

I want to say a word about Sufism, since Sufism and Islamic law are usually considered to be antithetical. Sufism is not strictly a denomination of Islam, like the four Sunni schools and the different Shi'i sects, but is a mystical/ascetic form of Islam. While modern Islam focuses on the practical, physical needs of this life, Sufism seeks oneness with the Divine. This is done by focusing on the more spiritual aspects of religion. Sufis strive to obtain direct experience of God by making use of man's "intuitive and emotional faculties" that one must be trained to use. The thoughtful Sufi would escape the world in his or her quest for an intimate mystical union with Allah. This is very much like what meditation is supposed to produce in Buddhism.

Through Sufism, a Muslim begins his journey toward the center—a journey known as the Path. As one progresses along this Path by meditating on spiritual things, the soul is beautified with virtue, which removes from it all its imperfections and takes away the veils that prevent the soul from becoming wed to the spirit. This Path of mysticism in Sufism is like the heart of a person's body: it is invisible from the outside but provides nourishment for the whole organism. It is the inner spirit that breathes in the outward forms of the religion and makes possible the passage from the outer world to the inward paradise. It is the Path leading directly to God. If a Muslim gets to the center, he is said to have reached the Truth. Muslims who seem to have reached this inner point are considered great saints and sages.

The Sufis' traditional woolen garment symbolizes this spiritual union and actually gives them their name Sufi, which means "wool weavers" or "wearers of wool." The popular term *whirling dervishes* points to their ritual dance that links their worship to the Divine.

Sufism has left a lasting imprint on Islamic poetry, philosophy, and academics as well as dance. It also serves as a cultural link between Asia and the Middle East, for its mystical beliefs and its emphasis on self-annihilation as a pathway to God joins it to Buddhist monism (all is one) more than to Islamic monotheism (one God).

Folk Islam

This is a blend of Islamic monotheism and animism. In spite of Muhammad's obvious hatred for idolatry, many of his early followers continued to open their hearts and homes to idols and other gods. Even today, the masses in many Muslim lands find Allah too distant and demanding to meet their personal needs. As a result, they practice their own form of earth-based spirituality through folk Islam. They turn to a pantheon of helpful powers—spirits, fairies, dead saints, and ancestors—for protection against spells, omens, the evil eye, and other ills caused by harmful spirits. These Muslims practice magic and pray to good spirits in their daily quests for the favor needed to battle evil spirits—the supposed source of illness, barrenness, and other painful conditions in life.

In much of the world, people have continued throughout the centuries to worship trees, stones, plants, and angels. Muslims in most Islamic lands may still communicate with spirits through dreams, visions, or by divination. They appeal to occult forces, using an assortment of amulets, charms, magic, astrology, sorcery, and witchcraft. To many, the waxing and waning moon—honored on numerous Islamic flags—plays a part in these rituals.

Consider these current examples:

- *Afghanistan.* The largest people group in Afghanistan are the Pashtun, a seminomadic people. They constitute the ethnic majority found within the Taliban. Their loyalty to Islam is fierce, but Pashtun culture seems often to supersede Islamic orthodoxy. Pashtun women pray regularly but are not allowed to go to the mosque. Consequently, they have woven their beliefs with superstition and animistic practices. Fearful of curses and evil spirits, they often wear amulets and charms for protection and good luck.

- *Baggara.* Many tribes of the Baggara—in Western Sudan and Eastern Chad in Africa—believe strongly in the evil eye and try to protect their cattle from jealous onlookers, even dwellers within their own villages. Their use of witch doctors is a second piece of evidence that ties the beliefs of the Baggara to that of folk Islam. Children who are ill will commonly wear either a bracelet or necklace tied to a small leather pouch that contains *Qur'anic* verses. This is a classic example of how Islam has been combined with African traditional religions.

- *Maduresse.* Nine million live on Java and the nearby island of Madura. There is much folk Islam among them, the belief of which focuses on seeking protection in life through magic by either appeasing or controlling the good and bad spirits. These people

> have a strong belief in spirits, the use of amulets, black and white magic, and the worship of ancestors.

I have given only three examples, but animism permeates Islam around the world. Many of its characteristics are universal; thus, folk Islam can be found across the spectrum of Islamic nations. It is plain that the beliefs and practices of ordinary Muslims frequently contradict many formal aspects of the Islamic faith.

Jihad

If you were to tune in tomorrow to a TV special on jihad having four Muslim speakers, you might hear four different answers to the question "What is jihad?" The first man might say that jihad is striving to lead a good Muslim life, praying and fasting regularly, being a good spouse and parent. The second might respond by identifying jihad as working hard to spread the message of Islam. The third might say it is supporting the struggle of oppressed Muslims in Palestine, Kashmir, Chechnya, or Kosovo. And none of these panelists would be wrong!

The fourth speaker, however, might admit, reluctantly, that jihad also means working to overthrow governments in the Muslim world that are not Islamic enough to suit the faithful—conquering and reforming these flawed nations—and even attacking America because of its lack of morals and its support of Israel. For America seems to be the major country standing in the way of Islam taking over the world, which is the true goal of Islam. Muslims believe that if the whole world were to become Muslim, then and then only could there be world peace.

In a glossary of Arabic Islamic terms, you can find two different meanings under the word *jihad*:

1. *Jihad*: Islamic religious war—that is, promoting the message of Islam by force of arms. (No mention of inward struggle.)

2. *Jihad*: Struggle. Any earnest striving in the way of God, involving personal, physical effort, for righteousness and against wrongdoing. "Lesser *Jihad*": in defense, fighting to protect Islam from attack or oppression. "Greater *Jihad*": internal struggle for the soul against evil (e.g., lust, greed, envy, etc.). Also, to strive to do actions that have great value in Islam, and that one has to overcome in oneself in order to do (e.g., to overcome the temptation to sleep when it is time to pray the morning prayer is a greater jihad).

In short, *jihad* basically means "to strive or struggle," and it is considered the sixth pillar of Islam by a minority of Muslim authorities.

When you talk about jihad with most Muslims or read about jihad in Muslim-written books, you will likely be told that in Islam the primary meaning is "striving to be a better Muslim" and that the prevailing meaning of "holy war" or "conquest by the sword" is *not* true—just something falsely created by us in the West. However, within Islamic jurisprudence (a body or system of laws), jihad is usually taken to mean military exertion—holy war—against non-Muslim combatants in the defense or expansion of the Islamic state. Its ultimate purpose is to establish the universal domination of Islam.

Just read the *Qur'an*, the act of which what I did! I found at least fifty-four verses in the *Qur'an* under the heading of Jihad, and all but one of them had to do with "promoting the message of Islam by force of arms." Not one verse had to do with "inward struggle."

Here are a few of the fifty-four verses (emphasis mine) in the *Qur'an* that have to do with jihad. Note their violent content:

- Surah 8:59–60: "Let not the Unbelievers think that they can get the better (*of the godly*). They will never frustrate (*them*). Against them make ready your strength to the utmost of your power, including steeds of war, *to strike terror into* (*the hearts of*) the enemies of Allah and your enemies" (Yusuf Ali).

- Surah 9:123: "O you who believe! *Fight the disbelievers* who are near to you, and let them find *a harshness in you.*"
- Surah 9:14: "*Fight* them! Allah will *punish* them by your hands and humble them."
- Surah 8:12: "When your Lord inspired the angels, (*saying*): 'I am with you. So make those who believe stand firm. I will throw *fear* into the hearts of those who disbelieve. Then *smite* the necks and smite of them each finger."
- Surah 8:17: "*You (Believers) slew them not, but Allah slew them.* And you (*Muhammad*) did not throw when you threw, but Allah threw, that He might test the believers by a fair test from Him."
- Surah 9:5: "When the sacred months are over, *slay* the polytheists wherever you find them, and take them (*captive*) and besiege them, and lie in ambush for them everywhere. But if they repent [apparently convert to Islam] and establish the Prayer ["There is no god but Allah and Muhammad is a messenger of God"] and pay the *Zakat* [tax], let them go their way. Allah is Forgiving and Merciful." (Islamic law stipulates that it is a Muslim's duty to wage war not only against those who attack Muslim territory but also against polytheists, apostates, and People of the Book [at first restricted to Jews and Christians but

later extended to Zoroastrians and other faiths] who refuse Muslim rule.)

The fact that Muhammad himself fought in twenty-seven battles and his generals in another thirty-two battles (either before or after his death) would seem to confirm what the *Qur'an* states—that it is holy war. It is worth noting that the words *fight* and *kill* appear more frequently in the *Qur'an* than does the word *pray*.

Islam teaches that humanity is divided into two distinct groups: the abode of Islam (*Dar al-Islam*), in reference to Muslims, and the abode of war (*Dar al-Harb*), in reference to non-Muslims. This means that men who belong to the abode of Islam are in a constant state of war with non-Muslims, who belong to the abode of war—until such a time that those non-Muslims convert to Islam. In other words, Muslims can never peacefully coexist with non-Muslims. Muslims can call a truce when they realize they are weak but may break it when they become strong.

Jihad, the only form of warfare permissible in Islamic law, may be declared against any non-Muslim who refuses to convert to Islam or submit to Islamic rule. *Jihad* is perpetual in nature; in theory, there can be no permanent peace with non-Muslim states, only truces, which can be repudiated when circumstances become favorable for the resumption of hostilities. War ceases only when Jews, Christians, and others submit by converting to Islam or agreeing to pay a poll tax (*jizya*) and a land tax (*kharaj*). If you don't, you lose your life.

The Muslim community is collectively required to engage in the struggle (jihad) to expand Islam throughout the world so that all of humankind may have the opportunity to live within a just political and social order. There are only a few persons who are exempt: those with mental problems, those who have the responsibility for aging parents, and women.

Muslims differ in regards as to who can declare a jihad. For the Sunnis, the caliph—with the support of the religious scholars (*ulama*)—has full authority to declare jihad. The Shi'ites view this power as residing only in the one who is the religious head. So in the absence of a mullah or an imam, only defensive jihad is considered permissible. But this has been gotten around by stating that all legitimate forms of jihad are defensive and, therefore, can be waged in the leader's absence.

However, there are some powerful Muslims, like Osama bin Laden, who feel that many of the leaders in Muslim countries are corrupt, which gives them the right to declare war against all the forces of evil in the world. This includes the overthrow of "un-Islamic" Muslim rulers. As to jihad against the West, revolutionary violence (including suicide bombers) and guerrilla warfare are not only legitimate but obligatory to battle against the sinners who ignore God's will and sovereignty.

So often in the press and public speeches the impression is given that only the fundamentalists—who are alleged to be just a small group in Islam—are for jihad and the rest of Muslims are peace-loving. But since jihad is so strongly proclaimed in the *Qur'an*, obviously it is the obligation of *all* Muslims to promote the spread of Islam by any means possible! It also needs to be remembered that the Wahhabis—who are the great majority of Muslims in Saudi Arabia, and in control of its government—are among the most fanatical Muslims there are. Wahhabis have a strong influence in many of the mosques in America because of the finances they have given to build those mosques and maintain them. (Osama bin Laden is from Saudi Arabia, and he acquired many of his ideas from the Wahhabis.) Thus, jihad is very much alive, even among Muslims in America. Wahhabis also control a lot of the mosques in England and other European countries.

There exists another serious problem that all the people of the world need to be warned about. I refer to the Muslim *madrasas*—religious schools for boys. (Strict Muslims do not allow girls to go to school.) The main curriculum in these schools is the *Qur'an*. There are no courses offered in world history, English, math, computer technology, or science—in other words, no general education.

The students start at the age of eight and spend four to eight hours a day for eight full years, focusing on the interpretation of the *Qur'an* and the *Hadith*. Many of the boys memorize the whole *Qur'an*, plus a generally extremist body of related traditions found in the *Hadith*. There are forty million Muslim youth worldwide in these schools today, including those in the USA.

Early in the training of these boys, their teachers focus these young minds on dozens of the *Qur'an's* extremely militant war verses, plus other texts that promise Paradise for Muslim martyrs. Hatred for Jews and Christians (largely synonymous with Israel and America) and a general dislike for all non-Muslims are deeply instilled in these pupils. The Bible is described as corrupted. Separation of Islam from political control is despised. (In other words, the Muslims don't want democracy.) These schools are breeding grounds for terrorists.

A good many of these schools are financed by Saudi Arabia and other rich nations and affluent Muslims. This material is taught to some Muslim children in America. As of this writing, there seem to have been halting steps taken by our government to urge the Saudi Arabian government to change some of the contents of the books used in America. The Saudi government has promised to change them, but I have yet to hear if they have. It is obviously difficult for the American government to have full access to these schools, for they are probably classified under the heading of religious schools.

Some Muslim authorities, especially among the Shi'a and Sufi s, distinguish between the greater jihad—which pertains to spiritual self-perfection—and the lesser jihad, defined as warfare, as mentioned a few pages earlier. Using these two expressions—lesser jihad for warfare and aggression and greater jihad for inward struggle—they can downplay jihad as it pertains to war.

But there is something very interesting that should be noted here. Granted that going to war, with the likelihood of being killed, is called lesser jihad and the inward struggle called greater jihad is presumably more important, why are the *Qur'an* and *Hadith* full of tremendous promises for those who are killed in holy war but not one single special promise is given to those who participate in a lifetime of greater jihad?

Here are some of the *Qur'anic* promises accorded to those who are martyred in the lesser jihad. Surah 3:157 says, "If you should die or be slain in the cause of Allah [jihad], His forgiveness and His mercy would surely be better than all that they amass." In other words, those who are killed in jihad have their sins forgiven.

But there is more. Surah 3:169 states, "Think not of those who are slain in the cause of Allah [jihad] as dead. They are alive; with their Lord they have provision." They go straight to Paradise.

The *Hadith* likewise provides many affirmations of the rewards for those who die for Islam in lesser jihad. Muslim tradition teaches that martyrs are distinguished from others in life after death in several ways: their self-sacrifice and meritorious acts render them free of sin, and therefore, they are not subject to postmortem interrogation by the angels Nakir and Munkar. Rather, they bypass the grave and the Day of Judgment (a necessity for all other Muslims) and proceed immediately upon death to one of the highest locations in Paradise, near the Throne of God. Also, as a result of their sacrifice, they can be buried in the clothes in which they died and do not need to be washed before burial. Most people have heard about the seventy-two virgins who are promised to this group of men.

But I read of no special rewards given to those who strive in the greater jihad. They will all have to go into the grave and experience the interrogation by the angels Nakir and Munkar. They will have to experience the Day of Judgment that takes place while kneeling around hell. They will be tried according to their deeds, and none of them can have assurance that the balance will be in their favor. Even if their "good" deeds outweigh their "evil" deeds, they have no assurance that it is Allah's will for them to go into Paradise. They will all have to go over the bridge spanning hell, with the possibility of falling into it forever. And if they do make it to Paradise, they don't know which one of the seven levels of Paradise will be their abode. Of course, no seventy-two virgins for them.

It seems quite clear that in Islam the main meaning of jihad is to participate in the spreading of Islam around the world by all means, even by force.

Many people are concerned about the scope of this worldwide disruption. What does the future look like? There is no one who hopes more than I that my assessment does not come to pass, but here is what I see. Let us take a look at recent history.

After World War, I the Muslim nations were defeated and poor. Many years earlier, some of them had become colonies of England, France, Portugal, Holland, Spain, etc. They were without much strength and badly divided. But after World War II, most of them became independent nations. Since they were not used to ruling themselves, they tried a number of different political ideologies.

Here is how one Muslim writer has described the situation: "Unfortunately, many governments in the Islamic world are weak, corrupt, and authoritarian. In countries where despotic regimes [those with a king or other ruler with absolute, unlimited power—autocratic, tyrannic, and oppressive] suppress all critics, and where illiteracy can reach over 60 percent among men and over 90 percent among women."

Some of these nations were socialistic and were friendly with the communists; most have been characterized by one-man rule. Many of the leaders of these nations were military men and remained in power by force or through fraudulent elections. Free elections seldom occurred. Muslims generally do not feel that democracy is an ideal type of government because it leaves the making of laws in the hands of citizens; instead, they prefer living according to Islamic law, which is supposedly based on the *Qur'an* and is the type of rule that Muhammad exhibited. Of course, under Islamic law, there is no freedom of religion and often no freedom of speech.

Some of these new governments could perhaps be classified as moderate when it comes to Islamic law. Hence, during this time, there occasionally were dissidents who felt these governments should be more Islamic, and these men started jihadist movements to cause change. This made it difficult for those in power; while they were Muslims and believed in the *Qur'an* to an extent, these jihadists were a threat to their governing. The rulers were against the jihadists not because of what they personally believed but because they were a challenge to their authority. Yes, not only are jihadists against Israel and any country that supports the Jews but also are against Islamic governments that they feel are not Islamic enough!

Then along came the oil crisis in the 1970s. Muslims discovered that they had power because of their possession of large oil deposits. A number of the Islamic nations became rich from this oil, especially Saudi Arabia. It began to use this oil money to spread Islam around the world. The majority of the mosques in America are currently financed by Saudi Arabia. The possession of oil was power—a power that could bring the rest of the world to its knees. This gave a new surge to Islam.

If there ever was much of a trend toward Western modernization and democracy, it was abruptly detoured, and probably completely halted, when Iran's Islamic revolution happened in 1978–1979 under the leadership of Ayatollah Khomeini. The leading modernizing governments in Iran, Egypt, and Lebanon seemed to be experiencing the revenge of God. Islamic revivalism produced a wave of fundamentalist movements, reaching from Egypt and Sudan to Iran, Pakistan, Afghanistan, and Malaysia.

From this time onward, religious revivalism and the role of Islamic movements became a major force in Muslim politics. Muslims became aware of the *ummah*, which is the worldwide community of believers. Islam was on the rise. The world became all of a sudden aware of the over-one-billion Muslims. There is a lot of internal strife among the different Muslim groups, but just like feuding brothers and sisters, they often pull together when faced by a common external threat. Now these weak Islamic nations could combine their power and once again focus on the goal of conquering the whole world and making everyone Muslim.

Then came the Afghanistan war when, in 1979, Soviet Russia invaded it. At this time, the Afghan tribal society consisted of fragile units divided into many tribes. However, the Soviet occupation provided a common enemy and mission. The call for a jihad offered a common Islamic religious identity and source of inspiration. The Muslims began fighting the Russians in guerrilla warfare. Many camps were set up in Afghanistan and Pakistan to train these jihadist fighters.

We have all heard of Osama bin Laden. In 1982, he entered Afghanistan and began setting up his own camps to train those engaged in this guerrilla war. Many Muslims came from other Islamic nations to help in the struggle, and by 1984, there were a large number of these fighters.

At first, these fighters were known as Arab Afghans in battle. Subsequently, al-Qaeda was organized. These activities were applauded by the Saudi government, which, along with the United States, had made a heavy commitment to supporting the jihadist movement against the Soviet Union. The Soviet troops withdrew from Afghanistan in 1989, and bin Laden returned to his home country, Saudi Arabia. But he did not feel that the government was Islamic enough, and he soon found himself in trouble with the government. So he went back to Afghanistan in April 1991.

In 1992, an Islamic state was formed in Afghanistan. But the country was gripped by a civil war that pitted the majority Pashtun population in the south and east against the ethnic minorities of the north. Pakistan and Saudi Arabia supported Sunni *mujahadin* (soldiers of God) groups while Iran backed an alliance of Shi'a minority organizations. The majority of Afghans found themselves caught in the middle of a prolonged civil war marked by heavy fighting, lawlessness, pillaging, rape, and plunder.

Late in 1994, as if out of nowhere, the predominantly Pashtun Taliban—a band of *madrasa* (Islamic school) students (*taliban*) who had been living as refugees in Pakistan— suddenly appeared. Within two years, they swept across Afghanistan. At first, the Taliban were hailed as liberators who promised to restore law and order, stability and security, and make the streets safe for ordinary citizens. They disarmed the population, cleaned up corruption and graft, and imposed *Shari'a*. At first, they enjoyed success and popularity as a reform movement. It was not until their capture of Kabul in 1996 that they revealed their intention to rule the country and to impose a strict puritanical form of Islam. With strong support from Saudi Arabia and Pakistan, by 1998, they had subdued 90 percent of the country and driven the Northern Alliance into a small area of northern Afghanistan. However, the Taliban government was recognized by only three nations: Saudi Arabia, Pakistan, and the United Arab Emirates.

When the Taliban came to power, they turned over many of their training camps to JUI factions, who in turn trained thousands of Pakistani and Arab militants as well as fighters from South and Central Asia and the Arab world in their radical jihad ideology and tactics. Very few people around the world, let alone those of us in the United States of America, had ever heard of the Taliban and these training camps for jihadists until 9/11. This is when everything changed.

Even after the invasion of Afghanistan by the USA and our apparent success, these training camps continued in parts of Afghanistan and in Pakistan. As of this writing, the Taliban are causing a lot of casualties, and these camps have indoctrinated many Muslims in jihadism and sent them back to the countries where they came from—and other parts of the world—with a hatred toward any Muslim who might be considered "moderate" or anyone favorable to the USA—since our country is the main backer of Israel—causing great contention in the Islamic world. (Could this be a partial fulfillment of the prophecy of Zechariah 12:3, "And it shall happen in that day that I will make Jerusalem a very heavy stone for all peoples; all who would heave it away will surely be cut in pieces, though all nations of the earth are gathered against it"?) I don't see this tension subsiding anytime in the near future.

Because of the increase in power among the Muslim nations, there is now a movement to try to get the UN to recognize all the Muslim nations as one nation and give them a place on the Security Council. There do not seem to be any strong movements or leaders for a more moderate Islam. (Note: it seems that the trend is to go back to a stronger Islamic state.) So with these many zealous trained jihadists, it looks like jihad will continue to be a threat, and Muslims will continue to increase and progress toward their goal of an Islamic world.

Another important factor is the high birth rate among the Muslims, which will greatly advance their numbers and, of course, their power.

Islam is out to convert and conquer the world, particularly the West—that is, Europe and the Americas. The means include proselytism, conversion, a change of certain laws, marriages with local women, and, above all, immigration. Another very subtle way Islam is winning in America is through the press and news agencies. In some cases, jihadists may use guns and bombs; in others, they use words and falsehoods—misleading statements—to increase the number of Muslims. We need to remember that Muslims typically give their loyalty to Islam more than to the country in which they live.

If we consider the fear that the jihadists have spread around the world and in America, the cost to the taxpayers for the armed protection of our liberties, the psychological impact of the threat of terrorism, and the political and judicial blackmail they have caused (for example, with oil), one might wonder if the West has not already entered into a state of subjection to Islam without knowing it! Random Muslim terrorism rules the world through fear. There is always that question, "Who is going to be attacked next?"

So how does this affect the Muslims in America?

Up until about twenty or thirty years ago, most Americans were not aware that there were Muslims here. The small population that lived here kept mostly to themselves and were not very visible. But things began to change in 1965 when the US government relaxed its immigration laws. Along with this came an influx of Muslim students to our American colleges and universities for both undergraduate and graduate degrees.

At first, the Muslims just met in unmarked houses, which kept them invisible. But as the number of immigrants and students began to increase, the Muslims started building mosques. Also, since it was around this time that Saudi Arabia came into its oil wealth, it started financing these mosques, paying also for the training of imams (spiritual leaders of the mosques) and then helping them to come to America and take charge of these mosques.

While the early immigrants to America were not too vocal and blended to a degree into the American society, when these students came from the Arab and other Muslim nations, they felt that the Muslims in America had compromised and were straying away from true Islam.

The students began to start extremist movements on many campuses and in these newly founded mosques. There are a number of even small towns that have a college or university with enough Muslim students and professors to enable them now to have a mosque, which has surprised many Americans. Big cities, yes, but not a mosque in a small town!

Most of us first became aware of the influx of people from India (some Hindu, some Muslim)—very visible because they began to run many of our gas stations and motels. Then around 1980, we began to notice a great increase in Muslim doctors, mainly from Egypt and Pakistan. Now in just about every town of any size, these Muslim professionals are very noticeable.

In these early days, there were many Islamic movements and charities set up here in America. These were organized, supposedly, to help poor Muslims in other countries. But it has turned out that quite a number of these so-called charitable organizations are bodies that have been raising money for the extremist jihadist movement. After 9/11, many of these organizations were forced to close down.

There is a tendency for these immigrant Muslims to live in areas by themselves, so they don't have a lot of contact with other Americans. And their social gatherings are centered around the local mosque. While most Muslims appreciate the freedom that we have in America and the opportunity to make much more money here than in their home country, they are not pleased with the American Hollywood society or with the American government, which is the leading backer of the nation of Israel. Also, there is an abundance of Arab-language newspapers produced by Muslims that foster the Islamic way of thinking instead of the American view. I have a friend who reads the leading Muslim English newspaper. He said that in all the time that he has been reading the newspaper, he does not remember coming upon one article favorable to the United States government.

Maybe in the past there were Muslim leaders who told their people, "We must Westernize." But if a Muslim leader has said this since the mid-1970s, he is a lonely figure. Indeed, it is hard to find statements by any Muslims—whether politicians, officials, academics, businesspersons, or journalists—praising Western values and institutions. They instead stress the differences between their civilization and Western civilization, the superiority of the Islamic culture, and the need to maintain the integrity of that culture against the Western onslaught. Muslims see Western culture as materialistic, corrupt, decadent, and immoral. Muslims refer to America as part of the "godless West."

The governments of Muslim countries are likely to continue to become less friendly to the West, and the Muslims living in America will go along with them.

For this reason, I doubt if there is much likelihood for the Muslims who live in America to become Westernized (in many ways, I hope they never do) and excited about democracy. Here is what many Muslims think of democracy:

> Today, one of the ugly examples of people taking the Divine Shari'a into their own hands, is the one related to the so-called democracy by taking people's opinion, directly or through their parliament, about implementing the Islamic Laws. The essence of this is subjugating the implementation of the Creator's Shari'a to the will of His creatures or rendering it to a mere choice like any human-set constitution or laws. This is total and clear disbelief. (Taken from a Muslim Website.)

There is already a push among the Muslims here in the States and other countries to be allowed to live under Islamic law, which is anything but democratic. If the Muslims in America were granted the right to be governed under Islamic law, then when a Muslim was found guilty of theft, his hand would be cut off. If two people committed adultery, they would be stoned to death. If a Muslim converted to another religion, he or she could be killed (most likely by a family member), and the killer would be guiltless. It would be a crime for anyone to try to convert a Muslim.

If a woman was raped and reported it to the authorities but did not have four witnesses (a virtually impossible situation!), that would be ignored under Islamic law.

The wide use of the Internet has been very influential in the spread of the *Qur'anic* type of Islam, which tends to be what we would consider extreme. The Muslims, and much of the news media, are trying to make us believe that the fundamental extremists are just a small minority and that most Muslims are moderate. This is not true. The *Qur'an* clearly teaches an extremist type of Islam. If a person is a "good" Muslim and is trying to follow the *Qur'an* and the *Hadith*, then that person is naturally an extremist. If truly a "moderate," that person would be considered by other Muslims to be a liberal.

We need to remember that Islam is not an individualistic sort of religion but a community, and the community can put strong pressure on all its members to conform to its community values. With the growth of Saudi Arabia's Wahhabism type of Islam and them financing the greater majority of the mosques here in America, there doesn't seem to be much of a possibility that most of the Muslims in America will become moderates.

I recently read something that was very frightening. The commentator asked, "Let's suppose there is only a very small group, say, five hundred extremist Muslims here in

America. But what would happen if just ten of those were to decide to become suicide bombers and go into action?"

I read something entered on the Internet by a moderate group of Muslims at www.reformislam.org that confirms the conclusions I have arrived at. Here is what I read:

The Need for Reform

Islam, in its present form, is not compatible with principles of freedom and democracy. Twenty-first century Muslims have two opinions: we can continue the barbaric policies of the seventh century perpetuated by Hassan al-Banna, Abdullah Azzam, Yassir Arafat, Ruhollah Khomeini, Osama bin Laden, the Muslim Brotherhood, al-Qaeda, Hizballah, Hamas, etc., leading a global war between *Dar al-Islam* (the Islamic World) and *Dar al-Harb* (the non-Islamic World), or we can reform Islam to keep our rich cultural heritage and to cleanse our religion from the reviled relics of the past. We can no longer allow Islamic extremists to use our religion as a weapon. We must protect future generations of Muslims from being brainwashed by the Islamic radicals. If we do not stop the spread of Islamic fundamentalism, our children will become homicidal zombies.

Accepting Responsibility

To start the healing process, we must acknowledge evils done by Muslims in the name of Islam and accept responsibility for those evils. We must remove evil passages from Islamic religious texts [meaning the *Qur'an* and *Hadith*], so that future generations of Muslims will not be confused by conflicting messages...Any set of beliefs that is spread by force is fundamentally immoral; it is no longer a religion, but a political ideology. [For the complete Manifesto, go to the Website.]

Jihad is something that affects all of us. It would be great if Islam was reformed, but it doesn't look like this is going to happen. It seems that Muslims are becoming more Islamic instead of more moderate.

7

Major Beliefs of Islam: Family Life, Women, Mosques, Angels, Jinn, Satan, Sin, the Prophets of God, the Holy Books, Jesus, the Death of Jesus, the Second Coming of Christ, Salvation

Family Life

THE BASIC UNIT of Islamic society is the family, which includes the extended family consisting of grandparents, uncles and aunts, cousins, and in-laws, as well as parents and children. Islam clearly defines the obligations and legal rights of family members. The father is responsible for both the economic welfare of the household and the preservation of the teachings of religion among its members. However, the actual religious instruction often depends on the mother, especially in the earlier stages, and Muslim women play a dominant role in every other aspect of home life as well as in the education of the children.

Usually, the father dominates in economic and social activities outside the home. It is the wife who reigns completely in the home, where the husband is like a guest. It is the wife who is central to family life and who provides most of the social bonding. She exerts much influence and wields great power through the family as wife, mother, and mother-in-law. The division of inheritance is specified in the *Qur'an*, which states that most of it is to pass to the immediate family, while a portion is set aside for the payment of debts and the making of bequests. The woman's share of inheritance is generally half of that of a man with the same rights of succession.

Marriage in Islam is a civil contract that consists of an offer and acceptance between two qualified parties in the presence of two witnesses. The groom is required to pay a dowry (*mahr*, bride price) to the bride, as stipulated in the contract. The is money is paid to the bride and not the family, and is due when the wedding occurs. In some Muslim countries, this dowry is quite expensive, and men may have to work for years to save up enough money. Sometimes, the men who live in exorbitant countries will seek brides from other countries where the dowry is less expensive.

The *Qur'an* states that a man can have up to four wives if he can properly care for them. Each wife is to live in independent living quarters of equal economic status. A woman can marry one man only. Divorce can be for any reason, but a woman cannot initiate divorce. In order for a husband to divorce his wife, he must first inform her of his desire to divorce her, using the word *Talaq*—"I divorce you"—three times. If said only once or twice, the divorce is revocable at the option of the husband but not when said *three* times. Even so, the divorce takes effect only after three months, not that instant; this is to make sure that the wife is not pregnant. If so, the divorcing husband will be required to meet his responsibilities for the new baby. Also, the three months can be useful as a "cooling-off period" in which the pair hopefully will seek a reconciliation. The couple must continue to live under the same roof but must abstain from sexual relations during that time.

A Muslim man is allowed to remarry the same woman twice, but after the third divorce, she becomes forbidden for him to marry again.

Women

Both the *Qur'an* and tradition give a lower status to women than to men. Surah 2:228 states, "Men are a degree above them [women]." The superior status of men is based directly on the *Qur'an*.

1. A Muslim man can be married to four women at the same time, but a Muslim woman can be married to only one man. "Marry (other) women of your choice, two or three or four" (Surah 4:3).

2. Men have the right to ask for a divorce, but not women (Surah 2:229).

3. Women may inherit only half of what men inherit (Surah 4:11).

4. Women may not serve as imams (spiritual leaders) and are not allowed to lead in prayer when men are present. (Men must always be above women, according to Surah 4:34).

5. A woman is not allowed to answer the door if her husband is not there, even if it's her brother or a relative (this is derived from Surah 33:53).

6. Women are supposed to stay in their houses. Many Muslim women cannot travel without the permission of their husband or father (Surah 33:33).

7. If a wife refuses to have sexual relations with her husband, he is permitted to beat her until she submits (Surah 4:34).
8. Islamic law requires that two women are needed to bear witness in civil contracts as opposed to one man.
9. Traditionally, a Muslim woman must wear a veil, stand behind her husband, and kneel behind him in prayer.

Muslim scholars currently disagree as to whether Islamic holy texts justify traditional Islamic practices such as veiling and seclusion (*purdah*). Starting in the twentieth century, Muslim social reformers have argued against these and other practices such as polygamy, with varying success. At the same time, many Muslim women have attempted to reconcile tradition with modernity by combining an active life with outward modesty. But certain Islamist groups and regimes like the Taliban zealously seek to continue traditional law as it applies to women.

Mosques

A mosque is a place of worship for Muslims, who often refer to it by its Arabic name, *masjid*. Its primary purpose is to serve as a place of prayer. The main meeting is on Friday afternoon, usually at 1:30 p.m., when a thirty-minute lecture or sermon is given, followed by a time of prayer that lasts about twenty minutes.

However, mosques are not solely for religious purposes. Islam is not merely a religion but a political and social entity. The imams have tremendous power in controlling the minds and sympathies of Muslims, and are able to inflame the congregations politically or spiritually. Jihad often comes out of the mosque. This presents a real problem here in America because the mosques operate as tax-free religious institutions, which the government feels it cannot suppress.

The mosque is also important to the Muslim community as a place to meet and study, and for social welfare activities. Some mosques have been successful in getting rid of the drug peddlers in the area. If a person converts to Islam, the mosque will give him money, help him find a job if necessary, and so forth. Should a single mom with children convert to Islam, the mosque will take care of her—provide child care, pay her rent, and help her to find work. They will not leave her to fend for herself. Members of the mosque who have financial needs may also be helped, but there is special consideration for new converts.

Egypt is the capital of Islamic education for the entire Muslim world. Al-Azhar University in Cairo sends imams as missionaries all over the world to spread Islam. Many of the teachers at this university are sympathetic to jihad.

If Muslims around the world have any questions on the *Qur'an* or about Islam, they may contact this university for an answer.

Angels

In the gap between Allah and humankind, there exists a hierarchy of numberless angels. They were created perfect; therefore, they cannot err or commit sin. Each human has two angels assigned to him or her, and they are stationed on the person's two shoulders: one to record the person's good deeds and the other to record the bad deeds.

Muslims believe in four archangels:

1. *Gabriel* (*Jibreel*). His function is to communicate the commands of Allah to prophets and messengers. Thus, he is known as the Angel of Revelation, and is said to hold the most prominent place.
2. *Michael* (*Mikaeel*). He is the controller of the winds and the clouds. He inflicts the wrath of Allah by creating violent storms, floods, and earthquakes. He is also the guardian of the Jews.
3. *Israel* (*Izra'il*). He is the Angel of Death. He has many angels under his supervision. These assistants are responsible, at the appointed hour, for extracting the soul from the body and transporting it to

its storage place until the Day of Judgment. A pair of angels, called *Munkar* and *Nakir*—the "Denied" and the "Denier"—are responsible for interrogating every deceased person in the grave.

4. *Israfil.* He is the one who summons people at the time of the resurrection for the Day of Judgment.

Jinn

Jinn are another group of created invisible beings at the bottom of the hierarchy of angels, and from jinn, we get the word *genie*. The jinn have a form made of smokeless flames and can transform themselves into any shape. Although animals such as dogs and donkeys can see the jinn, they are invisible to humans. Islam teaches that while angels are perfect and cannot sin, jinn are powerful, intelligent spirits who possess the freedom of choice between good and evil. It claims that the majority of them have sinned and therefore are working agents of Satan; their mission is to cause the destruction of humanity. They have the ability to think and reflect. They marry and reproduce among themselves. They are capable of appearing in human or animal form and are able to possess people.

The jinn existed for thousands of years before the creation of Adam and lived in the heavens. They had freedom and could travel anywhere in the universe without restriction.

Azazel was the father of the jinn, like Adam is the father of the human race. Azazel had a very high status in the heavens where he resided. When Azazel learned of the creation of Adam—who was appointed the vicegerent of Allah on the earth, a position he himself intended to inherit—he would not bow to Adam as commanded by Allah but rebelled, thus becoming Satan (*Iblis*).

Satan then was expelled from Paradise and was able to convert the majority of his offspring to his side. Thus, the majority of the jinn are known as devils. They may take on the appearance of cats and dogs and crawling creatures like snakes, scorpions, and rats. However, their favorite attire is that of a black dog.

Islam teaches that jinn now live on the earth, and most of them reside among ancient ruins and in places contaminated with ritual impurity, such as bathrooms, cemeteries, and animals' yards. Another favorite spot of theirs is wherever monetary transactions take place.

Islam further teaches that the jinn will die and ultimately be resurrected on Judgment Day.

Satan

In the *Qur'an*, Satan is called by the Hebrew word *Shaitan* and also by the word *Iblis*, which is a corruption of the Greek word *diabolos* (devil, accuser). There is a controversy among Muslims as to the origin of Satan. Since Islam teaches that angels can't sin but Satan obviously did, he could not be an angel. Therefore, many Muslim theologians have held the opinion that Satan belongs to the species known as jinn. Muslims believe that Satan was the first creature to disobey and has been at the source and center of evil even before the creation of Adam.

Sin

Muslims reject the doctrine of original sin. They believe that humans have a moral weakness rather than a sin nature. Because of disobedience, Adam and Eve were expelled from the Garden of Eden (which was located in heaven) but not separated from God. The Bible tells us that we, their descendants, are therefore born with a fallen nature, prone to resist God and want our own way. Moreover, we have a strong enemy who takes advantage of our fallen nature to tempt us to oppose and disobey God.

Islamic tradition, however, teaches that each child is born with an inclination toward religion, which is understood to be Islam. Children are perverted after birth by the environment. Sin cannot be transferred or inherited from person to person. The *Qur'an* teaches that the human race was given an innately pure nature called *fitrah*. Muslims state that though we were created weak, we are not separated from God by that weakness. A child is not responsible for his or her sins until the age of puberty. (A Muslim told me that when children do something wrong, parents should give them only a slight slap on the hand.)

Islam declares that all people commit sinful acts except the prophets of God, who are exempt. There appears to be a contradiction here, because the *Qur'an*—in Surahs 40:55, 47:19, 48:2, and 100:3—speaks openly of Muhammad's sins and his need to ask forgiveness. Whatever the case, sins are not due to our having a sinful nature but occur because of one's forgetfulness of God. Furthermore, by their own actions, humans can free themselves from any bondage to sin.

One Muslim wrote to me:

> Human beings are no more "fallen" than they are "saved." Because they are not "fallen," they have no need of a Savior. But because they are not "saved" either, they do need to do good works—and do them ethically; this alone will earn them Allah's mercy. Adam's disobedience was his own personal misdeed—a misdeed for which he repented and which God forgave."

In other words, Adam didn't really sin but only made a mistake. This is the central difference between Islam and biblical Christianity.

God has dealt with sin by mercifully sending the *Qur'an* to man. He commands Muslims to continue dealing with sin by *da'wah*, "calling all people to the path of Allah." Human nature is weak and easily led astray, so Allah saw it was necessary to set limits to human freedom of action. These limits are to be carried out in the community by the law (*Shari'a*) both religiously and politically to keep Muslims in the straight way. Islam functions as a theocracy. As creatures under law, human beings are perfectible but not perfect. The aim of communal allegiance is to discipline and educate people to deal with their human frailty. Salvation becomes largely a communal effort.

The fatalistic Islamic worldview, combined with an exaggerated view of the omnipotence of Allah, leads to fatalism in moral and ethical matters and a lack of any sense of moral responsibility. God is the source of all things, and nothing can happen (the Muslim argues) except by Allah's direct will. Consequently, Allah is the source of evil as well as good, and every action of man is in accordance with a preordained plan. The sinner can always say, "God made me this way. I was but walking in the path He ordered." This lack of a sense of responsibility is widespread.

The *Qur'an* doesn't say much about sin. An act is not intrinsically right or wrong. It is right only when God specifically decrees it to be so, according to His will. Nor does the *Qur'an* put much emphasis on the gravity of Adam's transgression. The Islamic view of sin is it comes from such things as ignorance, bad social contacts and companions, incorrect knowledge, poor habits, laziness, lack of judgment, and invisible influences that have an induced effect. Since man is not a sinner, there is no need for a Savior. Islam says that it is faith and action that determine our salvation.

In the *Qur'an* published by Why-Islam, you will find this enlightening comment on page 406, right after Surah 30:30:

> As turned out from the creative hand of God, man is innocent, pure, true, free, inclined to right and virtue, and possessed of true understanding about his own position in the Universe and about God's goodness, wisdom and power. That is his true nature, just as the nature of a lamb is to be gentle and of a horse is to be swift. But man is caught in the meshes of customs, superstitions, selfish desires, and false teaching. This may make him pugnacious, unclean, false, slavish, hankering after what is wrong or forbidden, and deflected from the love of his fellow-men and the pure worship of the One True God.

It would be wonderful if what the Muslims believe was true, but I have five children, so I know it is not true, because they began to sin at a very early age.

Here is my comment: If children are born pure and innocent, like Islam claims, and a sinful nature is not transferred
from parent to child, then commission of sin is something
that has to be taught or learned by watching others. Parents
have the greatest influence on children, especially when
they are small, so the blame for their sinful selfishness rests
squarely on their parents! Adult Muslims are supposed to
read and follow the *Qur'an*; they are to go to the mosque
and learn there about the will of Allah, and, ideally, they
should live in a country that is governed by *Shari'a*, the
law code of Allah. So there is no valid excuse for Muslim
parents not living an exemplary life, and the Islamic community everywhere should gradually become perfect! Why
hasn't it? What is wrong?

The Prophets of God

Prophets play a very important part in the theology of
Islam. They are needed for two basic reasons: (1) humans
are frail and need direction, and (2) God cares for His creatures. According to the *Qur'an*, God has sent a prophet to
every nation to preach the message of there being only one
God and to call people back to Himself.

According to Islamic tradition, 124,000 prophets have
been sent, even though only twenty-eight of them are mentioned in the *Qur'an*, and most of these are ones found also

BURNING QUESTIONS ABOUT ISLAM

in the BibleSlike Noah, Job, Abraham, Isaac, Jacob, Joseph, Moses, Aaron, David, Solomon, Jonah, Zechariah, John the Baptist, and Jesus.

Among the prophets, five are recognized to be in the highest rank:

- Muhammad (the apostle of God, who is reputed to be the greatest because he was the last; and while others were sent only to certain people groups, Muhammad was sent to the whole world; hence, he was "the seal of the prophets and belongs to all times and places")
- Noah (the preacher of God)
- Abraham (the friend of God)
- Moses (the speaker with God)
- Jesus (the word of God)

Surah 2:136 states, "Say (*O Muslims*): 'We believe in Allah and that which is revealed to us, and in what was revealed to Abraham, Ishmael, Isaac, Jacob, and the tribes; to Moses and Jesus and the (*other*) prophets by their Lord. We make no distinction between any of them, and to Allah we have surrendered ourselves.'"

While declaring that all the prophets proclaimed the same inspired message, Islam nevertheless claims that these prophets were sent to specific people groups and had a message just for them. However, the teaching goes, these peo-

. 199 .

ple groups gradually drifted away from God and corrupted the original message so that it was no longer recognizable. Therefore, there was a need for additional prophets. Islam declares that these prophets were infallible in that they did not commit sins or violate the Law of God.

The Holy Books

Four of the highest-ranking prophets were given books of divine revelation. The four are Moses (the Torah), David (the Psalms), Jesus (the Gospel), and Muhammad (the *Qur'an*.) Of these four books, Muslims contend that only the *Qur'an* has been preserved in an uncorrupted state. The others "have been greatly corrupted and cannot be trusted."

However, Muslims will utilize a number of verses of the Bible which they say predict the coming of Muhammad or support other appropriate teachings.

Jesus

Muslims believe in the virgin birth of Jesus and the fact that He performed many miracles. However, they do not believe that He was the divine Son of God. He was "a great prophet"—one of the long line of prophets sent primarily to the Jewish people—but was merely human. His title *Messiah*, they think, simply means He was one who went around from place to place preaching. Associating Jesus with God by calling Him the Son of God, they say, is blasphemy. (If this is true, then Muslims must condemn God the Father as being a blasphemer because twice—Matthew 3:17 and 17:5—the Father declared, "This is my beloved Son, with whom I am well pleased.")

Muslims openly declare that the greatest of all sins is *shirk*—the assigning of partners to God—which is what they accuse Christians of doing when we say that Jesus is the Son of God and equal to the Father and the Holy Spirit. The *Qur'an* sternly declares in Surah 4:116, "Surely, Allah forgives not that partners should be ascribed to Him. He forgives all save that to whom He pleases. Whosoever ascribes partners to Allah has strayed far indeed."

An enlightening comment follows this verse: "(This verse, and also a number of sayings of the Blessed Prophet on the same subject, expound the Muslim doctrine of God's mercy towards all sinners, save only those who were guilty of the greatest sin of all: polytheism [which they think includes Christians] and idolatry. If a man or woman dies with faith, he may be punished for his sins, or, because of his good deeds he may be saved, or Almighty God may forgive him absolutely. Believers may spend some time in hellfire before they are purged of their sins and impurities, and are admitted into the Garden of God's grace. But disbelievers will never have this chance.)"

In other words, to a Muslim, anyone who believes in the deity of Jesus Christ has absolutely no hope of going to one of the seven heavens, no matter how many good deeds he or she may have done.

Obviously, the biblical teaching that Jesus Christ was true God as well as true man is a massive stumbling block to all Muslims.

The Death of Jesus

To Christians, the death and resurrection of Jesus Christ is the very center and heart of the Gospel. Without this proven truth, Christianity has nothing to offer. We find this stated clearly in 1 Corinthians 15:1–8:

> Now I would remind you, brothers, of the gospel I preached to you, which you received, in which you stand, and by which you are being saved, if you hold fast to the word I preached to you—unless you believed in vain. For I delivered to you as of first importance what I also received: that Christ died for our sins in accordance with the Scriptures, that he was buried, that he was raised on the third day in accordance with the Scriptures, and that he appeared to Cephas, then to the twelve. Then he appeared to more than five hundred brothers at

one time, most of whom are still alive, though some have fallen asleep. Then he appeared to James, then to all the apostles. Last of all, as to one untimely born, he appeared also to me.

And in Acts 1:1–3, we read the following:

In the first book, O Theophilus, I have dealt with all that Jesus began to do and teach, until the day when he was taken up, after he had given commands through the Holy Spirit to the apostles whom he had chosen. To them he presented himself alive after his suffering by many proofs, appearing to them during forty days and speaking about the kingdom of God.

According to Islamic tradition, however, Jesus did not die on the cross. Instead, He was taken up to heaven, and someone who looked like Him (many Muslims say it was Judas) died in His place on the cross. This entire allegation is founded on *one* passage in the *Qur'an*, Surah 4:154–158, which states,

We took from [the Jews] a firm covenant…because of their disbelief and of their speaking against Mary a tremendous calumny. And because of their saying: "We slew the Messiah, Jesus son of Mary, Allah's messenger." They slew him not, nor crucified him, but it appeared so to them; and those who disagree concerning it are in doubt thereof; they have no knowledge thereof except pursuit of a conjecture; they slew him not for certain. But Allah raised him up to Himself. Allah is Mighty, Wise.

Here is a comment I found at this point in the *Qur'an* published by Why-Islam (page 102):

Allah saved Noah from the flood, Abraham from the fire, Muhammad from the traps of the idolaters, and Jesus from the wickedness of the Jews, who wished to crucify him. It was Judas Iscariot, who sought to betray Jesus, who was arrested instead, and crucified instead of the Prophet Jesus, upon whom be peace.

Muslims feel that it is disrespectful to believe that God would allow one of His prophets—and especially one of the most honored of the prophets—to be crucified. But surely this argument is very strange, for history informs us that a number of the caliphs of Islam suffered assassination. Why didn't Allah save those honorable men from such a cruel death?

There are quite a few things recorded in the Bible that make this statement in the *Qur'an* entirely impossible. In the first place, the Bible states that Judas went away and hanged himself even before Jesus was condemned by the governor, Pilate (Matthew 27:1–11). Furthermore, both the mother of Jesus and John, the beloved apostle, were standing by the cross, and Jesus had a conversation with them (John 19:25–27). Surely Mary and John would have known if someone else was speaking to them—especially if it had been Judas, whom they also knew! And again, since the Jewish leaders entertained such hatred toward Jesus and were present for the full event, surely *they* could not have been deceived—nor would they have let Jesus escape and another die in his place!

There are other reasons why such a belief is unreasonable:

1. It is contrary to the extant record of multiple eyewitnesses that the one crucified between the two thieves was "Jesus of Nazareth" (Matthew 27, Mark 15, Luke 23, and John 19).
2. Muslim substitution legends are contrary to the earliest extrabiblical Jewish, Roman, and Samaritan testimonies about the death of Christ.
3. There is not a shred of first-century testimony denying Jesus's death, given by friend or foe of Christianity.

4. The legends are unthinkable since they demand total ignorance on the part of those closest to Jesus, His disciples, and on the part of the Romans who crucified Him.

The Muslim denial of Christ's death by crucifixion is based on a theological misunderstanding. They contend that Allah would never "stoop to punish" such a great prophet for the sins of someone else, completely ignoring the fact that God has allowed many other of His faithful servants to suffer unjustly. How can they blindly overlook the Old Testament prophecies concerning the death and resurrection of the Messiah and the many times that Jesus clearly stated that He would "go up to Jerusalem, be crucified and the third day rise again"? The death and resurrection of Jesus Christ is spoken of more than 120 times in the Bible.

Muslims are very familiar with Surah 4:154–58, the one passage that denies the Messiah's death. However, there are other verses in the *Qur'an* that state that Jesus did die and was raised up from the dead and then taken to heaven.

Surah 3:55 reads,

> (*And remember*) when Allah said: "O Jesus! I am gathering you [literally, in the Arabic, "raising you up from the dead"] and causing you to ascend to

Me, and am cleansing you of those who disbelieve, and am setting those who follow you above those who disbelieve until the Day of Resurrection. Then to Me you will all return, and I shall judge between you as to that in which you used to differ."

(One Muslim I pointed this out to—one who could read Arabic—replied that it just said "Raising you up from the dead" and didn't specifically mention "crucifixion," and therefore, it didn't apply. But that is a weak objection.)

Surah 2:87 states, "And assuredly We gave Moses the Scripture, and after him We sent messenger after messenger. We gave Jesus son of Mary the clear miracles (*to serve as proof of Allah's sovereignty*) and strengthened him with the Holy Spirit (*the Angel Gabriel*). Is it so, that whenever a Messenger whose message does not suit your desires comes to you, you grow arrogant, denying some of them, and **slaying others**?" (Bold type emphasis added.)

And Surah 19:33–34 declares, "So peace be upon me the day I was born and **the day that I die and the day I shall be raised up to life** (*again*). Such was Jesus, the son of Mary; a statement of the truth about which they [the Jews] (*vainly*) dispute." (Bold type emphasis added.)

These verses point quite clearly to Jesus Christ's death and resurrection. But the Muslims have tried to play down these verses.

The Second Coming of Christ

Christians believe that Jesus Christ will one day return from heaven to earth. And so do the Muslims—but with a very strange twist. They say that Jesus, having never died, will return as "the true teacher of Islam" and will proclaim its message to all mankind. And when he appears he will kill the Antichrist, slaughter all the pigs, break the cross, destroy the synagogues and churches, and establish the religion of Islam. He will next do away with all the "infidels"—meaning all people who are not Muslims, including Jews and Christians. Finally, Jesus will select one of the sects of Islam (of which there are seventy-two) and will kill all Muslims who belong to the other sects. For instance, if he chooses the Shi'ites, then the Sunnis and all the rest will be killed. Since no Muslim knows which group Jesus will favor, obviously they are all in danger of being wiped away! They also teach that Jesus will live upon earth for forty years, get married, have children, and then die and be buried in the city of Medina beside the prophet Muhammad.

Muhammad died, and his grave is in Medina. Unlike Jesus, he was not taken directly to heaven. Yet in a book I was given by a Muslim, *Our Teaching*, printed by Islam International Publications, it states on page 13, "Muhammad excels Jesus by a thousand measures." Superior to Jesus? How can that be?

Salvation

When Christians speak of salvation, they usually mean a personal experience of heart conversion; to Muslims, however, the word only means "restoration"—a returning and a remembering of Allah. In Islam, the greatest challenge for earthlings is not so much to personally know God as to remember that there *is* one.

One Muslim has stated, "Inasmuch as sin in the *Qur'an* does not include a taint of nature, but only a proneness to wrong actions due to the weakness of man, the concept of salvation in Islam does not include the element of regeneration." Thus, salvation in Islam is, for the most part, a future state experienced only in the hereafter. It includes pardon from past sins and deliverance from hell as well as gaining God's favor and acceptance into heaven on Judgment Day.

The Means of Being Rescued from Sin

Salvation, in the hereafter, on the human side involves (1) belief or faith, and (2) action (good works). Salvation cannot be achieved without these two elements. As to "faith," there are three basic ingredients: (1) belief in the oneness of God, (2) belief in the Prophet Muhammad, and (3) belief in life after death. As to the "actions" that are required to obtain salvation, one must obey the five pillars of Islam, namely (1) reciting the *Shahadah* (the confession that there is only one God and Muhammad is His true prophet), (2) praying five times a day, (3) fasting throughout the month of Ramadan, (4) almsgiving, and (5) a pilgrimage to Mecca. Some writers include a sixth which is *jihad*. However, it is not enough just to *do* these things, they must be done in the "correct way" or else you gain no merit.

Muslims are given meticulous details about the correct way in which these religious duties should be performed. Islamic devotions are of two types, mainly (1) obligatory and (2) supererogatory—going beyond the requirements of duty. But even so, they may accomplish nothing.

The Uncertainty of Salvation

There is no assurance of salvation (going to one of the seven heavens) in Islam. Even if your good deeds outweigh your bad deeds on the Day of Judgment, if Allah does not will so, He can still send you to hell. (To most Muslims, this lack of assurance of salvation is not considered a weakness but a reality that should motivate one to continued obedience.) Some Muslims strive more than others, but no matter how hard one tries and succeeds in good deeds, there is no possibility of going to Paradise if one does not believe in the prophethood of Muhammad. In other words, anyone who is not a Muslim, no matter how good that person may be, will end up in hell because of his lack of faith in Muhammad! (However, Islam does teach that after time in hell many will pay for their sins then go to one of the seven Paradises. So it is almost like purgatory.)

While I was browsing one Muslim website that contained an article describing Paradise and hell, I came across this very frightening statement for all Muslims. It said, "Many texts indicate that nine hundred and ninety-nine out of every thousand of the children of Adam [which includes the Muslims] will enter Hell, and only one (in a thousand) will enter Paradise." Then it gave the following quote from the *Hadith* by al-Bukhari to show the source of this statement (found in the book mentioned in chapter 5 on page 126, vol. 1):

> Muhammad said: "Allah will say, 'O Adam!' Adam will reply, 'I respond to Your call, I am obedient to Your orders, and all good is in Your hands.' Then Allah will say to Adam, 'Send forth the people of the Fire.' Adam will say, 'How many are the people of the Fire?' Allah will say, 'Out of every thousand, take nine hundred and ninety-nine.'"

Imagine being in a religion where you have only one chance in a thousand of going to Paradise!

8

Major Beliefs of Islam: The Dead, the End Times, Resurrection, the Day of Judgment, Paradise, Hell

Where Are the Dead?

THERE IS QUITE a lot of confusion among Muslims about what happens between the time a person dies and the body is resurrected and appears before Allah on the Day of Judgment. I asked several knowledgeable Muslims what they had been taught but didn't receive a very clear answer. But here is the gist of what I was told.

Even though the dead are unconscious, in the grave there is still activity and some feeling of pain. Most Muslims believe that there are two angels—usually called *Munkar* and *Nakir*—who will visit the dead person to ask him a series of questions about his faith. Accounts do not agree on exactly what questions will be asked of the deceased. However, most versions indicate that after his entering the grave, the angels ask the dead person to sit up; they ask him who is his Lord, what is his religion, and who is his prophet. Of course, the correct answer is "Allah, Islam, and Muhammad." (If a person does not confess that Muhammad is a true prophet of God, there is absolutely no chance of that person going to Paradise and he will have to go to hell.)

For the believers who pass the test successfully, the angels make their graves more spacious (though they still suffer torment) and open a window through which they can gaze at the Garden and receive the winds and odor of Paradise. For unbelievers who fail the test, the angels open a door to hell's fire for them. Thus, the deceased one feels the heat and hot winds from hell, and "his grave narrows until his ribs merge into one another."

It is often suggested that the difference between the torment of the believer and that experienced by the unbeliever, besides its intensity, is that whereas the torment for unbelievers is a prefiguring of the final destiny of the wicked, the believer's torment is primarily designed to have a purging effect on the soul.

However, Islam teaches that those who die in jihad (holy war) go directly to Paradise when they die. Furthermore, the children of Muslim parents who die before the age of puberty go directly to heaven. From what I have read, it is unclear as to whether the young children of non- Muslims go immediately to Paradise or not.

The End Times

It is interesting to note that the teaching of Islam concerning the calamitous nature of the end times is quite similar to that found in the Bible. Surah 82:1–5 reads, "When the sky is cleft asunder, and when the planets are dispersed, and when the oceans are poured forth and when the graves are overturned, each soul will know."

Surah 81:1–3 comes quite close when it says, "When the sun is folded up, and when the stars fall, losing their lustre, and when the mountains are moved." The majority of Muslims believe that before the signs in nature occur, they will be preceded by widespread moral decadence. Based on the *Hadith,* it is believed that godly wisdom will suffer a complete extinction, there will be an increase in the usage of wine, and the committing of adultery and rape will be common activities. There will be a rise in injustice and moral corruption of all kinds.

It is interesting to note that according to many Muslim commentators, the most important sign of the closeness of the fateful hour is the coming of Christ and his destruction of the false Messiah (Antichrist). This will bring about peace and righteousness on earth, and Christ will then establish the true religion of Islam.

Resurrection

Muslims believe there will be a Day of Resurrection. They believe that this day is preordained by God, but its date is unknown to man. The trials and tribulations preceding and during the resurrection are described in the *Qur'an*. The *Qur'an* emphasizes bodily resurrection, a break from the pre-Islamic Arabian understanding of death. It states that resurrection will be followed by the gathering together of mankind, culminating in their judgment by God.

The Day of Judgment

The God of the *Qur'an* has decreed that there will be a day when all will stand before Him to be judged. The preaching of a bodily resurrection was a cornerstone of Muhammad's early ministry. Islam states that there will be a trumpet call.

Allah will resurrect everyone who has died, from the beginning of creation until the last moment of life.

On that day, which takes place while people are kneeling around hell, the divine judicial process is carried out by means of a scale, which is used for balancing the individual's good deeds against his evil deeds. Everything a person has done, including intentions and desires, will be brought forth on that day. Those whose good deeds outweigh their evil deeds will be rewarded with Paradise (seven different degrees), and those whose evil deeds outweigh their good deeds will be judged to hell (seven different degrees). Whether one's good deeds outweigh one's evil deeds is a subjective matter though, known only by Allah.

As a result, no Muslim has assurance that God will accept him or her. I had one imam tell me that there is a 100 percent possibility of every Muslim going to hell—at least for a while. The *Qur'an* teaches in Surahs 3:157 and 3:169 that only those who are killed in battle, fighting the holy war (jihad), are assured of going directly to Paradise.

The judgment is entirely up to Allah. Even if your good works outweigh your evil ones, if Allah does not like you, He can still send you to hell. Surah 11:119 states, "Except those to whom your Lord has shown mercy. For this end He has created them. The word of your Lord shall be fulfilled: 'I [Allah] will fill Hell with jinn and men altogether.'"

In the final analysis, Allah determines who goes to Paradise and who goes to hell.

One Muslim wrote me and explained it this way:

> Paradise and Hell have already been created. They will never come to an end or cease to exist. Allah created Paradise and Hell before the rest of creation, and He created inhabitants for each of them. Whoever He wishes will enter Paradise by His grace and mercy, and whoever He wishes will enter Hell as a result of His justice. Every person will behave according to that for which he was created, and his destiny will be that for which he was created; good deeds and evil deeds are foreordained for all men.

Islamic folklore includes a tale in which, while waiting to be judged, some people attempt to approach one or more of the prophets—like Adam, Noah, Abraham, Moses—but are not able to do so because they have sinned. But finally they go to Muhammad, and the Prophet answers, "I am the right one to intercede—insofar as God allows it—for whomever He wills and chooses." Then Muhammad makes a request to Allah and is granted permission to intercede.

The last phase of one's judgment is the crossing of the bridge over hell. Some believe that this bridge is like a narrow, sharp sword and is hotter than fiery charcoal. The more dedicated will be able to cross easily and very fast while others have to go slowly. But only those whom Allah feels are worthy of Paradise will be able to cross the bridge successfully.

However, no one who believes that God has a Son who is equal with the Father will be included in this group. The condemned will fall into the abyss of hell as they try to pass over this bridge. Some Muslims believe, however, that Muhammad will be given permission to intercede for certain people, and his intercession is so effective that many of those who had been originally condemned to Hell are released from there and taken to Paradise. But this is not found in the *Qur'an*.

Paradise

The best description I have found of the Islamic heaven mirrors what is found in the first two chapters of the book of Esther. There, we are told of the banquet that King Xerxes gave and are informed about his royal harem consisting of many beautiful young women—a scene of ongoing sensuality.

When Muhammad ruled in Medina, he fought a number of battles, and he attracted many young men to fight alongside him by promising them, in the next life, all the things that royalty can experience here on earth—if they should be killed in battle (jihad).

Muslim sources state, "The delights of Paradise surpass the imagination and defy description. They are like nothing known to the people of this world; no matter how advanced we may become, what we achieve is as nothing in comparison with the joys of the Hereafter. It is sparkling lights, aromatic plants, a lofty palace, a flowing river, ripe fruit, a beautiful wife and abundant clothing, in an eternal abode of radiant joy, in beautiful soundly constructed high houses."

Here is one description of Paradise found in the *Qur'an*, in Surah 37:41–48:

> For them there is a known provision, fruits. And they will be honored in the Gardens of delight, on couches facing one another; a cup from a gushing spring is brought round for them, white, delicious to the drinkers, wherein there is no headache, nor are they made mad thereby. And with them are those of modest gaze, with lovely eyes (*women*).

Many of us have heard about the promise in the *Hadith* that the faithful Muslim men who are killed in jihad will have the companionship of seventy-two young and beautiful virgins, *houris*. Surah 52:20 states, "They shall recline on couches ranged around. And We shall wed them to *hou-*

ris (*ladies of heaven*) with large and lovely eyes." (See also Surah 56:22, 55:72, and 44:54.)

Another description of Paradise is found in Surah 47:15: "The Garden [in Paradise] that has been promised to the righteous is such that rivers will be flowing in it, of unpolluted water, and rivers will be flowing in it of milk of unchanged flavour, and rivers will be flowing in it of wine which will be delicious to the drinkers, and of honey, clear and pure."

According to the explanation given in one *hadith*, the wine in Paradise will not have been distilled from rotten fruit, the honey will not have been drawn from the bees' bellies, but all these drinks will flow in the form of natural springs.

Islam teaches that those in Paradise are content, peaceful, and secure. They do not participate in idle conversation but experience only peace. None will ever taste death. Rather, they will enjoy gentle speech, pleasant shade, and all kinds of fruit, as well as cool drinks and any kind of meat they desire.

There are seven different levels in Paradise, and it depends upon one's good deeds and the mercy of Allah which one the Muslim will go to. Apparently, there is a great deal of difference in the levels, because it is stated that Muhammad said, "The people of Paradise will look at the people dwelling in the chambers above them in the same way that people look at a brilliant star shining far away on the horizon, in the East."

These chambers differ in sublimity and appearance according to the deeds of their occupants. Some of them will be more supernal than others. I read one Muslim book that stated, "What leads to Hell is easy to do, while what leads to Paradise is difficult to do." This is not very promising!

Some other facts about the Muslim Paradise found in the *Hadith* or the *Qur'an* are the following (this material was taken from the islamworld.net website under "Heaven and Hell" and based on the book *In The Light of the Qur'aan and Sunnah* by Dr. Umar Sulaiman al-Ashqar):

1. Those who fear their Lord will be given two gardens in Paradise.
2. Any Muslim who kills an infidel (one who believes that God has a Son) will never experience the fire of Hell.
3. There are many beautiful mansions in Paradise.
4. After the believers have crossed the bridge over Hell they will be kept on another bridge between Paradise and Hell, where they will be purified through the settling of any wrongs that existed between any of them in this world. So when they enter Paradise they will be pure and clean, none of them bearing

any ill will towards another or demanding anything of another. [This sounds like purgatory to me.]

5. The first person to enter Paradise on the Day of Judgment will be Muhammad. It is reported that Muhammad said, "I will come to the gate of Paradise and ask for it to be opened. The gatekeeper will ask, 'Who are you?' I will say, 'Muhammad.' The gatekeeper will say, 'I was ordered not to open the gate for Anyone else before you.'"

6. "The first group to enter Paradise will be as beautiful as the full moon. They will not spit, blow their nose or excrete. Their vessels will be of gold, their combs of gold and silver. Each of them will have two wives, the marrow of whose leg-bones will be visible through their flesh because of their extreme beauty."

7. "The wives of the people of Paradise will sing to their husband in the most beautiful voices that anyone has heard. What they will sing is: 'We are good and beautiful, the wives of a noble people, who look at their husbands content and happy. We are eternal and will never die, we are safe and will never fear, we are remaining here and will never go away.'"

8. The people in Paradise will have all they desire.

9. Muhammad said that seventy thousand of his followers will enter Paradise without being called to

account. (In other words, there would be no Day of Judgment for them.)

10. The *Qur'an* states that of the Muslims who enter Paradise more of them will come from early generations than from later generations. Surah 56:12–14 reads: "In the gardens of delight: a whole multitude from the men of old, but only a few from the later generations."

11. The poor will enter Paradise ahead of the rich. Some Muslim writings state that these will enter Paradise forty years ahead of other people, while in other places it states that it will be five hundred years.

12. In spite of the fact that Islam teaches that once a person goes to Hell it is for eternity, it also reported that Muhammad taught that because of his intercession some who go to Hell will eventually end up in Paradise. The account goes like this: "The people of Hell will remain there, never dying, and never living. But there are people who will enter Hell because of their sins, and will be killed therein, so that they become like coals. Permission will be granted for intercession to be made, and they will be brought forth in groups and spread on rivers of Paradise, and it will be said, 'O people of Paradise, pour water on them.' Then they will grow like seeds in the silt left by a flood." Strangely enough, this

group will include some who never associated in the worship of Allah and were not Muslims.

13. It is also reported in the *Hadith* that Allah will bring forth from Hell whoever has the weight of a mustard seed of faith in his heart. This will include people who never did any good deeds at all. When this happens, it is said, "They will be made to stand in the courtyard of Paradise and the people of Paradise will start to pour water over them until they begin to grow like seeds left by silt after a flood. All traces of the fire of Hell will disappear." It is further stated, "These people will come out looking like the wood of the ebony tree; they will enter one of the rivers of Paradise and bathe in it, then they will come out looking white like sheets of paper."

14. Another Muslim quote states, "Those who are guilty of major sins are subject to the will of Allah. If He wills, He will forgive them, out of mercy, and if He wills, He will punish them for their sins and then admit them to Paradise by His mercy." However, those who commit *shirk*—believe that God has a Son, like all Christians do—will never be forgiven by Allah.

15. But in spite of all that is written about one's good works having to be more than one's evil deeds in order to get to Paradise, Surah 39:53 reads, "(*O*

Prophet!) Say: 'O my slaves who have transgressed against their souls! Do not despair of Allah's mercy! Surely Allah forgives all sins; for He is the All-Forgiving, the Most Merciful.'"

16. Angels will be able to make intercession for those in Hell.

17. Muhammad described the last person to enter Paradise by saying; "I know the last people of Hell who will be brought forth from it, and the last of the people of Paradise to enter it. It is a man who will come out of Hell crawling, on all fours. Allah will say to him, 'Go and enter Paradise.' So he will come to it and will suppose that it is full. He will go back and say, 'My Lord, I found it full.' Allah will say, 'Go and enter Paradise, for there you have something like the world and ten times over.'"

18. Paradise has eight gates through which people will enter. Muhammad is reported to have said that the distance between two gates is the distance of forty-years walking, but there will come a time when a gate will become very crowded.

19. Islam teaches that there will be seven levels in Paradise and it depends upon your good works as to which one you enter. Those in the lower levels can see those above them. The e inhabitants of the high-est levels will enjoy greater pleasures than the peo-

ple below them. Those who die in *jihad* will enjoy the highest level.

20. Muhammad claims that he made a "Night Journey" to Paradise and is reported to have said, "There are four rivers in Paradise, two visible and two hidden. The two visible rivers are the Nile and the Euphrates. These are rivers of water, of milk, of wine, and of clear honey."

21. Those who enter Paradise are promised beautiful mansions built story upon story, beneath which there will be rivers flowing in these gardens of everlasting bliss. Beautiful fair maidens will reside there for the pleasure of the men.

22. Beside the mansions there will be tents, which Muhammad described thus: "The tent is a hollowed-out pearl, thirty miles high. The man will have a number of wives which he will visit in turn; none of these wives will see the other wives."

23. Muhammad stated that a believer could acquire more than one house in Paradise by building a mosque for Allah, even if it is as small as the nestling-place scratched out by a grouse for its eggs.

24. Paradise is filled with a pure and beautiful fragrance which can be discerned from a distance of fifty-years traveling.

25. The trees of Paradise are abundant, good, and of many kinds—like grapevines, date palms and

pomegranates. The fruit will hang low so they can be picked easily. These trees will not be seasonal but bear fruit constantly.

26. There are trees in Paradise so huge that it would take the rider of a swift horse one hundred years to pass beneath.

27. The trunks of the trees in Paradise are of gold.

28. There will be animals and birds there.

29. Only those who believe that Muhammad was a true prophet and that his revelations were from Allah will be allowed into Paradise. Surah 32:15 makes this plain. But not all believers (Muslims) enter Paradise. Only those who do righteous deeds and humble themselves in repentance and obedience before Allah will get in. Also, no believer in Allah who is on friendly terms with those who oppose Allah and Muhammad—even though they be their fathers, their sons, their brothers, or other kindred—will be allowed into Paradise. (However, as we see elsewhere, there are many exceptions.)

30. Islam teaches that the way to Paradise is very hard because it is a very high and lofty place. The way to Paradise is obstructed by hardships that go against human wishes and inclinations. (This is stated in spite of the fact that Islam teaches that man is basically good, and only giving in to outside influences

makes one do wrong.) Thus one needs strong determination and will-power. Muhammad is quoted as having said, "Hell has been veiled with [surrounded by] desires, and Paradise has been veiled with [surrounded by] hardships." Muhammad is also supposed to have said, "When Allah created Paradise, He told Gabriel, 'Go and look at it.' So he went and looked at it, then he came back and said, 'By Your glory, no one will hear of it but he will enter it.' So Allah surrounded it with hardships and said, 'Go and look at it.' So Gabriel went and looked at it, then came back and said, 'By Your glory, I fear that no one will enter it.'"

31. Some of the hardships include: striving consistently and patiently in worship, restraining one's anger, forgiving, being patient, giving to charity, being kind to those who mistreat you, resisting physical desires, etc.

32. Islam teaches two portions are given to each descendent of Adam, one portion in Paradise and one in Hell. Then whoever is destined to damnation will inherit the portions in Hell that had been allocated to the people in Paradise, and those of the people of Paradise for whom eternal bliss is decreed will inherit the portions of Paradise that had been allocated to the people in Hell.

33. This one is a real shocker! Muhammad said, "Some people amongst the Muslims will come on the Day of Resurrection with sins as great as a mountain. Allah will forgive them, and will pass their burden of sin to the Jews and Christians."

34. Muhammad is supposed to have said, "I stood at the gate of Paradise and saw that most of those who entered were poor and destitute. I stood by the gate of Hell and saw that most of those who entered it were women." (This is a strange statement, because according to Islam most adults do not enter Paradise until after the Day of Judgment, which is still in the future.)

35. There will be only a small number of women in Paradise according to the following statement. "Muhammad [supposedly] said, 'Look, can you see anything?' We said, 'We see crows, and one of them stands out because its beak and feet are red.' Muhammad then said, 'No women will enter Paradise except those who are as rare among them as the crow is among others.'" (In spite of the fact that Muhammad declared that the majority of those in hell are women and there will be only a few women in Paradise, yet each man is promised at least two or more wives in Paradise—which is impossible,

because there will not be enough for each man to have even one wife.)

36. Those who will enter Paradise before the Day of Resurrection are Adam and Eve, those who die in *jihad*, and the children of the believers who die before reaching the age of puberty. Abraham and Sarah will care for these children until they are given back to their parents on the Day of Resurrection.

37. A child who has passed from this life is allowed, by the will of Allah, to plead on behalf of his parents, asking Him to be merciful in His judgment. Since the child cannot bear to be separated from his parents in Heaven, when Allah is calling him to Paradise he can refuse to enter the gates of Heaven without his beloved mother and father. In this way, the child takes each parent by the hand and leads them towards Allah. Perhaps God will then take pity on the parents.

38. Islam's teaching as to what happens to the children of unbelievers is very vague. Some Muslims say they will go to Heaven and might be servants there. Others say they will go to Hell.

39. Muhammad said, "No one of you will enter Paradise by his deeds alone." They asked, "Not even you, O Messenger of Allah?" He said, "Not even me, unless Allah covers me with His grace and mercy."

40. Good deeds will be a *reason*, not the *price* for admission to Paradise.

41. This is an interesting statement: "Allah created Adam in His own image, ninety feet tall. People kept getting shorter and shorter after the time of Adam, but everyone who enters Paradise will be in the image of Adam, ninety feet tall."

42. The people who enter Paradise are hairless, age thirty-three and never grow older (but different ages are mentioned elsewhere), will not spit, blow their nose, or sleep. Women will be much more beautiful there.

43. The pleasures of Paradise are superior to those of this world. There the people can eat and drink all they like.

44. The food and drink of the people in Paradise does not produce any body-waste.

45. The clothing and jewelry of the people in Paradise will never wear out or fade.

46. The palaces of Paradise have been prepared and in their gardens are places to sit and recline, beautiful couches of delightful colors and high beds whose interiors are lined with silk brocade. There are cushions and splendid carpets laid out in the most delightful manner.

47. The people of Paradise will be served by boys whom Allah will create to serve them and who will be most

beautiful and perfect in form, boys who remain in that youthful form forever, never changing or advancing in age.

48. In Paradise there is a market to which the people will come every Friday; then a wind will come from the north and blow on their faces and clothes, and they will increase in beauty. They will then return to their wives, who will also have increased in beauty. Their wives will say to them, "By Allah, you increased in beauty after you left us." And they will say, "And you too, by Allah, you have increased in beauty since you left us."

49. The people of Paradise will visit one another, in delightful gatherings where they will remember their lives in this world and how Allah has blessed them by admitting them to Paradise.

50. The smallest number of wives that any one man will have in Paradise is seventy-two. The believer in Paradise will be given the strength of one hundred men.

51. The wives of the people of Paradise will sing to their husbands in the most beautiful voices that anyone has ever heard. What they will sing is: "We are good and beautiful, the wives of a noble people, who look at their husband content and happy." And they will sing, "We are eternal, and will never die, we are safe and will never fear, we are remaining here and will never go away."

Hell

In the *Qur'an*, there are at least 350 references to hell, and many of these verses offer quite a clear picture of the torments of the fire:

- Surah 25:11–12: "We have prepared a flaming fire for those who deny the Hour. When it [here the Fire is personified] will see them from afar, they will hear its raging and roaring."
- Surah 55:43–44: "This is Hell, which the sinners deny. They go circling round between it and fierce, boiling water."
- Surah 56:42–43: "(*Those in Hell will dwell*) amidst scorching winds, and seething water; in the shadow of pitch-black smoke."
- Surah 67:7–8: "When they are flung into it [Hell] they hear its roaring as it boils up, as though it would burst with rage."
- Surah 11:106: "As for the wretched, they shall be in the Fire, wherein there shall be for them a moaning and a sighing."
- Surah 4:56: "Surely, those who disbelieve in Our revelations, We shall expose them to the Fire. As often as their skins are roasted We shall exchange them for fresh skins, that they may taste the torment."

- Surah 14:16–17: "Hell is before him, and he is given to drink of festering water. He will sip but can hardly swallow it, and death will come from every side, yet he cannot die. A dreadful torment is his."
- Surah 14:49–50: "And you will see the sinners that day bound together in chains. Their garments (*are*) of liquid pitch, and their faces covered with fire."
- Surah 22:19–21: "As for those who disbelieve, garments of fi re will be cut out for them, while boiling water will be poured down on their heads. Whatever is in their bodies and skins are melted by it. And for them are goads of iron."

Hell has seven different levels; the lower the level in hell, the greater the intensity of the heat. Surah 6:132 states, "For all there will be ranks from what they did. Your Lord is not unaware of what they do."

Also, there are seven gates. Surah 15:43–44 reads, "And assuredly, Hell is the promised abode for them all. It has seven gates; and for each gate there is an appointed portion." Each sinner will enter a gate according to his or her deeds, and will be assigned to a level of hell accordingly.

Here are some further facts about hell based on Muslim writings:

1. In spite of the fact that Islam teaches that once a person goes there it is for eternity, I found this statement (this sounds somewhat like purgatory): "Those who will enter hell and be brought forth at a later time are the monotheists who did not associate anything with Allah, yet they committed many sins that far outweigh their good deeds. They will enter hell for a period known only to Allah; then they will be brought forth through the intercession of those who intercede, and Allah will bring forth, through His Mercy, people who never did any good at all." (Muhammad taught that in the future he—but not Adam, Noah, Abraham, Moses, or even Jesus—could intercede for some Muslims in hell and Allah would release them.)

2. Muslims have no definite guarantee of entering Paradise. One imam said to me, "There is a 100 percent chance that all Muslims go to hell." Allah may forgive them or punish them as He wills. They may do some righteous deeds that will save them from hell, or they may enter hell and remain there for as long as Allah wills, then be brought forth through the intercession of those who intercede and the Mercy of the Most Merciful.

3. Muslims will go to hell if they remain in a country that is not Islamic—the domain of unbelief—and let themselves be exposed to unnecessary trials and

temptations; this assumes that there are Muslim countries to which they could migrate and they refuse to do so. Surah 4:97–98 states, "Assuredly, as for those whom the angels take (*in death*) while they wrong themselves, (the angels) will ask: 'In what were you engaged?' They will reply: 'We were oppressed in the land.' (The angels) will say: 'Was not Allah's earth spacious enough for you that you could have migrated therein?' As for such, their habitation will be Hell, an evil journey's end."

4. The *Hadith* records Muhammad as conversing thus: "'No one who has an atom's weight of pride in his heart will enter Paradise.' A man said, 'But what if a man likes his clothes and shoes to look good?' He said, 'Allah is beautiful and loves beauty. Pride is rejecting the truth and looking down on people.'"

5. Many Islamic texts indicate that a large number of the human race will enter hell and few will enter Paradise. Surah 12:103 reads, "And though you try so eagerly, the majority of men will not believe."

6. The *Hadith* records Muhammad as saying, "An indication that large numbers of people rejected the call of messengers and will be in hell is the fact that the prophets will come on the Day of Resurrection, some with a small group (less than ten), and others with one or two, and some with no followers at all."

7. Many Islamic texts indicate that 999 out of every 1,000 of the children of Adam will enter hell, and only one in a thousand will enter Paradise. The *Hadith* states that Muhammad said, "Allah will say, 'O Adam!' Adam will reply, 'I respond to Your call, I am obedient to Your commands, and all good is in Your hands.' Then Allah will say to Adam, 'Send forth the people of the Fire.' Adam will say, 'How many are the people of the Fire?' Allah will say, 'Out of every thousand, take nine hundred and ninety-nine.'" So Islam asserts that the ratio of people admitted to Hell when all nations are taken into account is 999 in every 1,000.

8. The wisdom behind there being so many people in hell (this is not my statement but comes from a Muslim source), the reason so many people will be in hell is not that the truth failed to reach them all, wherever or whenever they lived. Allah does not blame anyone whom His call did not reach. Surah 17:16 reads, "When We decree that a population shall be destroyed, We (first warn and) command those of them that live in comfort, and yet they per-sist in sin so that the word is proved true against them, and then We destroy them utterly." Thus, Islam claims very few have responded to the mes-sengers that God has sent. Those who did not fol-

low the messengers will enter hell, excepting those whom the Message did not reach or who could not understand it because of the garbled form in which they heard it.

9. But not all Muslims will go to Paradise. As for those who claim to follow Islam, the true religion, many of them will also enter hell. These are the hypocrites who will be in the lowest level of the fire. Many of those who claim to follow Muhammad will be tested by ambiguities and doubts—these are the misguided inventors and followers of heresies. The *Hadith* states that the *ummah* (global community of Islam) will split into seventy-odd sects, all of which will be in hell except for one. So very few are saved, especially in latter times.

10. All who reject the *Qur'an* as God's Word will go to hell. Surah 11:17 states, "These believe in it, but for those of the factions that deny it [the *Qur'an*], the Fire will be their promised place."

11. Most of those who enter hell will be women. The *Hadith* records Muhammad as saying, "'O women, give in charity, for I have seen that you form the majority of the people of Hell.' They asked, 'Why is that so, O Messenger of Allah?' He said, 'Because you curse too much and are ungrateful for good treatment.'"

12. Here is another reason given why most women will be in hell: "Women will be few among the inhabitants of Paradise because in most cases they prefer the immediate pleasures of this life, as they are less wise and unable to keep the Hereafter in mind. They are too weak to strive and prepare themselves for it, and are more inclined toward this world. In addition to this, they are the strongest factor in this world that distracts men from the Hereafter, because men are inclined to desire them and they are not concerned with the Hereafter. They are quick to follow those who call them to deviate from Islam and reluctant to follow those pious people who call them to the Hereafter, and righteous deeds."

13. When the people of hell enter the fire, they become huge in size. Muhammad is recorded in the *Hadith* to have said, "The distance between the shoulders of the *Kaafir* [unbelievers who deliberately hide the truth] in hell will be like three days traveling for a fast rider [I would imagine, on a camel or horse]. The space he occupies will be as wide as the distance between Mecca and Medina [which is 270 miles]. This increasing of the body size will increase his suffering and torment. But in spite of the fact that the bodies will be huge, the fire will penetrate their bodies until it reaches their innermost depths."

14. As for the food in hell, it will be a bitter *daree* (a low-growing thorn fruit that does not nourish and thus does not satisfy one's hunger). Although this fruit tree is so vile and obnoxious, the people of hell will become so hungry that they will have no choice but to eat from it until they are full. However, when their bellies are full, this food will start to churn like boiling oil, which will cause a great deal of suffering. At that point, they will rush to drink a mixture consisting of boiling hot water. They will drink it like camels that drink and drink, but their thirst is never quenched. It will tear their innards. All this is for the purpose of making the people in hell suffer constantly with increasing punishment.

15. Here is a description of the dress of the people in hell, found in the *Qur'an*. Surah 22:19: "As for those who disbelieve, garments of fire will be cut out for them, while boiling water will be poured down on their heads." Surah 14:49–50 states, "And you will see the sinners that day, bound together in chains. Their garments (are) of liquid pitch, and their faces covered with fire."

16. Hell has various levels in which the torment and degree of punishment is greater than in others. The *Hadith* states, "There are some whom the fire will take up to their ankles, others to their knees, oth-

ers up to their waists, and others up to their collar-bones." Surah 4:145 states, "Surely, the hypocrites will be in the lowest deep of the fire, and you will find no helper for them."

17. Surah 40:70–72 has this to say about the punishment of unbelievers: "Those who have denied the Scripture and the Message with which We have sent Our Messengers will soon know: when with chains and shackles around their necks they will be dragged through boiling waters; then they are cast into the Fire."

18. The *Hadith* states that the sun and moon will be thrown into hell, and will be fuel for it, to punish those wrongdoers who used to worship them instead of Allah.

19. The evil deeds that lead one to hell are the following:

- associating partners with Allah in worship
- disbelieving in His Messenger
- ingratitude and disbelief
- malicious envy
- lying
- treachery
- oppression and wrongdoing
- promiscuity
- backstabbing

- cutting off the ties of kinship
- cowardice at the time of *jihad*
- miserliness
- inconsistency between what is in one's heart and the face one shows to people
- despairing of the mercy of Allah
- panicking blindly at the time of crisis
- pride and extravagance at the time of plenty
- abandoning one's duties toward Allah
- transgressing His limits
- violating His sanctity
- fearing a created being instead of the Creator
- showing off
- going against the *Qur'an* and *Sunna* in word or deed
- obeying a created being in some act of disobedience to the Creator
- blindly supporting falsehood
- mocking the signs of Allah
- rejecting the truth
- withholding knowledge and testimony that should be revealed
- witchcraft and magic
- disobeying one's parents
- killing any soul forbidden by Allah except for reasons of justice

- consuming the wealth of the orphan
- usury
- desertion from the battlefield
- slandering the reputation of innocent, chaste, believing women

After reading a list like this, I don't see how any Muslim could ever think of making it to Paradise because of his or her own good deeds! Is Allah truly "the Compassionate, the Merciful"? Or does He take gleeful pleasure in condemning whomever He dislikes?

In these three chapters devoted to the Major Beliefs of Islam—twenty-four topics in all—we have at times paused to point out how the particular *Qur'anic* teaching differs from the biblical teaching on the same subject. The question may have occurred to you: "Why are Muslims unwilling to give credence to what the Bible clearly teaches—especially since the Jewish and Christian Scriptures preceded the *Qur'an* by many centuries? What is their excuse for not believing the Bible?"

This bring us to our next chapter: has the Bible really been corrupted?—a truly vital question.

9

Has the Bible Really Been Corrupted?

THIS IS A very important chapter. Why? Because the primary means for any Bible-believing Christian to share the wonderful love of God through Christ is via God's infallible Word, the Bible. We Christians know that it *is* the Word of God, and the Holy Spirit uses it to bring conviction to a sinner's heart. He shows that individual that "Christ is the answer" because of His vicarious death on the cross and His resurrection.

Muslims, however, do not believe that the present-day Bible is the Word of God. They have been taught that though the original material came from God, it has now been greatly "corrupted"—changed, much of it lost—and it was "rewritten at a later date." Therefore, it is not accurate.

Muslims believe that the material given to Moses, David, and other prophets was lost at the time of the Babylonian captivity. They admit that later on God gave Jesus the Gospel—just as He supposedly gave Muhammad the *Qur'an*—but they contend this material too was lost, and about three hundred years later, the present four Gospels were written. Since they are much later, they too are not reliable. So the Bible is not worth reading!

In order to try to prove that the Bible is not reliable, Muslims will quote a number of Christ-denying liberal "Christian" theologians—"scholars" who have accepted the "higher-critical" teachings of Julius Wellhausen (1844–1918), Rudolf Bultmann (1884–1976), etc. Every Muslim I have met is familiar with some of these rationalistic arguments. Also, all the mosques I have visited have this anti-Bible literature.

However, if these Muslims were consistent, they would have to reject much of the *Qur'an* on the same basis, because the same so-called scholars that they quote to disprove the Bible also deny some of the things the *Qur'an* teaches— like the fact that Adam and Eve were real people, there was a literal flood, that Jesus was virgin-born, etc.

Since Muslims do not believe the Bible, then it cannot be used effectively until you are able to show them that what they have been taught is in error and the Bible really is reliable. This can be done by using the *Qur'an*. When Muhammad first started his ministry, he was trying to win the favor of the Jews and the Christians, so he said many favorable things about them and their writings—statements that you can use to show that the *Qur'an* does not condemn the Bible. That the Bible was largely "rewritten" is a myth that Muslim scholars later made up!

Fact: for a hundred years or more after the *Qur'an* was written, there was no Bible in Arabic, so the early Muslims were not aware of any major differences between what the *Qur'an* states and what the Bible teaches. All these anti-Bible arguments were created later on. The following material is designed to help you get your Muslim friend to see that the Bible truly is the Word of God.

By using the *Qur'an*, I am not putting my approval on it but just using it as a means to get across a very important point.

The popular view expressed by the theologians of Islam and accepted by most Muslims today is that the Bible has been corrupted, is no longer authentic, and is therefore unreliable. Admittedly, there are many major differences between what is taught in the Bible and the *Qur'an*, but this does not automatically mean that the Bible is in error and the *Qur'an* is accurate. Since these charges of corruption come from the Muslims, the burden of proof is on them to bring forth some concrete evidence to that effect!

In order to do this, the Muslim scholars need to produce ancient manuscripts of the Bible that can be compared with later manuscripts, for it is in these manuscripts that the corruptions supposedly appear. I need some proof before I can accept the argument of the Muslims that the Bible has been mischievously mutilated! In reality, there are over ten thousand old manuscripts of the Bible or portions thereof still in existence, and these are in full agreement on all major points. Not one manuscript has been found with any major changes.

Here are a few thought-provoking questions for Muslims:

1. Will you agree that God is able to protect His own Scriptures?
2. If He is able, would He not want to protect them?
3. Why might the Almighty have allowed finite men to corrupt His written revelations for mankind?
4. If you believe that the Scriptures of the ancient prophets have not been accurately preserved, tell me the following:

   a. When were they corrupted?
   b. Where were they corrupted?
   c. Who corrupted them? If you think Christians or Jews deliberately altered their sacred Scriptures, why did they do this?

    d. How was this achieved?

    e. What evidence can you present?

5. If God allowed humans to corrupt the books of His great prophets like Moses and David, how do you know that the book you trust hasn't suffered the same indignity?

6. Do you think the Judeo-Christian Scriptures were tampered with before or after the *Qur'an* was delivered?

7. If the Bible has been purposely tampered with, surely many scribes were involved, over a lengthy period of many years. The majority of these forgers would have had no contact with each other. Do you think this really could have happened?

The *Qur'an* States That God Gave the Biblical Scriptures

> And assuredly **We gave Moses** the Book (Scriptures) and after him We sent messenger after messenger. We gave Jesus son of Mary the clear miracles and strengthened him with the Holy Spirit. Is it so, that whenever a Messenger whose message does not suit your desires comes to you, you grow arrogant, denying some of them, and slaying others? (Surah 2:87)

He has revealed to you (*Muhammad*) the Scripture with truth, confirming that which was revealed before it, even as *He revealed the Torah and the Gospel.* (Surah 3:3, emphasis added)

O you who believe! Believe in Allah and His Messenger and the Scripture which He has revealed to His messenger, *and the Scripture which He revealed before (you).* Whoever disbelieves in Allah and His Angels and His Scriptures and His messengers and the Last Day, he assuredly has gone far astray. (Surah 4:136)

We send revelation upon you, as We sent it upon Noah and the prophets after him, and as *We sent revelation* upon Abraham and Ishmael and Isaac and Jacob and the tribes, and Jesus and Job and Jonah and Aaron and Solomon, and as We gave David the Psalms. (Surah 4:163)

Let the People of the Gospel [followers of Jesus] judge by that which *Allah had revealed therein.* Whoever judges not by that which Allah had revealed, such are corrupt. (Surah 5:47)

Allah has bought from the believers their lives and their wealth because the Garden will be theirs. They shall fight in the way of Allah, kill and be killed; that is a promise binding upon Allah in the

Torah and the *Gospel* and the Qur'an. *Who is more faithful to His promise than Allah?* (Surah 9:111)

Then We caused Our messengers to follow in their footsteps; and We caused Jesus son of Mary, to follow, and *gave him* the Gospel [*Injeel*], and placed compassion and mercy in the hearts of those who followed him. (Surah 57:27)

See also the following: Surahs 3:47–48, 3:65, 5:66, 5:110, and 17:55.

According to these references from the *Qur'an*—and many others—it is clear that the Torah, the Psalms, the Prophets (which constitutes the entire Old Testament), and the Gospel (the New Testament) proclaimed by Jesus Christ are all revealed truths given by God, and they must be obeyed. Further, these verses indicate that both the Old and New Testaments of the Bible are sound and that in them salvation is to be found. These passages obviously refer to the Scriptures that the Jews and Christians had in their possession at the time that Muhammad started writing. Therefore, the Bible could not have been corrupted before Muhammad! As a matter of fact, the *Qur'an* acknowledges the entire Bible, referring to it as "the Book," and calls upon Muslims to resort to it:

If you are in doubt regarding what We have revealed to you, then ask those who have been reading *the*

Book before you. The *truth* has come to you from your Lord, therefore *do not doubt it.*" (Surah 10:94, emphasis added)

Those who believe (*in the Qur'an and the Prophets sent before you*) Jews, Christians, and Sabaeans; whoever believes in Allah and the Last Day and does what is right; shall be rewarded by their Lord; no fear shall come upon them, neither shall they regret. (Surah 2:62)

Say (*O Muslims*): "We believe in Allah and that which is revealed to us, and in what was reveled to Abraham, Ishmael, Isaac, Jacob, and the tribes; to Moses and Jesus and the (*other*) prophets by their Lord. *We make no distinction* between any of them, and to Allah we have surrendered ourselves." (Surah 2:136, emphasis added)

The Qur'an puts the Christians, the Jews, and their holy books on the same level as the *Qur'an.* Thus, the Bible was not corrupted at the time of the writing of these verses!

The *Qur'an* Claims That It Confirms the Biblical Scriptures

He (*God*) has revealed to you the Scripture with truth, *confirming* that which was revealed before it, even as He revealed *the Torah and the Gospel.* (Surah 3:3, emphasis added)

And to you have We revealed the Scripture with the truth, *confirming* whatever Scripture was before it, *and a watcher over it.* (Surah 5:48, emphasis added)

And this is a blessed Scripture which We have revealed, *conforming* [*sic*] that which (*was revealed*) before it. (Surah 6:92, emphasis added)

This Qur'an could not have been invented (*by one*) apart from Allah, but it is a *confirmation* of that (*series of revelations*) which was before it, and a (*fuller*) explanation of the Book—wherein there is no doubt—from the Lord of the Worlds. A comment after this verse says, "(The Lord's revelation throughout the ages and to all peoples is one. The Qur'an confirms, fulfils, completes and further explains the one true revelation.)" (Surah 10:37, emphasis added)

This (*Qur'an*) is no invented tale but *a confirmation of the previous (Scripture).* (Surah 12:111, emphasis added)

Could anything be clearer!

The *Qur'an* Says That the Faithful Should Believe in the Biblical Scriptures

> The Messenger believes in what has been revealed to him by his Lord, and so do the believers. They all believe in Allah and His angels, His Scriptures and His messengers. "We make *no distinction* between any of His messengers—and they say: 'We hear and obey.'" (Surah 2:285, emphasis added)
>
> And argue not with the People of the Book [Jews and Christians] unless it be in a way that is better, save with such of them who are iniquitous; and say: "*We believe* in that which has been revealed unto us and *revealed to you*; our God and your God is One, and unto Him we surrender." (Surah 29:46, emphasis added)

According to the *Qur'an*, Allah did not expect the Jews to seek light and guidance from Muhammad alone, because the *Qur'an* leaves no doubt that the Torah had been given by God and remained reliable and uncorrupted, so light and guidance could be found therein. Muhammad never met any of the previous prophets mentioned in the Bible, but in the *Qur'an*, it is written that Allah instructed Muhammad to follow the guidance of the Torah, Psalms, Prophets, and the message of Jesus as He proclaimed the Gospel (*Injeel*).

> Those are they whom Allah guides, so *follow* their
> guidance. (Surah 6:90, emphasis added)

From where did this guidance come? Apart from
the reading of the Scriptures (Torah, Psalms, Prophets,
Gospel—the direct teachings of Jesus), there was no other
means by which Muhammad could have found guidance.
Sad to say, Muhammad did not follow this advice, which,
he claimed, came from God.

> If only they had stood fast by the Law [*Torah*], the
> Gospel, and the revelation that was sent to them
> from their Lord, they would have enjoyed happi-
> ness from every side. There is from among them a
> party on *the right course*: but many of them follow a
> course that is evil. (Yusuf Ali; Surah 5:66, empha-
> sis added)

From these words in the *Qur'an*, it is clear that Allah
wanted the followers of Islam, as well as those of us today,
to know that the Law and the Gospel, and all the truth
given by revelation to the People of the Book, is reliable.
Because the Bible was reliable, God has set it as the standard by which He expected all people to live.

What other law could be referred to in the *Qur'an*
except that which is contained in the Hebrew scriptures

of the Old Testament, and what other Gospel than that found in the New Testament? The clearest definition of the Gospel given in Scripture is found in 1 Corinthians 15:1–4 (NKJV, emphasis added), where we read,

> Moreover, brethren, I declare to you *the Gospel* which I preached to you, which also you received and in which you stand, *by which also you are saved...* For I delivered to you first of all that which I also received: *that Christ died for our sins* according to the Scriptures, and *that He was buried*, and *that He rose again the third day* according to the Scriptures".

Thus, the Gospel referred to so many times in the *Qur'an* is the death, burial, and resurrection of Jesus Christ. Without these three truths, there is no Gospel. Yet Islam clearly rejects the death, burial, and resurrection of Jesus. Why did Muhammad and Islam not follow the advice that he claims came from Allah?

> Say: "O People of the Book! You have no ground to stand upon [of true guidance] unless you stand fast by the Law, *the Gospel* and all the revelation that has come to you from your Lord." (Yusuf Ali; Surah 5:68, emphasis added)

Which Gospel is being referred to here? Surely the *Qur'an* would not be recommending a "corrupted" Gospel! And the Greek text of the Gospel that Christians were reading during Muhammad's times is no different from the Greek text of the Gospel that is being read today. The Bible has not been corrupted.

The *Qur'an* confirms the fact that the Bible is the standard that God expected Christians to live by. If there had been any doubt about the reliability of the Bible, why would God have given such a command? Since there is no evidence that the Bible has been corrupted, then we can be confident that those who follow it are indeed the "party of the right course." God should be able to recognize those on the right course, and we know that it is to them He will give the rewards that He has promised! It is interesting to note that there is nothing in the *Qur'an* that might indicate that Allah ever instructed Muhammad to consult the scriptures of the Buddhists, Hindus, Confucianists, Taoists, Zoroastrians, etc., only the Judeo-Christian Scriptures!

We have seen that the *Qur'an* clearly states that the Torah, Psalms, Prophets, and the Gospel was the truth that had been revealed by God. The Bible is the yardstick by which the *Qur'an* can be measured. Why then do the Muslims—who claim to love and follow the teachings of the *Qur'an* and Muhammad—wish to go contrary to the *Qur'an* and claim that the Bible has been corrupted? Surely Allah would not instruct the followers of Islam to follow what is written in a corrupted book!

Would God Allow His Words to Be Corrupted?

Not only has God made known His Word, but also He has promised that He would keep His Word from corruption. This is found both in the *Qur'an* and the Bible. First, some relevant quotes from the *Qur'an*:

> And recite (*and teach*) that which has been revealed unto you in the Book of your Lord. *No one can change His words.* You shall find no refuge beside Him. (Surah 18:27, emphasis added)
>
> He has revealed to you (*Muhammad*) the Scripture with truth, *confirming* that which was revealed before it, even as He revealed the Torah and the Gospel. (Surah 3:3–4, emphasis added)
>
> There is none that can alter the Words (*and Decrees*) of Allah. (Yusuf Ali; Surah 6:34)
>
> Perfected is the Word of your Lord in truth and justice. *There is nothing that can change His words.* (Surah 6:115, emphasis added)

The above verses from the *Qur'an* show that the Old and New Testament books of the Bible are sound, have been protected from corruption by God, and that in them salvation is found. They indicate that Muhammad upheld the Bible that was in existence in the day in which he lived, which is the same Bible that the Jews and Christians have today. So in the light of these verses, how can Muslim theologians continue to argue that the earlier Scriptures have been corrupted? If Allah could not preserve the earlier Scriptures as He promised, then how can Muslims or anyone else trust Allah to be able to preserve the *Qur'an* from corruption? Can we take Him seriously? Won't He fail the Muslims just as He failed the earlier Jews and Christians?

If Muslims are so sure that Allah has and can continue to protect the *Qur'an*, then why could He not have protected the earlier Scriptures? Did God previously lose His power and authority, or has He since lost His ability to protect His Word?

When Muhammad was engaged in his mission, Jews and Christians were scattered all over the earth, and tens of thousands were in possession of their Scriptures. If the Bible really is corrupted, the logical question arises: how could it be possible for all the available manuscripts of the Bible to be corrupted simultaneously without leaving a single uncorrupted copy somewhere?

Okay, so it wasn't actually simultaneous. I'll put the question this way: how could it be possible for the Jews and Christians to get together for the alleged purpose of changing their Scriptures?

The *Qur'an* says in Surah 2:113:

> The Jews say the Christians are misguided; and the Christians says it is the Jews who are misguided; although both are readers of the Scripture…Allah will judge between them on the Day of Resurrection concerning that wherein they differ.

The petty quarrels and enmity that exited between the Jews and the Christians would not have permitted enough agreement for such a disgraceful act. In addition, how could they have done such a thing without God's knowledge and gotten away with it since He had promised to protect His Word? Impossible!

The Word of God found in the Bible clearly teaches that God will protect the Word that He has revealed:

> God is not man, that he should lie, or a son of man, that he should change his mind. Has he said, and will he not do it? Or has he spoken, and will he not fulfill it? (Numbers 23:19)

Forever, O Lord, your word is firmly fixed in the heavens. (Psalm 119:89)

The grass withers, the flower fades, but the word of our God will stand forever. (Isaiah 40:8)

But the word of the Lord remains forever. (1 Peter 1:25)

It is very clear from the Bible that God has promised to preserve His revealed Word. If God is preserving it, then how can it be vitiated or lost? Muslims claim that the *Qur'an* has never been changed (however, there is evidence from Muslim writings that the *Qur'an* has been changed). If God can protect the *Qur'an*, then why can't God also protect His revealed Word in the Bible? If what Muslims claim about the Bible having been corrupted is accurate, then they must admit that God has failed to keep His promise. If God failed in the past and let the Bible be corrupted, then how can anyone be certain that He has not failed when it comes to the *Qur'an* also?

The *Qur'an* Does Not State That the Bible Has Been Corrupted

I have received and read much literature from Muslims claiming that the Bible has been corrupted, and I have discovered that many statements made are contradictory and not trustworthy.

In the book *Christian–Muslim Dialogue* by Dr. Hasan M. Baagil and published by Islamic Educational Services, on page 11, it states, "History has shown that the Bible suffered changes throughout the ages." After this charge, he tries to show contradictions within the Bible. Then on page 17, he writes, "None of these scriptures remain in their original form now."

This is the typical Muslim claim, but it has no ground to stand on. It can't be true because in another book written by a Muslim, titled *Where Do You Stand?*, Abdul Hye states on page 29, "The original manuscripts of the Bible are **not available**" (emphasis is in the text). My question is, Since we do not have the original manuscripts to contrast our present Bible with, then how can Muslims say they are not the same?

But does the *Qur'an* really state that the Bible has been corrupted? If so, where? Let us examine some of the verses that Muslims use and see what these verses really mean.

> Of the Jews there are those who displace words from their (*right*) places, and say, "We hear and we disobey," and "Hear, may you not hear," and "Ra'ina [Listen to us]," with a twist of their tongues and a slander to Faith. If only they had said, "We hear and we obey," and "Do hear," and "Do look at us," it would have been better for them, and more proper; but Allah has cursed them for their Unbelief, and but few of them will believe. (Yusuf Ali, Surah 4:46)

The gist of this verse is that some Jews came to Muhammad looking for answers to some questions, and Muhammad responded to them. But when they left him, they distorted Muhammad's replies. These Jews neither omitted anything from the text of the Bible nor added to it; all they did was to obscure the meaning of certain words by twisting their tongue.

> O people of the Scripture! Now has Our messenger come, to you, expounding to you much of that which you used to hide in the Scripture, and forgiving much. Now there has come to you light from Allah, and a plain Scripture. (Surah 5:15)

This verse has to do with some Jews who asked Muhammad his opinion regarding Deuteronomy 22:23–24 in the Torah:

> If there is a betrothed virgin, and a man meets her in the city and lies with her, then you shall bring them both out to the gate of that city, and you shall stone them to death with stones, the young woman because she did not cry for help though she was in the city, and the man because he violated his neighbor's wife. So you shall purge the evil from your midst.

We see that, according to the Bible, both fornicators were to be stoned. But the Jews twisted their tongues and changed the meaning of *stoning* to *lashing*.

Some Jews came to Muhammad about this problem of stoning.

One of the Jews said, "Our women are beautiful, thus stoning has increased among us. So to save life, we cut (*the commandments*) short and applied one hundred lashes and the shaving of the head." Then Muhammad ordered them to be stoned. Thus, the Scriptures themselves had not been changed or corrupted, but the Jews just did not obey them to the letter of the law.

And they measure not the power of Allah its true measure when they say: "Allah has revealed nothing to a human being.' Say (*to the Jews who speak thus*): 'Who revealed the book which Moses brought, a light and guidance for mankind, which you have put on parchments which you show, but you hide much (*thereof*)." (Surah 6:91)

"Hide much" does not mean changing the text of the Bible but rather misrepresenting the facts by withholding some of the text of the Torah. The Jews proudly showed what was written on their Torah scrolls. However, they also hid much of what was written on these parchments, deceitfully withholding it from the people.

Of course, this was not proper conduct for these Jews, but "hiding much" is entirely different from "substituting texts."

Now (*O company of believers*), do you then hope that they will believe in you, when some of them have already heard the word of Allah and knowingly perverted it, after they had understood its meaning?" (Surah 2:75)

This verse does not say that the Torah's text had been changed but simply confirms the fact that some of the

Jewish rabbis interpreted the Torah according to their own desires. A comment in my favorite *Qur'an* is very enlightening. It reads the following:

> (Rabbis subsequent to Moses changed the Torah and interpreted it according to their own desire. Even today there are some Muslims who like to interpret Scripture according to their own preference. According to a *hadith* we are told that whoever interprets the *Qur'an* according to his own human opinion shall enter Hellfire.)

This comment obliquely confirms the fact that the *Qur'an* was not accusing the Jews of actually changing the text of the Bible but interpreting it in a way that suited them. Interpreting the Bible falsely and changing the very text are two vastly different things.

Please note that all the above verses from the *Qur'an* have to do with the Jews. There is not one single verse in the *Qur'an* that accuses the Christians of distorting the Gospel. Even so, we Christians are commonly tarred with the same brush.

So the corruption mentioned in the *Qur'an* does not mean that the revealed text had been changed. Rather, it charges that certain people cast doubts on the reading of the text—misrepresented the true meaning of the words by falsely rendering them and resorting to verbal tricks—as has been done down through the ages by heretics when confronted with texts that conflict with their particular views.

From the evidence presented thus far, there is only one valid conclusion that an honest person can come to: God has preserved the Bible from corruption, and its teachings are true and valid today.

Does Evidence of Corruption Exist?

Disputatious Muslims have taken the arguments of the enemies of Christianity—liberals, atheists, and cultists—and passed them on as true. However, there is absolutely no evidence that the Bible has ever been corrupted. Since the Old Testament reveals the true nature of the coming Messiah—foretelling His sacrificial death, His resurrection, His ascension to heaven, and His exaltation—we can be positive that these are accurate and true teachings and not something that was devised at a later date. These prophecies concerning Christ were written down over thousands of years by various Hebrew prophets. They were not conjured up in New Testament times!

The *Qur'an* states that the Bible available at the time of Muhammad was accurate and that God had preserved His

Holy Word. So we come to a major problem, an enigma. How can the *Qur'an* clearly imply that the Bible can be trusted, claiming that God protects His Word from corruption, and then at the same time say that the Bible has been corrupted because it differs with the *Qur'an* on many major issues?

There are only two possible conclusions: (1) The *Qur'an* *contradicts* itself and (2) The corruption of the text refers to the abuse or misuse of the text—simply the concealing of part of it, mistranslating or misinterpreting it. In all cases, the text itself has remained intact. Surely the thought that bodies of Jews and Christians everywhere would be able to unite not only in altering their sacred Scriptures but in agreeing on what should be changed is absurd—a virtual impossibility. Nor is there evidence to support the contention made by some Muslims that the *Qur'an* has abrogated the Bible or that the Gospel was taken to heaven with Jesus and is no longer available.

I would like to point out some things found in the *Qur'an* that are not found in the Bible:

1. God commanded the angels to prostrate themselves before Adam, but *Iblis* (the devil) refused (Surah 15:30–31, 20:116).
2. After Cain killed his brother Abel, Surah 5:31 states that "Allah sent a raven scratching up the ground, to show him how to hide his brother's naked corpse."

3. According to Surah 11:42–43, one of Noah's sons was drowned in the flood when he refused an invitation to enter into the ark.

4. In Surah 2:125–127, we are told that Abraham and his son Ishmael resided in Mecca and reconstructed the "Ka'ba," the holy place of worship for Muslims (Islam claims it was originally built by Adam but was destroyed in the flood). No proof is offered.

5. Surah 12:31 states that a group of women were so amazed when they saw Joseph that they cut their hands.

6. Surah 27:16 declares that Solomon was "taught the language of birds."

7. Surah 5:60 says that because certain men served idols, Allah's wrath was poured out upon them, and He "turned some to apes and swine" (I guess this is reverse evolution!).

8. Surah 5:110–115 (expanding on 3:47–49) tells us that Jesus performed these confirming signs: as an infant, he spoke from his cradle; later, he molded clay into the likeness of a bird and breathed life into it; and as a prophet, he asked Allah to send down to his disciples a miraculous table, spread with heavenly food, to help them believe in him.

9. Here is an obvious error: in Surah 19:27–28 Mary, the mother of Jesus, is identified as the "sister of Aaron." But Aaron predated Mary by nearly 1,400 years.

Differences between the *Qur'an* and the Bible

1. In Surah 11:44, it says the Ark came to rest on Mount Juki, while the Bible says it rested on Mount Ararat (Gen. 8:4).

2. According to the *Qur'an*, Abraham's father is Azar (Surah 6:74), but the Bible says his name was Terah (Gen. 11:26).

3. Surah 28:9 states that Pharaoh's *wife* adopted Moses, whereas Exodus 2:5 says it was Pharaoh's *daughter*.

4. The *Qur'an*, in 28:6, has Haman living in Egypt during Moses's time, but the Bible says that he lived in Persia during King Ahasuerus's time, almost a thousand years later (Esther 3:1).

5. The Bible says Aaron ordered the construction of the golden calf, but the *Qur'an* states in Surah 20:85 that it was Samiri who led them astray.

6. Zachariah, the father of John the Baptist, according to the *Qur'an* in Surah 19:10, could not speak "for three nights," but the Bible says in Luke 1:20 he could not speak until the child was born, about nine months.

7. Surah 19:23 states that Mary gave birth to Jesus under a "palm tree," while Luke 2:7 says it was in a stable.

These are important differences between the Bible and the *Qur'an*, but the major problem comes with the teachings of Islam concerning the character of God, the identification of Jesus Christ, and His death, resurrection, exaltation, and coming again. While the *Qur'an* mentions these things, Islam greatly demotes God and the Lord Jesus Christ.

Concluding Thoughts

Muslims are inconsistent when it comes to their use of the Bible. Though they claim that much of the Bible has been lost or corrupted, they do not reject all of the Bible as being unauthentic. In fact, Muslim apologists will often use certain Bible passages to support their belief that Jesus did not claim to be God or that he was sent only to those of the Jewish race, not all men. But their selection of authentic passages is arbitrary; they use only the ones that they feel are suited to prove their doctrinal interests. If passages seem to support Islamic doctrines, they will be declared authentic; if, on the other hand, they contradict Islamic beliefs, the scholars automatically pronounce them corrupt. But these unauthentic passages have the same manuscript authority as the authentic ones.

The whole Islamic concept of corruption (*tahrif*) has no historical footing. The Bible has overwhelming manuscript support that predates Muhammad by centuries. There is more manuscript evidence for the New Testament than for any other book of antiquity. No other book from the ancient world has as small a time gap between its composition and the earliest extant manuscript copies as the New Testament. Muslims need to be made aware that for an ancient book (first-century AD), the New Testament is the most accurately copied book in the world!

There is widespread misunderstanding among Muslims and others about the so-called errors in the biblical manuscripts. Reputable scholars have estimated there are two hundred thousand of them. These are not really "errors" but only variant readings, the vast majority of which are strictly grammatical. These readings are spread throughout more than 5,300 manuscripts so that a variant spelling of one word in one verse in 1,000 manuscripts is counted as 1,000 errors. The famous textual scholars Westcott and Hort estimated that only one-sixtieth of these variants rise above trivialities." The resultant text is therefore 98.33 percent pure. The great scholar A.T. Robertson said that the real concern is only with a "thousandth part of the entire text." This means that the New Testament is 99.9 percent free of significant variants.

The noted historian Philip Schaff calculated that, of the 150,000 variants known in his day, only 400 affected the meaning of the passage, only 50 were of real significance, and not even one affected "an article of faith or a precept of duty which is not abundantly sustained by other and undoubted passages, or by the whole tenor of Scripture teaching."

In summary, the *Qur'an* states that God *gave* the biblical Scriptures, the *Qur'an* claims that it *confirms* the biblical Scriptures, the *Qur'an* says that the faithful should *believe* in the biblical Scriptures, and the *Qur'an* does *not* actually state that the Bible has been corrupted. We have also seen positive proof that the Bible has not been altered.

Conclusion: Muslims have a choice. Either (1) Allah has failed to keep his promise to preserve the Bible, or (2) Muslims are not telling the truth when they state the Bible has been corrupted.

10

Why Having a Meaningful Conversation with Muslims Is Difficult

UNLIKE MOST WESTERNERS, Muslims are not averse to discussing religion. But I warn you: be prepared.

Muslims might not know much about their own religion (as one Muslim remarked to me), but every Muslim whom I have met is very familiar with the arguments against Christianity! It is important to be aware of these argument and understand a little of what you are up against when you attempt to reach out to Muslims.

Muslims will tell you that they believe in the Torah, Psalms, Gospel, and all the prophets found in the Bible, and that they honor Jesus highly. The only trouble is they do not believe in our present Bible as it has been written. Nor do they believe that Jesus is the Son of God or that He actually died on the cross. They claim that Jesus was "only" a prophet in a long line of 124,000 prophets. Thus, the Christian's standard approach of presenting the message of salvation—using the Bible and pointing to the Deity of Christ and His death and resurrection for our sins—is not effective from the outset.

I will give you the typical arguments that Muslims raise against Christianity so that you can prepare yourself. Here is how some of their arguments go:

1. Jesus came as the Messiah (which is stated in the *Qur'an*), but He never said he was God. He was the way to God before Muhammad came, but after that, all Christians should become Muslims.

2. We believe that Jesus was simply a prophet and not God's son. He will come back, and everyone will see which side he joins. I hope this happens in your lifetime so you can join our beautiful religion and see the true light.

3. I believe that God is One and has never been or looked like a human. If anyone thinks of God as existing in human form, then he or she is a great blasphemer.

4. Jesus never was crucified; the very thought is non-sense! If you tell me God sacrificed His only dear, unique son, then I ask you, isn't God great enough to be able to tell people what He requires, and delete their sins, without having to sacrifice His dear son and torturing him? The whole sinner thing makes no sense to me.

5. You Christians are so blind that you believe that God cannot save His own son from being crucified. This is to say God has limitations and is so weak that He let His son be humiliated and killed by humans. Anyone who has a limitation is weak and should not be called God. God has all the power. He is the one and only, and nothing is equal to Him.

6. What happened to the people who were born and died before God decided to send His son only two thousand years ago? It seems that the Christian God is a poor planner and a late thinker—because it took Him thousands, if not millions, of years to find a way of forgiving the sins of mankind.

7. I would like to know how you Christians explain the term *justice* in light of the statement that "Jesus died in our place, for our sins." Does this mean I will not be held accountable for the wrongdoings I commit during my lifetime?

8. If Jesus shed his blood on the cross to save people from their sins, doesn't this nullify the purpose of the Day of Judgment?

9. I do not believe in the New Testament. I only believe in the original testament. I do not believe any words from God can be edited and rewritten.

10. What I believe and know is that the Bible is mostly fake right now and is unreliable, since all its books were manipulated. Your Bible is a corrupted book that has been rewritten, changed, added to and reedited from the beginning to match your sick beliefs. The Bible was corrupted centuries and even millennia ago, and most, if not all, of the New Testament is complete hogwash—created by a false prophet named Paul. Therefore, to quote the Bible, to me, is a waste of time. Aren't there different versions of the Bible? Which is the correct one?

11. The *Qur'an* is the greatest miracle ever sent to a prophet! There is nothing like it. Can anyone create one verse that is similar, or even close? You would never be able to, even if you were the most fluent person and spoke a high level of Arabic. There is nothing in the world that comes near to the greatness of the *Qur'an*.

12. I do not believe it is possible to reach a proof-positive conclusion regarding ultimate truth.

13. God sent down prophets to tell us that He is One. Why don't you Christians listen and accept His Word? Why do you have to identify each one of the prophets as individuals when you could unite them into one?

14. Christians say that Allah cannot forgive anyone arbitrarily because His hands are tied by His own laws. Why would our most merciful Creator prevent Himself from having the capacity to forgive His servants who ask for forgiveness? Why would He place such a constraint on His mercy? Even if He were to make such a law, He could break it immediately as He is all-powerful.

15. The most important things in faith are having belief in one true God, doing good, avoiding evil acts. These are our salvation.

16. If you want to save yourself from hell, then follow the fastest-growing religion in the world.

I believe that before a person can be effective in presenting the claims of Christ, he or she needs to do some pre-evangelism. This is done by showing an interest in the individual as a person and asking questions about Islam that are off the beaten path. But instead of finding Muslims who are interested in answering questions about Islam, you ordinarily will be confronted with anti-Christian literature and facts that are not true, but gleaned from those who hate Christianity and are trying to destroy it. Sadly, most Muslims are basing what they believe about Christianity on this anti and false literature, and have no idea as to what true biblical Christianity teaches and practices.

But the problem becomes even more complicated. Instead of them showing an interest in what biblical Christianity actually teaches, you—a born-again Christian—will be told what you believe as a Christian! Muslims get very upset if they think you are saying something about Islam that is not accurate, but it doesn't bother them to make statements very forcibly about Christianity, which are not factual but based on false information.

Also, when they are going on about the evils of Christianity, they will not pause and give you an opportunity to object. If you sit there and just listen without trying to correct them, they will assume that you agree with them. You must repeatedly cut in to let them know that you are not agreeing with them. This may seem rude, but it is necessary.

If perchance a Muslim should ask you a question about Christianity, he will often tell you to make your answer short, and will not give you adequate time to explain. I regularly try to get the point across that I am willing to answer any question that someone might have about Christianity, but he must be willing to give me time to explain! I tell them that Muslims already have enough misunderstandings about Christianity, so please give me time to explain matters properly so that I don't add to the misunderstandings they already have.

I am not writing these things to discourage you from reaching out to Muslims but to let you know realistically what you are up against. The better we know the tactics of our opponents, the more effectively we can present the wonderful truths found in Jesus Christ.

11

The Muslim View of Christianity

WHEN COMMUNICATING WITH Muslims, it is very important to understand their thinking toward Christianity. They have a completely different comprehension of Christianity than what biblical Christianity really is. By understanding the thinking of the Muslim, you might be able to present Christianity in a more plausible way. Like the two disciples on the road to Emmaus who had a mistaken understanding of the true purpose of Jesus's life, so do the Muslims are in ignorance of what Christianity is all about. It will take much love, patience, and prayer to show them what the true Christian faith is all about, but it will be worth it.

Probably the biggest problem comes with Muslims not understanding the biblical concept of sin. Islam teaches that man is born pure and innocent, without a sin nature, and that sin cannot be transmitted from one person to another. Man is born pure but with a weakness, and it is the influence of human society and a forgetfulness of God that causes man to sin. Thus man is really not responsible for his sin, but society is. The *Qur'an* is a book of rules that are to be followed, and if men followed them fully, there would be no sin in the society. Therefore, Islam has set up its *Shari'a* (Islamic law), which is supposed to keep man on the right path. There are many moral laws set down that are rigidly enforced by the community.

Muslims also feel they can merit God's favor. They realize that they are not perfect but feel that because of their faith (their belief in one God, Allah, and in Muhammad as His prophet; praying five times a day; their giving 2 1/2 percent of their wealth to the needy; fasting during the month of Ramadan; and going on the pilgrimage to Mecca) this will somehow cancel out their sins and make them acceptable in the sight of Allah. However, no Muslim has assurance that he or she will be accepted into Paradise when the verdict is declared by Allah on the Day of Judgment. One's acceptance into heaven, in the final analysis, depends upon Allah's mercy and sovereign choice.

Muslims do not realize that not only are we born with sin but also we choose to sin of our own free will; and that sin produces spiritual death. Therefore, if one's sin is not removed by the blood of Christ, the sinner will be separated from God eternally.

Another serious problem enters in. Due to their concept of Islamic law, with its strong influence on their political leaders and their civil laws, Muslims think of America as being a Christian nation. But when they look at our low morals and Hollywood style of living, they feel that Christianity has failed to produce a moral society, in contrast to what the Islamic state has done. Yes, our religion should have a good influence upon society, but the Christian faith is primarily a personal relationship with God through Jesus Christ. Jesus came to make us not just moral on the outside but also holy on the inside. However, the Muslims consider themselves righteous and view Christians as sinners who need repentance.

The basic concept of Islam—that Allah is a master and humans are His slaves, and that governments that use Islamic law have been set up to help God enforce these laws, aided by mullahs—makes it even more difficult for the Muslim to understand Christianity. To a degree, the Muslim can understand the Jewish faith, because for a while the Jewish people had their own nation with its own laws and God sent prophets to them to enforce those laws. However, after a while, Israel ceased to be a nation and did not have leaders to help enforce the laws.

Then along came Christianity. Christ did not set up a national government. He did not appoint magistrates to rule over the people. In fact, Christianity did not attain imperial status for three hundred years. During those centuries, it was a persecuted minority—with its followers recognizing and paying their civil duty to the Roman Empire, and defying it only when they felt that the empire was incompatible with their first allegiance—to God. It was not until the time of Constantine that Christianity became the religion of the state and had laws to enforce its beliefs. (We know this repressiveness was not true Christianity.) Islam, by contract, started out with Muhammad, who from the outset was its Constantine, as well as its prophet. Muhammad immediately established Islam as a city-state in Medina. It was a form of rule as well as of worship. Then it expanded greatly, not simply as a creed but as an allegiance, a state, with sovereignty. Thus, the Muslims feel that both the nation of Israel and Christianity have failed, whereas Islam succeeded!

Christianity sees itself as a fulfillment of the Old Testament in the coming of Jesus Christ to provide salvation to all who believe, sealed by His death on the cross and His resurrection. But Islam looks at it much differently:

it believes that Islam has arrived whereas Christianity has fallen short. Muslims believe that if we want to know what the religion of the Prophet Jesus truly was we should go not to the existing Gospels, which the Muslims claim have been corrupted by the disloyalty of Christians and the deviation of their impure faith, but to the *Qur'an*. Islam claims that the Christian church has misconstrued the mission of Jesus. These "errors," Muslims feel, involve the central points of the Christian's understanding of Jesus— His Incarnation, His death upon the cross, and His resurrection. The Muslim sees Islam as correcting the Christian "distortion" of Jesus and of God; of course, the Christian sees it as nullifying the heart of Christianity.

Muslims do not recognize any glory in the cross but look upon it as a sign of weakness. Jesus was not able to keep the religious leaders from bringing Him to trial, and He was not strong enough to keep the Romans from putting Him upon the cross. In the eyes of a Muslim, this devalues Jesus. They do not see His crucifixion as the ultimate triumph over sin, death, and hell.

Another thing that is very confusing to a Muslim is that basically Christianity is an individual religion. We cannot be forced into it by any outside will. It is our own personal choice to accept Christ. We might have been born in a Christian environment, but each one individually needs to make a choice. Our faith ought to have an influence upon our environment, but it is individuals who make up the society. On the other hand, Islam is a communal religion. You do not operate as an individual but as part of the whole, and the whole has a very strong influence in making you conform to the teachings of Islam.

When discussing these issues with Muslims, we need to remember that the differences will not be eliminated so much by our arguments as by our patiently building a meaningful relationship with them. We need to stimulate each Muslim to study the New Testament, where he will come face-to-face with all it contains. What matters most is not that Muslims think ill of Christianity but that they have forfeited the wonderful salvation provided through Christ.

The fact that Jesus is mentioned a number of times in the *Qur'an* seems to be more of a hindrance than an advantage to the cause of Christ. While there are a few facts about Jesus presented in the *Qur'an* that are correct—like His virgin birth, and that He actually performed miracles—most of the facts have been greatly twisted and distorted. He is presented merely as another prophet in a long list of prophets and not as "the Savior of the world."

Because there are references to Jesus in the *Qur'an*, the real Jesus as a person is unknown to the Muslim. The secret of His significance remains undiscovered. The part, in fact, obscures the whole; the partial truth blinds the Muslim to the full truth, which actually becomes untruth. It withholds more than it tells about Jesus. Since Muslims are completely ignorant of the biblical Christ, it will take a lot of love, time, patience, and understanding to explain Him. This can best be done by letting Him live through our lives, and only then judiciously using our lips.

Another stumbling block to many Muslims is the Crusades. Though Islam was spread mainly by the sword, it seems that Muslims have forgotten this and are able to justify their bitterness about what occurred during the Crusades. While the motives of those who undertook the Crusades might have been worthy, the Crusades are a piece of Christian history unworthy of the name and nature of Christ. It is not that the Crusades in themselves were wrong, but they were blemished by the way they were conducted.

The Crusades were generated in contradiction and pursued in ambition. The relations between Western and Eastern Christendom, and between individual leaders within the forces, were for the most part lamentable. Self-seeking, stupidity, and plain human frailty have left a black mark on the true church of Christ. It was not the regaining of Jerusalem that should have been most important, but a positive and uplifting testimony to the cause of Christ is what was needed.

If a Muslim actually does read the Bible and puts forth an effort to understand it a little, he finds a variety of books of independent authorship, stretching over more than 1,400 years. Within the New Testament, he finds four different Gospels and a list of various Epistles. All this is in contrast to his holy book, the *Qur'an*, which is supposedly a revelation from God to one man, Muhammad, over a period of thirty-three years and contains only the history of Mecca and Medina.

It is difficult for the Muslim to comprehend why there should be four Gospels since he has been taught that the Gospel entrusted by God to Jesus the Prophet was reputedly a single book. The assumption is that because there are four, none of them is valid.

There is a reasoned Muslim explanation for this. Islam states that the early church lost the original Gospel that was supposedly revealed to Jesus by God, so several leaders set themselves to make good the deficiency, with the result that they differed from each other—and they were all wrong.

But for the Muslim, the teaching of Jesus as originally revealed has happily been safeguarded in the *Qur'an*. (It is sad to note that while in the *Qur'an* the word *Gospel* occurs a number of times, it never explains what this supposedly lost Gospel really was.) Muslims do not realize there is only one Gospel and that the life and teachings of Jesus were written by four different inspired authors to give various slants on the same ministry.

To a Muslim, the Epistles are mystifying. How can personal correspondence be divine revelation? If Paul chose to address himself to the Christians in Galatia, how can that constitute a piece of a preserved volume in heaven? The answer to this problem is very important. The Epistles of the New Testament are the clearest evidence that biblical revelation cooperates with human experience in order to complete and fulfill itself. For the revelation is not simply of a law to be followed, or a set of facts to be believed, or even a history to be accepted. It is the offer of a *relationship*.

The Epistles do contain a law to be obeyed, and this involves facts and history, but they speak essentially of a relationship to be received and experienced. The New Testament's doctrine of God means fellowship with God; its doctrine of man means repentance, forgiveness, and regeneration. The Epistles show in detail the nature of the recipients' faith, its impact upon their character and behavior, its import as a break with the past and a promise concerning the future.

The Old Testament is not as great a problem to the Muslim, for it contains a lot of rules and regulations given by prophets and then enforced to a degree by the "state." However, Muslims miss the fact that it is not primarily a book of laws involving prophets and a nation but a book that foretells the coming of a Savior and prepares the way for His coming.

The Muslim just cannot imagine that the differences between the Bible and the *Qur'an* could be Muhammad's lack of knowledge, or perhaps his own design or intent of purpose. They cannot conceive of the likely fact that Muhammad deliberately changed the truth of the Bible or that he received false information and did not check it out. (There was an abundance of both true and false information about Christianity available to Muhammad.)

Muslims also find the numerous present-day versions of the Bible bewildering; it only seems to confirm that there is a great discrepancy among Christians as to what the original Bible was like. They do not realize that these translations are based upon well-researched Hebrew and Greek texts. The issue is not what does the original text state but how it is going to be expressed to reach today's audience. (I must admit that the many versions can be bewildering, but this does not mean that the true message of the Bible is in doubt. Rather, an abundance of enlightening discoveries has given us an even more accurate Bible.)

It should be remembered that only recently has the *Qur'an* been translated into non-Islamic languages. It was felt that the only language the *Qur'an* could really be understood in was Arabic, and therefore, it is untranslatable. However, there are now a number of translations of the *Qur'an* into English, and some of them vary widely in clarity of meaning. A number of them have attempted to make the *Qur'an* more palatable for the Western mind, and some also have explanatory notes under the verses.

Another problem that has arisen has to do with the insistence of Christians that there are many fulfilled prophecies about Christ in the Bible, but nothing like this is found in Islam. On this point, the Muslims make a counterargument. In spite of the insistence of Islam that much of the Bible has been corrupted and most of the original has been lost, Muslims insist there were prophecies about the coming of Muhammad in the Bible, but they were suppressed, and most of them were removed.

However, Muslims now insist that they were not all removed and claim that they find places where Muhammad is truly prophesied in the Bible. (These are set forth and examined in appendix 5 of this book.) The *Qur'an* exhorts the Muslim to take advantage of the Scriptures that were written before in order to confirm the message of Muhammad. A Muslim will gladly point out to the Christian where our Bible foretells, describes, and commends Muhammad. Of course, quite a number of these scriptures clearly point to and were fulfilled in Jesus and have absolutely nothing to do with Muhammad. But somehow, the Muslims do not see the contradiction in their argument, and it seems to appease their conscience that Muhammad, supposedly, is found in the Bible.

But probably the hardest belief in Christianity for a Muslim to accept is that pertaining to the person of Jesus Christ: that He is both the eternal Son of God and was manifested in the flesh. Surah 112:1–3 states, "Say: 'He is Allah, the One! Allah, the eternal Besought of all! *He begat none. Nor was He begotten.*'" This is a formal rejection by Islam of the doctrine of Christ as the Son of God. To allow such a doctrine is to associate a man with God, to deify the human and so lift it to the status of worship that belongs only to God. To believe that God has a Son is to commit the supreme sin, *shirk*, for it contradicts the basic assertion of the Muslim that "there is no god except God."

The *Qur'an* acknowledges the Virgin Birth of Jesus, but it is unwavering in its opposition to the belief that the One so born is Divine. Also involved in this problem is another misconception that Muslims have. They feel that for God to have had a son He would have had to have sexual relations with a woman. Of course, this is not true. Jesus Christ is the eternal Son of the Father.

These are not easy problems for Muslims to overcome. At the crux of the matter is their thinking about sin. Since Muslims do not feel they are grievous sinners, they do not think of themselves as needing a mighty Savior. All they feel they need is guidance that comes through the *Qur'an* and their being a part of Islam. You need to emphasize the fact that you personally face the problem of sin in a more realistic way than a Muslim does.

Whereas Muslims do not believe they are great sinners before God, we with the Christian influence realize that we were born with a sin nature and by our own choice have sinned. We believe that God is holy and perfect and that He requires perfection, not just being 51 percent good. We know that we cannot satisfy God's righteousness by our own efforts, and except for the intervening of God with His mighty power and His providing salvation for us, we would be hopeless.

I have often used the following illustration with those in the cults, and it might be helpful here:

> Say you needed ten thousand dollars in a week. You might be able to borrow this amount from your parents, family members, relatives, or friends and then over a period of time be able to pay it back. But if the amount goes up to one hundred thousand dollars, your possibility of obtaining the sum is more difficult. What happens if it goes up to a million dollars? What about a billion dollars or a trillion dollars? What about one hundred trillion dollars? Of course, there is absolutely no human who could be of any help to you. The debt could never be repaid.

Then I explain that I am a hundred-trillion-dollar sinner, and I ask, "What does your religion have to offer? Only God is able to solve my problem, so to me, Jesus Christ being the eternal Son with the Father is no problem—because this is the only possible assurance that I have of not spending eternity in hell but rather of going to the seventh heaven to be with God for all eternity!" (I don't believe in seven heavens, but the Muslims do. The seventh heaven is the highest, where God dwells, so I use it for the sake of the Muslim I am speaking with.)

Muslims believe in the sovereignty of God. God is able to do anything that He wants. Is the Muslim not putting limitations on God's sovereignty by saying that it is unthinkable that God should have a Son and then be willing to give Him to provide mankind with eternal salvation! Muslims believe that God's word, the *Qur'an*, is eternal and was sent to earth to guide mankind back to Yahweh. Thus, the Muslim does believe that God has revealed something of Himself, at least in letting mankind know what His will is.

"Why is it so unthinkable to you Muslims that God would not reveal Himself in an even more personal way than just through the *Qur'an*—that is, by having His eternal Son, the living Word, come to earth, not just to show the way to God but actually provide the way to God by paying the penalty for our sins!" Without going into a long and profound explanation about Jesus as the Son of God, we need to reemphasize the fact that "God reveals" and that "God is Sovereign." It takes God to *reveal* God. If God is personal, then knowledge of Him must be a personal revelation; what better way to do that than to send His eternal Son into the world, not only to reveal God but also to provide eternal salvation? God Himself has taken upon Himself the responsibility to solve the problem of sin in an absolute, certain way and has not left it up to us to maybe merit God's favor.

I had an interesting experience along this line. I had gone to a particular mosque a number of times and had become acquainted with a certain Muslim. He kept asking me questions about Christianity, and I tried to answer them the best I could. I noted that he was somewhat different from the other Muslims I had met in the mosque, because he could think a little more logically. I had tried to explain to him that we are all sinners and therefore stand condemned before God and are hopeless in ourselves. But I went on to explain that God has taken matters into His own hand and sent Jesus Christ in order to pay the price for our sins.

After several weeks, he said to me, "If I understand you correctly, what you are telling me is that a man is brought into the courtroom. The judge is God Himself. The sinner is tried before God, found guilty, and the fine declared. Then it is at this point that the Judge, God, stands up, comes down from the bench, and stands alongside of the guilty man, and pays the fine for the one He had just condemned."

When I heard this, I commended him, saying that it was one of the best illustrations I had every heard regarding what God did for us in sending Jesus Christ to pay the penalty for our sins.

Let me summarize the major problems Muslims have in understanding Christianity and thus considering accepting Christ as their personal savior:

1. The *Qur'anic* view of Allah is that He is transcendent, and this cuts the Muslim off from a true knowledge and understanding of God. They feel God merely revealed His law but not Himself. He appears to be distant, essentially unknown and unknowable. Therefore, the idea of a personal relationship with God through Christ is very foreign to them. In the final analysis, Allah remains only the lawgiver and the final rewarder or punisher.

2. Islam has suppressed the true knowledge of the sinfulness of man. The *Qur'an* denies that we all have a depraved sin nature and willfully sin, making us guilty sinners before God, and that this sin needs to be paid for. Thus, Muslims do not realize that God requires not just partial obedience but complete holiness, which can be obtained only through the shed

blood of Jesus Christ. Islam claims we need only submission, not a new nature.

3. Islam has greatly distorted the true Christian teachings. Most Muslims are acquainted with the distortions found in the *Qur'an*. Above and beyond that, there has been a lot of anti-Christian material printed and distributed by leaders in Islam, so most Muslims have a false impression of Christianity. They have been taught that biblical Christianity posits three different gods—the Father, Son, and Mary—and that we teach that the Son is the result of God having sexual relations with a woman. They don't realize that the Son is eternal. Even though the *Qur'an* itself never makes such charges against the New Testament, Islam still teaches that much of the Bible has been lost and the rest has been greatly corrupted.

4. The average Muslim associates Christianity with America and the West, with its Hollywood moral standard. In Islamic countries, they have rules against such things and the power to enforce them. Therefore, they feel that Christianity has failed to come close to the moral standard that Islam sets and see no reason to convert to Christianity.

Here are some of the many misconceptions that Muslims have as to what they would have to do if they became a

Christian. They not only do not see their need for a Savior but also do not understand what it takes to get integrated into Christianity (I have to confess that many Christians also hold these false impressions and have passed them on):

1. Change one's given Muslim name, like Ahmad, to a Christian name like John.
2. Get baptized immediately and tell everyone about it, especially one's own family, which, of course, would cause him or her to be disowned.
3. Give up kneeling, like Muslims do when they pray, and instead sit on a chair or in a pew when speaking to God.
4. Start attacking Islam, Muhammad, and the *Qur'an*.
5. If a woman, she would have to hang a golden cross around her neck, wear short skirts and sleeveless dresses.
6. Eat all the pork that they like, because they are now free.
7. Live without restrictions and do anything they want, because their sins are all forgiven.
8. Be careful not to have any slips of the tongue by using the Muslim greeting "Peace to you."
9. See Arabs and Muslims as enemies, calling their God a demon and their prophet Muhammad a terrorist and a demon-possessed self-claimed prophet.

10. If living in America, become a Republican, support capitalism, democracy, and the Religious Right. Become as Westernized as possible.

I have not presented these misconceptions to try to discourage anyone from trying to reach out to Muslims but to explain realistically the task before them. I feel that too many of the books I have read have oversimplified the situation and have not faced it realistically.

12

***

Sharing Your Faith Introduction

BEFORE YOU ATTEMPT to share your faith in the Lord Jesus Christ with a Muslim, you need to have a clear understanding of the Islamic mind-set and the usual Muslim customs and reactions. If you are not aware of these and you break the rules, you will be greatly hindered in your presentation of the Gospel.

In our Western society, "individualism" is the norm, and we ordinarily experience guilt when we sin. In Islamic culture (as in many others), the collective community (the *ummah*) is most important, honor is paramount, and shame takes priority over all other feelings. Though the act itself may be sinful and even grievous, it is not nearly as cutting as the shame of discovery—being caught in the act—which brings dishonor not only on oneself but also on one's whole family and the community.

The Islamic community obviously has a powerful influence and usually controls one's thinking, his actions, and the enforcement of the established standards of right and wrong, based on *Shari'a*. It is therefore a gross dishonor to the community and family when a Muslim leaves Islam and converts to another religion, particularly Christianity, for this is looked on as treason. So honor must be maintained, and the way this is done is ordinarily by killing the one who has renounced Islam, often carried out by a family member.

The more honorable a family is, the better public positions its members will be able to get; they will also have more influential friends and likely be able to arrange better marriages for their children. For this reason, you, an outsider, if you wish to be accepted, need to be very careful that you do not do anything that will bring shame or dishonor upon your Muslim acquaintances.

The following chart lists some of mankind's most significant cultural values. It reveals the distinct difference between the thinking of the Eastern and the Western worlds.

Cultural Value	Eastern/ Muslim Society	Western Society
Honor	All important	Helpful, but not essential
Relationships:	People are more important than events	Events are often more important than people
Time orientation	The past (traditions)	The future
Family	Extended	Immediate
Time usage	Punctuality not important	Punctuality very important
Blame	Avoided, transferred	Okay to accept blame
Hospitality	Essential and honorable	Nice but not essential
Change	Of little value (often shunned)	Highly valued
Sin	An external mistake	An internal moral failure
Status	Usually inherited	Usually earned
Discipline	Internal (shame administered by the family)	External (physical administered by the parents)

Aging	Leads to greater respect and increased decision-making	Usually leads to less respect and decision-making
Rights	Society is most important	The individual is most important
Confrontation	Usually indirect (by a third person or through a story)	Usually direct (one-on-one)

It is important to note here that even though Christianity is often thought of as a Western religion, the Bible is not a Western book; rather, its origin, its stories, and its way of expression are Eastern.

As we explore some of the ways to reach out to Muslims, it is good to keep in mind 1 Corinthians 9:22–23, which reads, "To the weak I became weak, that I might win the weak. I have become all things to all people, that by all means I might save some. I do it all for the sake of the gospel, that I may share with them in its blessings."

It should not, therefore, be the desire of any Christian to make a Muslim Western—a follower of our customs—but rather to present the claims of Christ to each Muslim in such a way that he or she can understand the Gospel from within his or her own background. (I take it that this is the reason you have read this book.)

Sometimes, Western Christians feel that Christianity is actually Western and all outsiders should be willing to enter Christianity on our terms and conform to our ways. This is a great mistake, and this type of thinking is a great hindrance in presenting the Gospel. How much are we willing to adapt in order to reach Muslims for Christ? (To adapt, I say, not compromise! As a missionary in Japan for thirty-five years, I had to make a lot of adjustments yet not in the message I proclaimed but in my methods. This attitude can work for you too!)

The Initial Meeting

Not too many years ago, most Americans had never met a Muslim, let alone talked to one for any length of time. But things have changed. More and more, as we go to doctors' offices, malls, convenience stores, garages, gas stations, etc., we come into contact with Muslims. There are likely some who live in your neighborhood, or maybe you work with one. It may even be that a Muslim man has married into your immediate or extended family (Muslim women are not allowed to marry non-Muslims). All these individuals are potential contacts who need to hear the claims of Christ.

"To have friends, you must show yourself friendly." Let's say that a Muslim family moves into your neighborhood.

You ought to try to meet these newcomers casually as they are out in the yard, or perhaps you can go purposely to their house and welcome them to the neighborhood.

Shaking hands is a polite way of greeting a Muslim. But always do so with your right hand, never the left. The left hand is used for "unclean" functions, so extending it to others is considered an insult. However, a man should never take the initiative if the other party is a woman; some Muslim women feel they should never physically touch a man who is not their husband or an immediate member of the family. If a woman feels free to shake hands with a man, she will usually reach out her hand.

When good friends meet, they are likely to embrace and kiss each other on the cheek, perhaps several times—but always men with men and women with women. If you are eventually greeted in this way, it is a wonderful sign.

Following your initial contact, you might want to take over a plate of homemade cookies. Hospitality and generosity are two of the most valued attributes in Eastern culture.

As your friendship deepens, plan to invite the couple over for some light refreshments. For this occasion, you ought to use your best dishes and serve fruit, nuts, sweets, and tea or coffee. Usually, Muslims do not make short visits, so you should be prepared for them to stay several hours. And don't be the first one to suggest that the visit is over; that is something that is usually done by the guest.

When you meet a Muslim, do not start witnessing or right away offer to have a Bible study. You need to build up trust. Listening attentively can do this. Find out what kind of problems they may have. Then you can let them know that you have experienced the same sort of problems and can relate how you handled them. *But don't give advice.* Let your friends know that you are on the same level as they are (you want to get into the same boat they are in). Let them know that you really understand their situation. Once you have identified with them in their plight, hopefully they might ask how you overcame the difficulty and got the victory. If you are invited to their place, when visiting for the first time, you should take along a gift, such as flowers or candy. The Muslim will ordinarily reciprocate with a gift since your hospitality has put him under an obligation, and Muslims will do almost anything not to be a debtor to you.

You might next want to invite your Muslim acquaintance over for a full meal. Muslims believe that the very best food should be served when entertaining. When this is done, once again, use your best dishes and silverware. You should be aware of the fact that Muslims do not eat pork or drink alcohol, so these should never be served. Some Muslims will eat only "safe" foods, which are referred to as *halal* or "permitted."

In most of the Islamic world, dogs are considered dirty. They can only be used for hunting or as watchdogs, not kept as pets. For this reason, if you have a dog, it is best to keep Lassie outside when you invite a Muslim family to your house.

You need to realize that proper clothing is important to Muslims. For this reason, if you invite them to your house or you are invited to their house, you ought to respect their standards and dress accordingly. Men should wear long pants, not shorts; and always wear a shirt, even in the summer. For women, the dress code is even stricter. They should wear things like a long skirt with a loose-fitting blouse, or a dress with long sleeves; definitely nothing sleeveless. No shorts, no low-cut necklines.

Note: In the Middle East, when someone says something only once, it is usually a polite statement or request, but it's not intended to be fulfilled. The person on the receiving ends knows this. To a Muslim, repetition intensifies a request. If an offer is genuine, it will be repeated. Thus, when you invite a Muslim to your home, don't be afraid to repeat the invitation so they know they are genuinely wanted.

Nonverbal communication, such as body language or tone of voice, often carries more weight than spoken words. This means that when verbal and nonverbal cues don't match up, people tend to believe what is really spoken by the *nonverbal* element. Keep this in mind, especially if you are disagreeing with a Muslim friend. Many Americans tend to look stern, or even frown, when presenting an opposing idea. One person familiar with Muslims offers this piece of advice: "You can say anything to a Muslim if you say it with a smile on your face."

Talk about Matters of Common Interest before You Bring Up Religion

It is best not to start witnessing right away. During a get-acquainted conversation, the Muslim will usually tell you he is a follower of Islam, and you can tell him that you are a Christian, but it is best not to carry it further than that in the early stages of building a relationship.

Some subjects of common interest that you can safely talk about are the following:

1. Raising children ("Do you ever do things in front of your children that you do not allow them to do?")
2. The economy
3. Society in general
4. Financial matters
5. Travel experiences
6. What it is like living in a foreign country
7. How the school systems compare (Education in the Eastern world is based more on rote memory than on the assimilation and application of relevant facts.)

8. Health
9. Family
10. Character
11. Behavior
12. Work ethics

Build a Friendship

Compared to our Western relationships, friendships with Muslims take longer to develop, and trust is given more slowly; but once friendships are made, they are lifelong.

The majority of Muslims will be very friendly, but they can often have a hidden motive. They may have some kind of request in mind, or perhaps, they are seeking to witness to you about Islam. Muslims are generally urged to move into areas where other Muslims live, but if they cannot, they are to make friends in order to convert those who are not Muslim.

Even though you do good things for them, they may not trust you, because they may feel you are doing the same thing to them as they are doing to you. Therefore, it is important to take your time and build a genuine friendship.

If they offer you something or invite you to a meal, you should not refuse it. If you refuse a meal or such gifts, they will feel you are not their friend.

There is a real battle going on worldwide between Muslims and Christians. When they find out you are a Christian, they may begin to bombard you with anti-Christian literature and bring up things they have heard against Christianity. They want to get to you before you get to them. But do not give up in cases like this. However, be aware that many Muslims see Christians as their perpetual enemies.

When they give you anti-Christian literature or start telling you how bad Christianity is, tell them you already know the facts about Christianity, so you don't want to talk about it. "But I do want to learn about Islam!" (Usually, before you can successfully present biblical Christianity to outsiders, you first have to get them to question their own religion. That is why it is best to start with the thought-provoking questions I give in the next chapter.) Tell them you desire to know how good Islam is! If, of course, they do have genuine questions about Christianity, they should feel free to ask them; but you don't want them to *attack* you. So be careful not to drive inquirers away. Once you have done so, it is very hard to get them back. First impressions are very important to Muslims.

When you ask questions, don't make them argumentative. Put them this way: "Can you explain such and such to me?" "Would you please help me to understand this?"

You want to love them into the Kingdom. This is done by learning to be a friend.

You might offer to help them with their English if they haven't been in America for a sufficient time. This is a project that a church might undertake if there are a number of Muslims in the area. In order to reach out to the children, a group of you might have a summer camp at the church for them. Since Muslims believe in most of the prophets mentioned in the Bible, you can use stories like those about David, Daniel, the three men in the fiery furnace, Jonah, John the Baptist, etc. Muslims are used to using stories to get points across.

Witnessing about Christ

Don't start by telling Muslims that they are sinners, because according to their estimation, they are not. Be careful not to give the impression that, since you are a Christian, you are better than they are. Should they do something wrong, Muslims feel it was the circumstance that made them do it, so they are not really responsible for their sin. Allah already knew that they had a weakness at that point, and He understands and will not hold them guilty.

Muslims are taught in the *Hadith* that there are three circumstances in which it is okay to lie:

1. *During war.* Deception is no sin.
2. *In times of dispute.* You can tell a lie about another person in order to bring about peace.
3. *To your spouse when you have been unfaithful.* This is in order to keep peace in the family.

Muslims lie on other occasions also: When seeking a job, being untruthful about one's education and age is acceptable. So they might falsify a birth certificate or a passport. Regarding marriage, under Islamic law, a couple can get married by an imam but need not register it with the government. This makes it easier for the man to divorce his wife: he just says "I divorce you" three times, and that is it. But if they had registered the marriage, getting a divorce would be complicated, especially in the West.

In Holland, people are able to get financial assistance from the government. But they can receive more aid if they are single than if they are married. So the husband will divorce his wife the easy way, and they will then apply for assistance as two single people—yet they remain living in the same house, together, as man and wife. So deception is justified in this circumstance.

Don't be surprised, therefore, if sometimes you are lied to. But let's get back to the topic of witnessing about Christ.

After you have built a relationship with your Muslim friend, you might say something like this: "I don't know a lot about Islam, and I have many questions. I hope you will be willing to help me find answers to some of my questions. But first, would it be okay if I explained to you how I became a Christian? You may think that all Americans are Christians. That is not true! Many people are just nominal Christians, and I suspect there also are nominal Muslims. But each true Christian has had a personal encounter with God as Savior. Would it be okay if I told you my own private story as to how I came into this relationship with God?"

I have given my personal testimony many times to members of other religions. A testimony is an excellent way to present the whole plan of salvation if you tell your story in an interesting way. Muslims are fond of stories, so this is a good way to get facts across to them.

Since Muslims generally do not understand Christianity, you must be careful not to rattle off, without explanation, standard Christian terms. Expressions like "Jesus saves," "substitutionary atonement," "born-again believer," "I'm bound for heaven," "grace," "trusting Jesus" will be foreign to them and may need some explanation. As I mentioned earlier, Muslims do not understand sin, so don't just say, "God convicted me of my sins." You need to name specific, inward sins. Go very slowly when you give your testimony, and be sure to explain all your terms. Here I will give my testimony, which goes like this:

I was born in Clearfield, in the central part of Pennsylvania. My parents were not Christians then, but my father always took us to Sunday school. Once, I asked my mother a question about the Bible. She couldn't answer me, so I felt I couldn't get much help from my parents when it came to spiritual things.

One night, when I was six years old, as I lay in my bed, I thought, *What would happen if I died in my sleep?* I didn't know anything about the way of salvation at the time. I felt that I needed some special preparation to get into heaven, but I didn't know what. In order not to die in my sleep, I decided not to go to sleep. Of course, eventually I did fall asleep!

The same question came to me every night for a week. Though I was only six, it was very real to me. From that time on, I realized I was carrying a heavy burden because of my sins. Every time I sinned, it became heavier. As my years in grade school progressed, the burden on my heart became even heavier. I wanted to get rid of this burden but didn't know how.

When I asked some people as to how I could get rid of this heavy burden, they said, "Just do the best you can, and since God is a God of love, everything will be okay." This didn't satisfy me. If the way to get to heaven was to do more good things than bad, it seemed I naturally always did more bad deeds than good ones. It was a hopeless situation.

Once I entered junior high school, not only was I carrying this heavy burden of sin but also I could not see any reason for living. After all, why was man put on earth? I was not satisfied with life and had few examples of people who were. Everyone seemed to be going in circles with no long-range goal.

In the summer of 1942, we moved to Chester, Pennsylvania, where my father got a job working in the shipyard during World War II. The pastor of a small community church came visiting one August afternoon shortly after we moved in, and he invited our family to church. My father, four brothers, sister, and I went the next Sunday. This was a gospel-preaching church where people diligently studied the Bible. I enjoyed going to Sunday school and soon became active in the young people's group.

The next year in October, there was an evangelistic campaign in our city. The Saturday night before it began, our young people's group went downtown and gave out invitations to the meeting. I went to the meeting on Tuesday night, and about three thousand people showed up. I was elated because maybe some people were there because I had given out invitations.

The evangelist began to speak on sin, but in a different way than I had ever heard it before. He did not talk about war, drunkards, thieves, etc., but said that pride, self-centeredness, selfishness, anger, wrath, lying, cheating, gossip, jealousy, covetousness, backbiting, disobedience to parents, fighting with brothers and sisters, etc., were awful sins before God. He didn't say we were just tainted with sin but we were all ungodly, wicked sinners before God. This did not go down well with me. I was considered a good boy in our area because my father was a strict disciplinarian. I knew I was not perfect, but to be called a wicked, ungodly sinner made me so angry I didn't hear anything else the evangelist said. As I left the meeting that night, I determined that I would not go back to any more meetings that week. I wanted to forget everything that rude evangelist had said. But God had other plans.

As I went to bed that Tuesday night, I recalled thirteen actual sins. I wasn't proud of this, but I also didn't think thirteen sins for a fourteen-year-old boy was too bad. Wednesday night as I went to bed, the Holy Spirit brought more sins to my mind. My list grew from thirteen to twenty-five. Thursday night, I began counting at twenty-six and got up to fifty. That night, I thought, *Maybe that evange-*

list was right about my sins and I was wrong. Well, on Friday night, I settled the issue. I continued on from fifty-one and got up to one hundred. Then my whole past life exploded, and the recollection of many more sins came pouring in upon me. These were not just general sin categories but actual sins. For the first time in my life, I realized what a sinner I was before the holy and righteous God of the Bible. It was very humbling.

Fortunately, the next night, I found the answer to my sin problem. Twice a month on Saturday night, many young people from various churches in our city got together for a meeting. I went, and was glad I did. The speaker's message was on sin, but this time, I could not argue with him because God had revealed part of my sinful heart to me. "The Bible tells us," he said, "that Jesus Christ came into this world to save sinners. If we will acknowledge our sins and believe that Jesus Christ died on the cross for them, then we can be saved."

As I sat there, I said to myself, "Am I really hearing what this man is saying? He said I am an ungodly sinner. I know that's true. He also said Jesus Christ died for sinners. Since I am a sinner, then I qualify for the salvation that Jesus Christ is offering."

Right there I bowed my head, confessed my sins, and asked Jesus to come into my life and save me from my sins. At that very moment, I felt the burden of my sins lifted. For the first time in my life, I was free from the burden of sin. Then I realized what was missing in my life. God had created me to have fellowship with Himself, but sin had come in and separated me from God. I hadn't known the reason I had been created. That's why I lacked any purpose for living. When God took away my sins, He brought me into a living fellowship with Himself. I left the meeting that night with a light heart and a reason for living.

The next day, Sunday, as I went to church, it had a new and deep meaning for me. I will never forget how they talked about God being our Father—because now I knew Him in a personal way. Monday, as I entered school, I realized I was a different person and that God was going with me.

Having been taught that when you know Christ as your Savior you are to read your Bible and pray every day, this is what I began to do. What I read in the Bible surprised me because it was such a personal book. It was as if it was written just for me. I didn't realize till then how God knew my heart so well. Of course, the Word of God began to convict me whenever I knowingly committed a sin and had a cleansing effect on my life. And Jesus Christ has been my daily guide ever since.

I have found that giving your personal testimony will help the outsider understand Christianity a little better, and it is something they will likely remember for a long time.

As you are giving your testimony, or later witnessing, when you use the Bible, it is best to quote from memory instead of reading the words from the Bible. Also, as you quote the Bible, don't mention that it is from the Bible. There is a good reason for this. As I've mentioned elsewhere, Muslims do not have any respect for the Bible and believe that it has been corrupted, so they are not familiar with the Bible. But as they hear parts of the Bible quoted, they hopefully will recognize the beauty of what you have quoted and may ask you where it came from. Then you can tell them, or maybe even show them, the passage in the Bible. In this way, they might come to realize the Bible is not like they have heard it to be. And they will be more open to the truths found in it as you progress in your relationship with them.

Do not invite a Muslim to your church right away. There are too many common things that can have a negative effect on a Muslim, such as the association of men and women together, the image of young people holding hands, the image of their dress, the practice of people wearing shoes inside the church, the cross in the front, and perhaps the style of music. You have to first build up friendship and trust. If there is a fellowship of former Muslims in your area, you might want to take your neighbor there first. But whatever you do, talk about your church in a positive way; don't say anything negative.

If there is a wedding, a funeral, a baptism, etc., these could be points of attraction. Such events might get them interested. If you mention that such an event is coming up, they might ask if they could come along.

Words Guaranteed to Start an Argument

Certain words or phrases can trigger emotional responses, whether we intend for them to or not. Some Muslims will react negatively to words that we Christians often use, like *church, convert, baptism, cross, crusade, Son of God, Savior, Israel, Jew, Christmas*—even the term *Christian*. Be careful.

Here are some alternative words you can use:

Instead of	Use
Church	Place of worship
Convert	One who enters the Kingdom
Baptism	Identification with Christ

Cross	Means of Roman execution
Crusade	Campaign
Savior	Rescuer
Israel	Palestine
Christmas	Feast of Christ's birth
Christian	Followers of Jesus (*Isahi*)

Important Dont's

1. Don't debate. No one wants to lose, so this is not a proper way to witness. Explain to your Muslim acquaintance that discussions are for friends and debates are for opponents.
2. Don't let the Muslim you are dealing with get you into a purely defensive position. You will never win a battle by merely defending.
3. Don't use the Bible at the outset. First, you must get your friend to doubt what Islam teaches.
4. Don't start saying bad things about the *Qur'an* or Muhammad.
5. Don't start by discussing Jesus as the Son of God.
6. Don't start by bringing up the Trinity. If he brings it up, however, be prepared.
7. Don't remain silent. Muslims are often more vocal in their beliefs than American Christians are. We Westerners believe that we should politely wait for

a pause by the other person before we interrupt and interject our own thoughts. However, if you just listen to a Muslim and do not interrupt and say something, he is likely to feel that you are agreeing with him. Or he'll conclude that you have nothing important to say on the subject. Muslims are often amazed at how wimpy—how uncertain and ashamed—Christians are of their beliefs. I have learned—even though I don't like to do it—that you have to continually interrupt when a Muslim says something you don't agree with and let him know your true feelings. But whenever you disagree, say it with a smile.

Aids in Sharing Your Faith

Using the Jesus film has been an effective way of helping Muslims understand who Jesus truly is. It is available in many different languages, and these DVDs can be obtained from Multi-Language Media, Inc., PO Box 301, Ephrata, PA 17522. Telephone number: (717)738-0582. Hours: 9:00 a.m.–4:45 p.m. (Eastern time).

Ask your friend to watch the film and to comment on it. This should not be a problem, because Muslims claim they believe in Jesus and hold him in high regard. (As explained elsewhere, the Jesus of the Muslims is not the Jesus of the Bible, so this is a good way to let them know about the true

Jesus.) A calendar that has Scripture verses written in the birth language of your friend would be a valued gift. He and his relatives will read these verses and come to respect the Bible. If you give a Muslim anything written in Arabic, he will never throw it away.

Don't Give Up if You Don't See Immediate Results

We need to remember that the success or failure of our witnessing to Muslims is not to be measured in numbers. Reaching out to Muslims requires patience. Often we do not see the full consequences of our efforts. It is the Christian's obligation to faithfully present the Gospel in a simple and loving way. We want our unsaved friends to see the beauty of Christ in our lives and actions. The results are up to God.

Commandments for Sharing the Gospel with Muslims

1. *Be constantly in prayer.*

    It is the Holy Spirit who wins men to Christ. Seek His guidance and power as you present the Word.
2. *Be a genuine friend.*

    Saying, "Hello, how are you?" isn't enough. If you really care, show it by inviting them to your home, sharing your time, and helping with their problems.

3. *Ask thought-provoking questions.*

Help them to reach their own conclusion about the Gospel. There are many of these questions in this book—see the next chapter. Here are a few short and simple ones that you might begin with:

- What does the *Qur'an* teach about forgiveness?
- Do you have assurance that God will accept you?
- What makes a person clean or unclean in Islam?
- I have heard that animal sacrifices are important in Islamic culture. Why is this so? (At the end of the pilgrimage to Mecca, all are supposed to sacrifice an animal.)
- When the animal is sacrificed, what deeper meaning does this have? (You might be able to refer to the animal sacrifices in the Old Testament that pointed to Jesus. Let them know that John the Baptist, whom all Muslims accept as a prophet, said in John 1:29 concerning Jesus, "Behold! The Lamb of God who takes away the sin of the world!")
- How is sin removed from a person in Islam?
- In Islam, how can people know for certain that God will allow them to enter Paradise on the Day of Judgment? (The only way a Muslim can be assured of going to Paradise is to be killed or kill himself in jihad.)

- In Islam, what things are considered honorable and what are shameful?
- Jesus is known as the Messiah in both Islam and Christianity. Why do you think Jesus, and only Jesus, has this title? What do you think it means? (This title is found eleven times in the *Qur'an* and is used only of Jesus and no one else. I have never met a Muslim who had any idea of its meaning. You should explain that it means "the Anointed One," "the expected deliverer.")
- No other prophet had this designation; could this be a significant fact? Since Jesus did not deliver the Jewish people from the rule of Rome, then what did He deliver His followers from? Might it not be deliverance from the dominion of sin, like the Bible states?
- Do you know that the angel Gabriel revealed to the prophet Daniel that the "Messiah shall be cut off , but not for Himself" (in 9:26) and that he even gave the *exact date* when Jesus would be "cut off," pointing clearly to His death?
- How do you account for the fact that the angel Gabriel mentioned this about the Messiah over six hundred years before Jesus was born? (Muslims believe that Gabriel is the revealer of

truth.) When Jesus lived here on earth, He also foretold His death. Should these facts be ignored?

- Since the book of Daniel was not written until after the Babylonian captivity of the Jews was almost over, it could not have been corrupted, like some mullahs claim happened to the rest of the Old Testament. What excuse do you Muslims have for not believing it and the other Bible books written after the Babylonian captivity?

4. *Listen attentively.*

When you ask a question, courtesy requires that you listen to the answer no matter how long it takes. You'll be surprised at how much you'll learn.

5. *Present your beliefs openly.*

After your friendship has been firmly established, state what you believe clearly and without apology, showing Scripture passages that support those teachings. This places the responsibility for doctrine where it belongs—on the Word of God.

6. *Talk about sin and how it affects our lives.*

Say, "Sin is the biggest problem in our world today. How do we deal with sin?" (A person who is living in sin hates himself. He is an enemy to himself. Most Muslims recognize that they are living in sin, but they don't know how to get forgiveness. Explain to them how Jesus forgives sins.)

7. *Reason, don't argue.*

Argument may win you a point but can lose you a hearing. There are some points on which you can argue forever without achieving a thing, except closing a mind.

8. *Never denigrate Muhammad or the Qur'an.*

This is as offensive to them as speaking disrespectfully about Christ or the Bible is to us.

9. *Respect their customs and sensitivities.*

Don't offend by

a. putting your Bible (a holy book) on the floor;
b. speaking too freely about sex (Muslims don't speak about sex; it is considered dirty);
c. appearing too familiar in casual relationships with the opposite sex;
d. refusing hospitality;
e. wearing shorts or other inappropriate dress; and
f. making jokes about sacred topics such as fasting, prayer, or God.

10. *Use the Word of God.*

As you build a friendship and respect, you can use the Bible more freely. You might be able to start a

Bible study with your Muslim friend. Make sure he has a Bible that is accurate and easy to understand. The Gospels are the best portions to start with, particularly Matthew and Luke.

11. *Persevere.*

Muslims have a lot of rethinking to do when they are confronted with the Gospel, but rest assured that the Word of God will do its work in His good time.

Above all, be humble. Speak with love. This will make a way for you. My cry and my prayer to the Lord Jesus Christ is that He might draw millions of Muslims into His kingdom.

Major Obstacles in Muslims Coming to Christ

The law of apostasy (*ridda*). In Islamic society, everyone must conform to the "law of God," so leaving the faith is considered apostasy. Therefore, conversion to the Christian faith triggers a rejection mechanism. According to *Shari'a*, an adult male apostate is to be given a short time to recant, and if he does not, he will suffer the full severity of the law. Upon being tried and convicted, he is stripped of all civil rights so that anyone is free to kill him, his marriage is declared null and void, his children are taken from him, and his property becomes spoil to the Muslim community.

Since his family is dishonored, it is often a family member who will kill him. The female apostate is to be imprisoned until she recants, however long that takes. Sometimes, she too is killed by her family. Often, the convert's only recourse is to seek refuge abroad.

Earlier in the twentieth century, Muslims who became Christians were treated more leniently. But now, with the return of the fundamentalist spirit, we seem to be witnessing a return to the full severity of the law of apostasy. This law is in effect in most Muslim countries, even where it is not explicitly written into the constitution. This is one of the leading reasons for more Muslims not being willing to take a stand for Christ.

Is honor killing likely to be carried out? Not in the United States and other Western countries where Muslims are a clear minority, and where the killer would be arrested and tried for murder. (Even so, the threat remains.) But one could be in danger if he were to visit relatives back in his Islamic homeland.

The treatment of Muslims who leave the faith and become Christians is certainly a major problem, and those working with Muslims need to do a much-better job of helping converts relate their new faith and life to their culture. I would not advise a new convert to go home and tell his family that he has become a Christian and then begin attacking Islam. Nor do I feel converts ought to be baptized immediately. I believe that it is better to work with the Muslim convert so that he may grow in his Christian faith and have real changes for the better in his life. As his acquaintances begin to realize that he is now gentle in his speech, has become honest, is more patient with people, and possesses a real joy and peace, they will note this difference—and instead of *him* having to tell people that he has become a Christian, they will begin to say, "I note that there has been a real change in your life. What happened to you?" Then the convert can explain patiently that he has become a Christian, and hopefully, he will not be rejected so severely.

When I was a missionary in Japan—a Buddhist country—I found that one of the hardest and the rudest things for a Christian to do was to not bow before the coffin at a funeral. Because Buddhists pray for and to the dead, we taught our Christians that this was something that God disliked and they could not do it. But we gave them an alternative. Knowing that after the funeral a meal would be served for the family and friends, we said the Christian should go to the family *beforehand* and politely explain that because of his beliefs as a Christian he could not attend the funeral and bow. But then he should offer to bring food for the meal, and to help with the serving and the cleaning up. This would show that the Christian had not only convictions but also a caring heart.

This way, his convictions did not so blatantly break his fellowship with members of his former community. And it helped reduce the misunderstanding and pain, which one's loyalty to Christ necessarily caused among his Buddhist friends, his birth community. Similarly, converts from Islam need much Spirit-led guidance. I feel it is important that we Christians give new converts adequate help in relating their faith and life to their culture in their tension-filled or traumatic transition from Islam to Christianity. The convert needs to separate from the Islamic faith but does not need to be taken out of the community. I feel it is a mistake to insist that a Muslim convert be baptized right away, take a Western name, hang a cross around one's neck, or completely change his or her style of dress.

In America, the transition of a Muslim into Christianity is nothing compared to what is normally experienced by those who live in Islamic-ruled countries. Yet even here in America, there needs to be serious thought given regarding converts. For most of them, attending the average American church is a great shock because of the slovenly way so many of the people are dressed and their frequent lack of decorum. I heard of a Muslim who went to a Christian church, and during the service, there was a young couple hugging and flirting. This is something that Muslims just do not do in public. For this reason, it is best to start off with a group Bible study in which the new convert can safely grow.

A Change in Approach to Evangelism

Few churches have spontaneously shown hospitality to Muslims. If a "seeking" Muslim were to show up in your church, would he be welcomed. or would he be mistrusted? Many churches do not readily welcome outsiders who are not our kind of people, let alone someone from another culture or another religion—especially if he is of the militant Islamic faith. Sadly, there is often a great reluctance to show genuine friendship.

If the church ever intends to make a real impact on the Muslim community, it is going to have to completely change its approach to evangelism. As it stands now, most evangelism of any kind is done on either Sunday morning or evening. In many cases, an evangelistic sermon will be preached and an invitation is given to come forward to accept Christ and make a public profession of faith. Some churches will immediately baptize those who respond, and they become church members without any discipling or having any idea of what it means to be a true Christian or a church member. Muslims are not saved in fifteen minutes and shouldn't be baptized immediately, because of the cost involved.

Winning Muslims is a long process that starts with building a meaningful relationship. It takes time to earn the right to present Christ in words. But we Christians need to remember that while we may not be able to present Christ in words at first, we are presenting Christ if we are openly living a life that shows the sweetness of Christ. It is always much harder and takes a lot more time and patience to show a Muslim what a Christian is truly like than just to tell him.

There is a cost to be paid in order to see Muslims come to know Christ. The question remains: is the average Christian and church willing to pay that price, in the sacrificing of themselves, in order to see these needy, religious souls come to know Christ as their Savior and Lord?

13

Important Questions
for Muslims

THE NORMAL WAY of witnessing is to start with the fact that the person is a sinner—and properly so—going on, then, to the sinner's need of repentance. At that point, the Christian opens his Bible and reads verses that show how a sinner can come to know Jesus Christ as personal Savior.

However, when one witnesses to Muslims, this is not a very effective approach, for the following reasons:

1. Muslims have an entirely different concept of sin than what the Bible presents. They believe they have the true commands of God in the *Qur'an*, and if they

are following some of them faithfully, they feel they are righteous. And they think those of us here in America are the sinners because of the Hollywood style of living that so many of us have. Muslims have been taught that all Americans are Christians, and so they associate this sinful style of living with Christianity. In the Muslim's mind, therefore, the Christians are the sinners and need to change, and the way to do that is to become a Muslim.

2. Muslims completely deny the fact that God has a Son and that Jesus is the Divine Savior of the world. They believe that He was just another in a long line of prophets and was sent only to the Jewish race; thus, He can't offer anything to Muslims, except be respected as a prophet—but certainly not as a Savior. So to them, Jesus can't be the answer to the problem of sin.

3. Muslims do not believe that someone can die vicariously for another person's sins. They deny that Jesus died on the cross, and the *Qur'an* declares that someone else died in His place. They believe each person has to take care of his or her own sins, so talking about Jesus forgiving their sins is foolishness to them.

4. Muslims do not believe that the Bible we presently have is accurate. They say that just about all of it is

different than the original—some parts deleted and other parts corrupted. Thus, you cannot use the Bible as your authority.

So how do we witness to Muslims? It is necessary to do some pre-evangelizing. You can do this best by asking thought-provoking questions about their religion. They must begin to have some strong doubts about Islam before you can present the Gospel effectively. Furthermore, you will not be able to address head-on the subjects of the Trinity, the Sonship of Christ, or His death as the vicarious atonement for the sins of mankind. Most Muslims are very well acquainted with the typical arguments of Christians on these subjects, and you won't make much progress because there will be a lot of resistance. But you definitely do need to discuss the issue of the Bible being corrupted.

In light of this, the questions that are presented in this chapter and elsewhere have been designed to try to get the Muslim you are speaking with to question his or her own religion. Later, you can sidle up to the teachings of the Trinity, the deity of Christ, the death of Christ, etc., via the back door—where Muslims are not prepared and they may not realize what you are doing.

Of all these points for discussion, I have found three to be the most telling:

1. The fact that Muhammad taught that, at the best, "only 1 in 100 Muslims will go to Paradise."
2. The fact that the angel Gabriel is never identified in the *Qur'an*, so no one can be sure as to where the *Qur'an* came from, which undermines its authority.
3. The claim that the Bible has been corrupted. On this issue, Muslims have two choices:

   a. Allah has failed to keep His *Qur'anic promise* to preserve the Bible.
   b. Muslims scholars are not telling the truth when they claim the Bible is no longer reliable.

The following questions do not need to be used in any particular order. I have presented all these matters to Muslims and have not yet received reasonable answers back from them, but I do know that in some cases I have gotten my point across and made them think.

May the Lord bless and encourage you as you seek to share the wonderful love of God and Christ to your Muslim acquaintance.

1. How Did Cain Learn to Murder?

Here is a problem that I stumbled upon in my study of Islam. I am still looking for an answer.

I was doing research about the Islamic concept of sin. In the *Qur'an* (one published by Why-Islam), the note under Surah 30:30 reads,

> As turned out from the creative hand of God, man is innocent, pure, true, free, inclined to right and virtue, and possessed of true understanding about his own position in the Universe and about God's goodness, wisdom, and power. That is his true nature, just as the nature of a lamb is to be gentle and of a horse to be swift. But man is caught in the meshes of customs, superstitions, selfish desires, and false teaching. This may make him pugnacious, unclean, false, slavish, hankering about what is wrong or forbidden, and deflected from the love of his fellow-men and the pure worship of the One True God.)

I have also read that Muslims do not believe that Adam and Eve really sinned but just "made a mistake"—thus, they remained pure and innocent once they repented. Their inner nature was not changed. If we assume this to be true, then Cain (*Qabeel*) and Abel (*Habeel*) obviously were born in a pure environment. Right? There was then no "mesh of customs," no "uncleanness," no "falseness," no "slavishness," no "hankering about what is wrong or forbidden."

Everything they knew about God was pure, because up to this point, no one had actually drifted away from God.

So my question is this: Since man is basically pure and innocent, there were no bad examples in the world, so why did Cain kill his brother Abel? Was this just a mistake on his part? Was it an accident? Taking this a little further, since in the beginning everything was perfect and sin only comes because of bad examples and influence, then where did all this bad influence come from?

I think I smell a contradiction. Don't you?

If your answer is "Satan is responsible," then who influenced Satan to sin? Didn't he once exist in a perfect environment? And wasn't his nature changed drastically when he fell?

2. What Is the Gospel?

Surah 5:46 in the *Qur'an* states, "And in their [the prophets'] footsteps We sent Jesus son of Mary, confirming that which was (*revealed*) before him, and We *bestowed on him the Gospel* wherein is guidance and a light … a guidance and an admonition to the Godfearing." (The word *Gospel* is also found in Surahs 3:3, 48, 65; 5:66, 110; 9:111; 48:29, and 57:27.)

Would you please tell me what this Gospel, *Injeel* ("Good News"), consists of? What actually was revealed to Jesus by Allah and then proclaimed by him? Surely, it must be important.

3. Who Died in Jesus's Place?

The *Qur'an*, in Surah 4:157, states that it was not Jesus who died on the cross but someone else. Would you please identify this person from the *Qur'an*? (I don't want what the scholars think but what the *Qur'an* clearly states.)

4. What Proof Is There That Someone Died in the Place of Jesus?

In just about any court of law, it takes more than one witness to condemn a person. The Bible says, "At the mouth of two or three witnesses." In the *Qur'an*, only one time (in Surah 4:157) does it claim that it was not Jesus who died but someone else died in his place. But in order for a truth to be established, you need two or three witnesses. In light of this, would you show me three places in the *Qur'an* where this dire charge—that an impostor died in the place of Jesus—is made?

5. Who Are the "We" in the *Qur'an*?

Hundreds of times, the *Qur'an* speaks about "we" doing certain things, in which Allah has to be one of them. So please identify, by just using the *Qur'an*, who are meant when it speaks about "we." (I don't want the answer that it is like a king using a plural to include his subjects or the nobles of his royal court. I don't believe the *Qur'an* ever identifies Allah as a king. Please, I don't want speculation. I want the *Qur'an* to identify the other parties.)

6. In the *Qur'an*, Where Is the Messenger Who Delivered Allah's Words Clearly Identified?

Where in the *Qur'an* does it specifically identify, clearly, the one who appeared to Muhammad and gave him his messages, either at the very beginning or on previous visits? Don't tell me what the scholars or commentators say as to who that person was; I want to read the very words of the *Qur'an* where that person is identified! I have a good reason for this request. The Bible over and over clearly identifies the one who is speaking with a heavenly message.

Here are some examples.

In Genesis 6:13 (emphasis mine), we read, "And *God* said to Noah." So the one speaking is identified, and the one spoken to is identified.

> Now **the Lord** said to Abraham. (Gen. 12:1)

> After these things **God** tested Abraham and said to him, "Abraham!" And he said, "Here am I." **He** [God] said, "Take your son, your only son Isaac, whom you

love, and go to the land of Moriah [in Palestine], and offer him there as a burnt offering on one of the mountains of which I shall tell you. (Gen. 22:1–2)

When the Lord saw that he turned aside to see, *God* called to him out of the bush, "Moses, Moses!" And he said, "Here I am." (Exodus 3:4)

Then in verse 14, God identifies Himself clearly: "God said to Moses, 'I AM WHO I AM.' And he said, 'Say this to the people of Israel, I AM has sent me to you.'"

In the sixth month *the angel Gabriel* was sent from God to a city of Galilee named Nazareth, to a virgin betrothed to a man whose name was Joseph, of the house of David. And the virgin's name was Mary. And he come to her and said, "Greetings, O favored one, the Lord is with you!" But she was greatly troubled at the saying, and tried to discern what sort of greeting this might be. And the angel said to her, "Do not be afraid, Mary, for you have found favor with God. And behold, you will conceive in your womb and bear a son, and you shall call his name Jesus. He will be great and will be called the Son of the Most High. And the Lord God will give to him the throne of his father David. [This inauguration will occur in the future.] And he will reign over the house of Jacob forever, and of his kingdom there will be no end." And Mary said to the angel, "How will this be, since I am a virgin?" And the angel answered her, "The Holy Spirit will come upon you, and the power of the Most High will overshadow you; therefore the child to be born will be called holy—the Son of God." (Luke 1:26–35)

He [Saul of Tarsus, who later became the apostle Paul] heard a voice saying to him, "Saul, Saul, why are you persecuting me?" And he said, "Who are you, Lord?" And he said, "I am *Jesus*, whom you are persecuting. But rise and enter the city, and you will be told what you are to do." (Acts 9:4–6)

In the Bible, the one who is speaking is usually identified right in the text, so we don't have to speculate as to who spoke. (I could give many more examples, but these show you what I mean.)

My request again is, "Please show me in the actual text of the *Qur'an* where it clearly identifies the one who is said to be speaking to Muhammad." (I know what the Muslim scholars speculate, but I want the very words of the *Qur'an*.) Where is the proof that it was Gabriel?

7. No Original *Qur'an*

Muslims keep claiming that Islam has an unaltered *Qur'an*. This is impossible and can easily be proven—all from sources inside Islam.

1. The original *Qur'an* existed in the mind of Muhammad. He had it memorized. Muhammad is dead, so it is impossible to have the original *Qur'an.*

2. Since Muhammad was illiterate and could not write, he had to dictate the words to someone else. Now it becomes secondhand.

3. What was written down was scribbled on pieces of papyrus, stones, palm leaves, animal shoulder blades, ribs, or bits of leather. The material on which these portions of the *Qur'an* were written are not available today, so there is no way to determine if it was copied correctly. Also, most of this material is perishable and, therefore, very obviously not available today.

4. One of the reasons for someone compiling the first complete copy of the *Qur'an* was because much of it was memorized and only in the heads of various followers. But a good number of them were dying in battle, and it was felt that some of the *Qur'an* might be lost. The evidence is clear that it was not all writ-

ten down before Muhammad died. So there is no original *Qur'an*! Wouldn't you agree?

8. Was Zachariah Dumb for Three Days (the *Qur'an*) or for Nine Months (the Bible)?

Let us assume the reliability and accuracy of the *Qur'an*, that it has never been altered. In Surah 19:7–10, we are told that Zachariah, the father-to-be of John the Baptist, was made voiceless for three days because he did not believe the words of the messenger who appeared to him. Three full days! (See also Surah 3:39–41.) But when we turn to the Gospel account (Luke 1:5–20, 57–64), the story is quite different. [Read this account, noting especially verses 20, 59, and 64.] For some good reason, it seems, the Christian authorities deliberately rewrote the story—they changed the three days and nights to nine months plus eight days. How come?

"An inconsequential matter," you may say. "What's the point?"

Well, we have two possibilities: either Muhammad (or his listeners) made a clear mistake when he declared that "three days and nights" was the confirming sign or Christian scribes, for some obscure reason, must have deliberately altered—falsified—their holy Scriptures! Why would they do that? Which of these two possibilities is easier to believe?

If the *Qur'an* is not inaccurate here, what could have motivated early Christians to maliciously alter the original Gospel account? I would like to know.

Tell me, why shouldn't I believe that the *Qur'an*, not the Bible, is wrong?

9. Why Do Muslims Say That Only Parts of the Bible Were Preserved?

Muslims claim that the original Bible has been "corrupted, changed, and much of it lost." Whenever there are things in the Bible that differ from what is written in the *Qur'an*, then automatically "the Bible has been corrupted" in these spots, they say. However, at the same time, Muslims will use certain verses from the Bible when they try to prove that Muhammad's coming was foretold in Scripture. Yes, and other parts of the Bible are also taken to be authentic if they seem to contradict a theological teaching Muslims dislike! Muslim scholars reject what they want but take whatever they think will help their cause.

The Bible either has to be either taken as a whole or rejected as a whole, not divided up in a way that might suit one's fancy. So I ask, is it authentic or is it not?

10. Did Allah Fail to Preserve the Bible Like He Promised?

The *Qur'an* very clearly states that the Gospel is something that was revealed by Allah Himself and thus should be considered to be the Word of God. Here are some verses of the *Qur'an* that state this fact (it doesn't take a scholar to determine this):

> And in their footsteps We sent Jesus son of Mary, confirming that which was (*revealed*) before him, and We *bestowed on him the Gospel* wherein is guidance and a light, confirming that which was (*revealed*) before it in the Torah—a guidance and an admonition to the Godfearing. (Surah 5:46)
>
> He has revealed to you (*Muhammad*) the Scripture with truth, *confirming that which was revealed before it, even as He revealed the Torah and the Gospel.* (Surah 3:3)
>
> If they had observed (*practiced*) the Torah and the Gospel and *that which was revealed to them from their Lord.* (Surah 5:66)
>
> Say, "O People of the Scripture! You have nothing (*of true guidance*) till you observe the Torah and the Gospel, *and that which was revealed to you from your Lord.*" (Surah 5:68)

> Then We caused Our messengers to follow in
> their footsteps; and We caused Jesus, son of Mary,
> to follow, and *gave him the Gospel, and placed compassion and mercy in the hearts of those who followed him.*
> (Surah 57:27)

It is quite clear from the above quoted verses of the *Qur'an* that God was the one who revealed the Gospel to the Lord Jesus Christ; thus, what He taught should be considered "the Word of God"!

Now we come to the real problem: God has not only made known His Word by revelation but also promised that He would keep His Word from passing away, being corrupted or changed. The following verses from the *Qur'an* proclaim this:

> And recite (*and teach*) that which has been revealed
> unto you in the Book of your Lord. *No one can
> change His words.* You shall find no refuge beside
> Him. (Surah 18:27)
>
> There is none to alter the decisions of Allah.
> (Surah 6:34)
>
> Perfected is the Word of your Lord in truth and
> justice. *There is nothing that can change His words.*
> (Surah 6:115)

> Theirs is the good news [the Gospel] in this world and in the Hereafter. *No change can there be in the words of Allah.* This is the supreme triumph. (Surah 10:64)
>
> This is the way of Allah that has been followed in the past, *and you find no change in the way of Allah.* (Surah 48:23)

The *Qur'an* clearly states that the Gospel is something that was revealed by God. And the *Qur'an* further teaches that Allah is going to protect His word so that it cannot be changed, altered, or lost. Since Muslim scholars claim that much of the Gospel is now extinct—has been destroyed, lost, or altered—then the only conclusion I can come to is that Allah has failed to keep His promise to protect that which He revealed to Jesus in the Gospel. Would you agree?

11. Allah's Low Moral Requirements

I've had quite a number of Muslims tell me that Allah will "multiply their good works ten times." I also read this claim in a book. Let us now take a clear look at what Islam teaches. The *Qur'an* states that on the Day of Judgment, each man's good works and evil works will be put on scales, and if one's good works amount to at least 51 percent and the evil works to only 49 percent—and if Allah is favorable—then you will go to one of the seven heavens. But if the balance is the other way around, then you go to hell.

Let's examine this teaching. If the multiplication principle is really true, then a Muslim actually has to be only 5.1 percent good in order to have the possibility of making it into heaven. For if we multiply 5.1 by ten, it means that individual's good works will actually amount to 51 percent, which would tip the scale, and therefore, he has the possibility of going to heaven.

Does it seem right that a person can be so utterly sinful and still get to heaven?

12. What Does Islam Have to Offer Sinners?

What does Islam have to offer people who want to be 100 percent sure of going to live with God the very moment they die? Can Islam give me 100 percent assurance that there is no possibility of my going to hell?

13. Two Eternals?

Islam teaches that the *Qur'an* is eternal and has always existed unchanged in heaven. How can that be possible? It also teaches Allah is eternal and has no equal. But if both the *Qur'an* and Allah are eternal, then Islam has two eternals. Doesn't this mean that Allah has an equal? How is it possible to have two eternals?

14. Why Was the *Qur'an* Written in Arabic?

Muslims claim that the *Qur'an* is the final Word of God and that it is for all nations. If this is true, why was it written in Arabic? Muslim scholars declare that Arabic cannot properly be translated into any other language so that the true meaning comes out! Why was the *Qur'an* not written it in a language that could be translated so everyone would have the same advantage? It seems that Allah is partial to the Arabs! Why should that be?

15. Why Hasn't Islam Changed the Environment?

Surah 30:30 states that "man by nature was created upright." A comment under this verse states the following:

> (As turned out from the creative hand of God, man is innocent, pure, true, free, inclined to right and virtue, and possessed of true understanding about his own position in the Universe and about God's goodness, wisdom, and power. That is his true nature, just as the nature of a lamb is to be gentle and of a horse to be swift. But man is caught in the meshes

of customs, superstitions, selfish desires, and false teaching. This may make him pugnacious, unclean, false, slavish, hankering after what is wrong or forbidden, and deflected from the love of his fellowmen and the pure worship of the One True God.).

Thus, Islam teaches that man is basically good, and it is the *environment* that causes people to go wrong as they forget about Allah. But the environment within Muslim countries ought to be improving so that in them there is not this bad influence and environment.

The first thing Muslim children hear when they are born is the *Shahadah*. Many of these children go to *Qur'an*-oriented schools. They memorize the *Qur'an*. From an early age, they see their parents praying five times a day. These Muslim parents surely ought to be a good example to their children and not teach their children to sin. Once a year, they fast daily during the month of Ramadan. The *Qur'an* is held in high respect. The call from the mosque to prayer should constantly remind these families of Allah, so there is no excuse for forgetting Him. The parents and children go to the mosque and hear the talks by the imam that should keep them on the straight and narrow path.

In some Muslim countries, like Saudi Arabia, no other religion is allowed to be taught. No Bibles or other holy books are permitted to enter the country. Islam is the only religion, and the *Qur'an* is the only religious book that can be read. Thus, there should be nothing to "deflect from… the pure worship of the One True God." TV and the radio are controlled. Many Muslims live in countries that are ruled by *Shari'a*, and the government is able to enforce the laws. I am told that "*Shari'a* is Islamic law, formed by traditional Islamic scholarship." In Islam, *Shari'a* is the expression of the divine will, and "constitutes a system of duties that are incumbent upon a Muslim by virtue of his religious belief." "Islamic law covers all aspects of life, from matters of state, like governance and foreign relations, to issues of daily living." Therefore, those who stray out of the way and would corrupt the environment can be removed.

Muslims also have the *Sunna* to tell them how to act in most situations. Muhammad is considered the ideal man. One Muslim writer wrote (emphasis mine),

> It is this idea of the imitation of Muhammad that has provided Muslims from Morocco to Indonesia with such a uniformity of action: wherever one may be, one knows how to behave when entering a house, which formulas of greeting to employ, what to avoid in good company, how to eat, and how to travel. *For centuries Muslim children have been brought up in these ways.*

Another paragraph written by a Muslim states,

> MORALITY AND ETHICS IN ISLAM. Islam
> is a comprehensive way of life and morality is one
> of the cornerstones of Islam. Morality is one of the
> fundamental sources of a nation's strength. Islam
> has established some universal fundamental rights
> for humanity as a whole, which are to be observed
> in all circumstances. To uphold these rights, Islam
> has provided not only legal safeguards, but also a
> very effective moral system. Thus, whatever leads to
> the welfare of the individual or the society is mor-
> ally good in Islam.

With all these advantages of supposedly having divine
guidance for their life under law, often organized as a
political expression, it seems to me that the environment
of Muslim-dominated countries should gradually improve
so that there will be no "bad influence." They should evolve
into a perfect human society that ought to be an example
for the rest of the world!

With so much evil influence in other countries—and
especially in the West—I would assume that people all over
the world would be flocking to these Muslim countries
where the most pure form of life can be lived out! However,
the truth is that most people of the world, including many

Muslims, are pressing to migrate to the countries of the West. How amazing!

Would you please explain to me why none of the Muslim-dominated lands have become places such as described in the *Qur'an* and the *Hadith* so that in them sin is gradually being eradicated?

16. Comparing Muhammad with Jesus

Muhammad accepted the fact that Jesus performed many miracles to prove the divine origin of his message, such as his healing of the sick, raising the dead, etc. The *Qur'an* states in Surah 5:110, "Then will Allah say: 'O Jesus, son of Mary! Remember My favor to you;…you did heal him who was born blind and the leper by My permission; and how you did raise the dead, by My permission; and how I restrained the Children of Israel from (*harming*) you when you came to them *with clear signs*.'"

However, Muhammad refused to do any of these signs. Do you not realize that this makes it very difficult for the followers of Jesus to believe that Muhammad is superior to Christ as an apostle of God and a prophet?

17. The Example of Muhammad

The *Sunna* (traditions recorded in the *Hadith*) set forth the actions of Muhammad that Muslims are expected to follow. It tells Muslims how they are to dress themselves, along with many other activities and actions. If Allah really desires Muslims to follow the example of Muhammad (see Surah 33:21), then surely in all aspects the leader needs to be a perfect example.

But there is one situation where, if a Muslim followed the example of Muhammad, he would openly violate the *Qur'an*. According to Surah 4:3 of the *Qur'an*, a man may have up to four wives: "Marry women of your choice, two or three or four."

However, Muhammad had at least *eleven* wives and two concubines. Why would Allah make an exception and permit someone to violate His commandments if that leader was meant to be the perfect example?

18. Confessing the *Shahadah*

Would you kindly take a few minutes in order to help me understand one of the most important teachings in Islam? My question has to do with the *Shahadah*. You are very familiar with it: "There is no god but Allah, and Muhammad is His messenger." I understand the first part but not the second part—for the following reasons.

I understand that Islam teaches that there have been 124,000 prophets, starting with Adam. Also, according to Islam, all these prophets have proclaimed the same message. Even though these prophets were supposed to be perfect (according to some scholars), they were still just humans. The *Qur'an* states that Muhammad was just a messenger along with the other prophets. Muslims also claim—even though he is never identified in the *Qur'an*—that it was the angel Gabriel who brought the message from Allah down to the various prophets, including Muhammad. Therefore, it seems to me that the angel Gabriel, who was involved in bringing the one true message to the 124,000 prophets, should receive some recognition.

1. Why does the angel Gabriel not receive any recognition in the *Shahadah* for bearing the message from Allah to the prophets but a mere *man* does?
2. Why does the *Shahadah* just recognize Muhammad and not any of the other 123,999 prophets since they brought the same message?
3. Also, can you tell me why it is so important to have a human messenger recognized along with Allah? I would think that Allah should receive all the glory!

19. Who Are These Virgins (*Houris*) in Heaven?

I have read most of the verses in the *Qur'an* on the subject of Paradise, and I keep coming across the promise of *houris* to the men who go there. Would you kindly explain to me exactly who these *houris* are? They are variously described as "ladies of heaven, fair females, lovely-eyed women, dark-eyed virgins, beautiful virgins, bashful dark-eyed virgins, young maidens of equal age with firm breasts (pointed breasts), perpetual virgins, lovely companions, maidens with swelling (protruding) bosoms."

What is promised to men in Paradise is described this way in the *Hadith*:

> There is in Paradise an open market wherein there will be no buying or selling, but will consist of men and women. When a man desires a beauty, at once he will have intercourse with them as desired.

Since these sexually available individuals include men as well as women, is homosexual intercourse permitted in Paradise?

My research became more complicated after I read another *Hadith*:

Every man who enters Paradise *shall be given 72 (seventy-two) houris*. No matter at what age he has died, when he is admitted into Paradise he will become a thirty-year-old and shall not age any further. A man in Paradise shall be given virility equal to that of one hundred men.

It would seem that if each man is given seventy-two *houri*s, there must be a vast number of them!

So my question, simply stated, is this: Exactly who are these *houris*, and where do they come from? Are they of both sexes? Did they all live on earth at one time? If so, when? Or are they a new species of humanity who never lived on earth? And what special privileges do Muslim women who go to Paradise receive? (I find it curious that, evidently, the Prophet never addressed this subject.)

20. Allah's Will and the Killing of Apostates

On a Muslim website (islamworld.net) explaining the teachings of Islam about Paradise and hell, I found the following statement:

Allah created Paradise and Hell before the rest of creation, and He created inhabitants for each of them. Whomever He wishes will enter Paradise by

His grace and mercy, and whomever He wishes will enter Hell as a result of His justice. Every person will behave according to that for which he was created, and his destiny will be that for which he was created; good deeds and evil deeds are foreordained for all men.

The teaching that Allah does whatever He pleases is found in many surahs in the *Qur'an*:

Surah 2:253. "Allah does what He will."

Surah 3:40. "'Such is the will of Allah,' He replied, 'who does what He will [pleases].'"

Surah 11:107. "For your Lord [Allah] is Doer of what He wills."

Surah 14:4. "But Allah leaves in error whom He will and guides whom He pleases. He is the Mighty, the Wise."

Surah 14:27. "Allah leads the wrongdoers astray. Allah does what He will."

Surah 22:18. "Assuredly, Allah does what He will."

Islam teaches that when a man comes into this world his future had been clearly determined by Allah. Allah's will is that some will be led in the right path and do good deeds, enabling them to go to Paradise. Others Allah

WILBUR LINGLE WITH ROBERT DELANCY

"leads astray" so that they will make wrong choices and go to hell—so that it shall be full, like He promised! If this is true, then why in Muslim countries that are ruled by *Shari'a* do Muslims kill those who leave Islam and convert to another faith? It would seem that this desertion truly was the will of Allah, that these people should leave Islam! When Muslims put to death someone who has converted to another religion (an apostate), are they not then punishing a person for doing what Allah's will has decreed? Are they not resisting the will of Allah?

21. What Makes Islam Superior?

Among the theistic religions with their various divisions and branches, why do you feel that Islam is superior to all the others? Most Muslims claim that a person has a better chance of entering into Paradise by adhering to Islam than by following any of the other faiths. Also, since there are at least seventy-two different sects in Islam, what does your group have to offer more than the others? I am an outsider, and would like to know and understand your thinking on this very important subject.

I am not interested in negative remarks about the other religions but rather what you have to say positive about Islam that makes you feel it is superior to other religious groups. (Merely pointing out errors in other groups does not prove that yours is the true religion. Agreed?) The more specific you can be, the better.

As I analyze Islam, I cannot distinguish the difference. Here are the marks that most religions (with the exception of biblical Christianity) have, and I believe, they are also contained in Islam:

1. There is a belief in a God or in gods.
2. They had a charismatic founder or leader.
3. Followers must have faith in the founder as someone sent by God.
4. They possess sacred writings that must be adhered to.
5. But these writing cannot be understood by the average follower and must be interpreted by a certain group of men who would be considered scholars.
6. They have distinctive beliefs and practices that make the adherents feel superior.
7. Only its followers will go to Paradise.
8. Submission is required. Whatever the leaders declare is to be followed without questioning.
9. These leaders have a set of moral teachings and directions that must be followed.
10. They refuse to admit that humans are born with a fallen nature, inherited from their parents.

11. It teaches that temptation to sin is something that humans can overcome by their own power, with a little bit of help from God.
12. Teaches that a person's good works will be weighed in the balance, and they need to be at least 51 percent in order for him to have a chance for a blissful life in the next world.
13. They have a belief in a future Day of Judgment.
14. Since one's future is dependent upon the amount of good works compared to evil deeds, a person can never be sure of his or her eternal destination. This will be determined only on the Day of Judgment.
15. They have built-up traditions, which the adherents believe have brought more meaning to their religion.
16. The worst sin that a person can commit is to disassociate him or herself from that group. Such people are given absolutely no hope of a blissful afterlife when this happens. But not only that, the apostates are shunned in this life. Some may even be martyred.
17. The followers of this group are taught that they are superior to the people in other groups.
18. They will use bait—such as giving money or showing unusual kindness—to get people into their religious group. Once a person is hooked, the kindness can be discontinued and the person needs to show

submission. The person is just to follow without thinking for himself or herself, or asking questions.

So I ask, what does your religion have to offer that makes it different from other faiths? In what ways is it superior?

22. While Wanting Allah to Show Mercy, Why Don't Muslims Show Mercy?

When talking about sin, Muslims continually speak about how merciful Allah is. His heart of mercy, they feel, will cause Him to be forgiving, and perhaps He will overlook their sins. Even though good and evil deeds are said to play a part in determining a Muslim's eternal future, in the final analysis, it is up to the mercy of God. Of course, most Muslims feel that Allah will be merciful to them, and so they have a chance of ending up in one of the seven levels of Paradise.

Here is where I have a real problem: while Muslims want Allah to be merciful concerning their sins, why is there absolutely no mercy expressed in Islamic law? Under *Shari'a*, if a person steals something, off goes his or her hand; if a Muslim commits adultery, the designated punishment is carried out; if a Muslim leaves Islam and converts to another religion, he or she is put to death.

When it comes to religious freedom in Muslim-dominated nations, it is extremely limited! There is absolutely no room for mercy under *Shari'a*. *Shari'a* is said to be based on the contents of the *Qur'an*, which is held to be the eternal Word of God.

So my question is this: why do Muslims believe that Allah is very merciful and always seeking ways to forgive Muslims of their sins, and at the same time Muslims under *Shari'a* here on this earth rarely show mercy?

23. Why Is "Lesser Jihad" More Rewarding than the "Greater Jihad"?

Jihad, which is defined as "struggle," is a topic that is on many people's minds these days.

Jihad is divided into two classes. The first is known as lesser jihad, which is defined as "promoting the message of Islam by force of arms." The second is greater jihad, and it is defined as "the internal struggle of the soul against evil, such as lust, greed, envy, etc." It could include overcoming the temptation to sleep when it is time to recite the Morning Prayer. Also included in the greater jihad is working hard to spread the message of Islam. It is stated that the greater jihad is of greater value because one has to overcome one's self.

It seems that most Muslims I have spoken to, and the books by Muslims I have read, play down the meaning that associates jihad with war and state that the basic meaning of jihad is "striving to become a better Muslim." This is where I have some questions and would like your help in finding the most accurate answer.

Though it is called *lesser* jihad, it seems that there are far more and greater rewards for participating in the lesser jihad than in the greater jihad.

Surah 3:157 promises, "If you should die or be slain in the cause of Allah [jihad], His forgiveness and His mercy would surely be better than all that they amass." In other words, those who are killed in jihad automatically have their sins forgiven. But there is more. Surah 3:169 says, "Think not of those who are slain in the cause of Allah [jihad] as dead. They are alive; with their Lord they have provision." They go straight to Paradise!

Furthermore, the *Hadith* provides many details about the rewards awaiting those who die for Islam in lesser jihad. Muslim tradition teaches that martyrs are distinguished from others after death in several ways: their self-sacrifice and meritorious acts render them free of sin, and therefore they are not subject to a postmortem interrogation by the angels Nakir and Munkar. Rather, they bypass the grave and the Day of Judgment and proceed immediately upon

WILBUR LINGLE WITH ROBERT DELANCY

death to one of the highest locations in Paradise, near the Throne of God. Also, as a result of their sacrifice they will be buried in the clothes in which they died and do not need to be washed before burial.

I read of no special rewards given to those who strive in the *greater* jihad. They will all have to go into the grave and experience the interrogation by the angels Nakir and Munkar. They will have to endure the Day of Judgment, which takes place while kneeling around hell. They will be tried according to their deeds, and none of them have any assurance that the balance will be in their favor. Even if their good deeds outweigh their evil deeds, they have no assurance that it is Allah's will for them to go into Paradise. They will all have to go over the narrow bridge spanning hell and risk the possibility of falling into hell forever. And if they do make it to Paradise, they don't know which one of the seven levels of Paradise they will be placed in. Of course, there's no promise of seventy-two virgins!

Here are my questions:

1. Why do those who participate in the lesser jihad, and are killed in battle while doing so, receive such astounding rewards instantaneously (their sins are forgiven, they go immediately to the highest places in Paradise and are promised all the sensual pleasures one could desire) while the Muslims who participate

daily and over years in the struggle of the greater jihad receive absolutely no special promises?

2. There are at least fifty-four verses in the *Qur'an* dealing with jihad. Of these verses, all but one has to do with taking up arms and fighting in the cause of Allah to spread Islam. If the true and primary meaning of jihad really is "striving to become a better Muslim," why is there not one single verse in the *Qur'an* mentioning this, while there are so many verses that explain jihad as participating in *war* for Allah? (If a person just read he *Qur'an*, he or she would surely come to the conclusion that jihad refers only to "promoting the message of Islam by force of arms.")

3. Are the rewards of lesser jihad enticing to you? If not, why not?

24. Was the Death of Jesus Foolishness?

Muslims say that it is not reasonable but foolish to believe that someone (Jesus) should die as a substitute—to pay for other people's sins. They feel that surely they can take care of their sins by their own good deeds if they don't commit too many evil deeds to off set the good ones!

The *Qur'an* states in Surah 17:15, "Whosoever goes right, it is only for the good of his own soul that he goes right; and whosoever goes astray goes astray to his own loss. No soul can bear another's burden. Nor do We punish until We have sent forth a messenger (*to give warning*)." Then there is a comment that follows this verse: "The doctrine of vicarious atonement is condemned. Salvation for the wicked cannot be attained by the punishment of the innocent. One man cannot bear the burden of another; it would be unjust, and reduce the sinner's sense of accountability."

As a Muslim in America, have you ever thought about the fact that we are living in a nation that has liberty and freedom because there were patriots who were willing to shed their blood in order to gain independence for America? I know this happened several hundred years ago, but if those thousands of men had not fought and died, we would not have the freedom we have today.

You should also be aware that America later fought a war in which thousands of Northerners gave their lifeblood so that black slaves could be free. They too were risking their life to gain freedom for someone else.

Americans went over to Europe and fought the Germans—twice—to keep other nations from being enslaved, and myriads of Americans gave their lives for people who reside in other lands. The same happened with the many men who died while fighting against Japan—to free those in the Philippines, Burma, and other conquered nations—to give them their freedom.

Since humans are willing to give their lives to gain freedom for other people, why should it seem strange to you—and foolish—that a loving, compassionate, holy God should be willing to send His Son into the world to die and shed His blood for the sins of the world so that we could be freed from the power of Satan? God's Word states that Jesus came to turn mankind "from the power of Satan to God," and declares that "He [God] has delivered us from the domain of darkness [Satan] and transferred us to the kingdom of His beloved Son [Jesus Christ]."

This was something that was not forced upon the Son, for Jesus said, "No one takes it [my life] from me, but I lay it down of my own accord. I have authority to lay it down, and I have authority to take it up again. This charge I have received from my Father." This was done so that we can live a life of holiness that is in harmony and fellowship with God on this earth and then go directly to heaven at the time of physical death and spend all eternity in a close relationship with God.

Here is an additional thought. Jesus said, "Greater love has no one than this, that he lay down his life for his friends." But beyond this statement, God's Word declares, "But God shows his love for us in that while we were still sinners [enemies and ungodly], Christ died for us." Therefore, by rejecting the death of Jesus Christ to save you from your sins, you are rejecting the greatest love that is possible to be known! I have experienced it, and know just how wonderful it is!

As a Muslim, you are aware that the greatest promises in the *Qur'an* are for those men who die in the cause of jihad for the spread of Islam. Those people go directly to the highest Paradise. They do not have to wait in the grave. They do not have to appear at the Day of Judgment. They are promised seventy-two virgins. These rewards are all exclusive—to a limited number, to martyrs. But Jesus died to save all mankind—all who will believe—from an eternal Hell and provides assurance of going to heaven the very moment one leaves this life. Truly, because of who He is—the incarnate Son whose life on earth was sinless—He is capable of doing this!

Just as you, a Muslim, believe that God will not forget those who die in jihad, God the Father will not forget His Son who shed His blood for the sins of the world. God's Word says,

> And [Jesus] being found in human form, he humbled himself by becoming obedient to the point of death, even death on a cross. Therefore God has highly exalted him and bestowed on him the name that is above every name, so that at the name of Jesus every knee should bow, in heaven and on earth

and under the earth, and every tongue confess that Jesus Christ is Lord, to the glory of God the Father.

One of the best known verses of the Bible is John 3:16: "For God so loved the world, that he gave his only Son, that whoever believes in him should not perish but have eternal life." Is it any wonder that those who truly believe in Jesus as Savior love Him?

Do you still think the death of Jesus Christ is foolishness?

25. Can a Man Really Have More than One Wife in Heaven?

Reading Muslim material can be very confusing. If you read the following—taken right from the Islamic website islamworld.net—you will soon see the contradiction. The following quotes state that there will be more women in hell than in Paradise. But at the same time, Muhammad promised men in Paradise two or more wives. Of the world's population—now and throughout history—there have been just about an equal number of women as men. Since Muhammad taught that there will be more women in hell than in Paradise, then there could not be enough women for each man to have even *one* wife in Paradise, let alone two or more!

The only solution to this enigma that I have heard from any Muslim is that there are simply a vastly greater number of women than men in the world. But this is not true. (Go to an almanac and look it up for yourself.) I am rather good at math, but this is one problem I am not able to figure out.

Please take a few minutes to read the following quotes, obtained from the two standard *Hadiths* (taken from the Islamic website islamiworld.net), and help me out by giving me a believable answer (no speculations):

> *Al-Bukhari* and *Muslim* report from Usaamah ibn Zayd that the Prophet said, "I stood at the gate of Hell, and saw that *most of those who entered were women*."

> *Al-Bukhari* and *Muslim* report from Abu Sa'eed al-Khudri that the Prophet said, "*O women*, give in charity, for I have seen that *you form the majority of the people of Hell*." They asked, "Why is that so, O Messenger of Allah?" He said, "Because you curse too much and are ungrateful for good treatment."

> *Al-Bukhari* and *Muslim* report from Ibn 'Abbas the same incident: "I saw the Fire of Hell, and I have never seen anything so horrific or terrifying. I saw that *the majority of its inhabitants are women*."

> *Most* of the sinners amongst the monotheists [Muslims] *who enter Hell will be women*, as is reported in *as-Saheehayn*, via Ibn 'Abbas: In the

Khutbah [Friday noon sermon] given during a solar eclipse, the Prophet said, "*I saw Hell and I saw that most of its inhabitants were women.*"

Here are statements about Paradise:

Shaheed said that Muhammad said: "The smallest number of *wives* that any one man will have in Paradise *is seventy-two.*"

These [heavenly] pavilions are wondrous tents, made of pearls, each one is made from a single, hollowed-out pearl. They are sixty miles high; according to some reports they are sixty miles wide. Al-Bukhaari reports from 'Abdullaah ibn Qays that the Messenger of Allah said, "The tent is a hollowed out pearl, thirty miles high: *in each corner of it the believer will have a wife* whom no one else can see."

Allah has prepared for His believing slaves in Paradise that which no eye has seen, nor ear has heard and has never even crossed the minds of men, such that even the person who has the least blessing in Paradise will think that he is the most blessed among them. Abu Sa'eed al-Khudri (may Allah be pleased with him) said that the Prophet (peace and blessing of Allah be upon him) said: "The lowest of people in status in Paradise will be a man whose face Allah turns away from the Fire towards Paradise, and shows him a tree giving shade. He will say, 'O Lord, bring me closer to that tree so that I may be in its shade…Then he will enter his house [in Paradise] and *his two wives* from among al-hoor al-'iyu will come in and will say to him, "Praise be to Allah who brought you to life for us and brought us to life for you." Then he will say, "No one has been given what I have been given."'" (Narrated by *Muslim*, no. 275)

Could these statements, recorded in the *Hadith*, supposedly from the mouth of the Prophet, be in error? If not, what is your explanation?

26. Can Sinning Be Blamed on Forgetfulness?

Since Islam does not believe in original sin, it has tried in various ways to explain why humans habitually sin. One of the reasons given by Muslims for the extensiveness of sin is "outside influences," such as an evil society, the wrong friends, Satan, etc. But there is another explanation that Muslims also give about the commonness of sinning that puzzles me greatly: "When Adam and Eve fell from paradisaical perfection they became tainted with the forgetfulness that characterizes fallen human beings." So the reason that man sins is simply because he forgets the laws and prohibitions of God.

This is very hard for me to accept for the following two reasons:

1. The first thing a newborn Muslim child hears is the *Shahadah*. The child hears portions of the *Qur'an* quoted five times a day when his parents pray. Moreover, a large percentage of Muslim children are educated in *madrasas*, where their primary textbook is the *Qur'an*. Many of the forty million children in these schools memorize the complete *Qur'an*, along with key parts of the *Hadith*. (I understand that even Muslims who do not go to these schools often have the complete Qur'an memorized.) The calling to mind of the *Qur'an* and elements of the *Hadith* continues throughout one's adult life. Here is my question: How can a person who has memorized the entire *Qur'an*, or a large part of it, claim that his or her sin is because of forgetfulness of the laws of God? These laws remain in one's head and can be recited even after the person has transgressed them. Therefore, it is impossible for me to accept the logic that deliberate sin is simply because a person has "forgotten" what he or she has memorized, and

can continue to recite even after sinning! Would you please explain how this is possible?

2. The second reason why it is very difficult for me to accept the argument that sinning is a result of forgetfulness is because Islam claims that humans by nature are pure and innocent. Here is what the *Qur'an* teaches in Surah 30:30, followed by a comment on this verse:

> So set your purpose (*face*), (*O Muhammad*) for religion as a man by nature upright (*the nature framed*) of Allah, in which He has created mankind.

> Comment: (As turned out from the creative hand of God, man is innocent, pure, true, free, inclined to right and virtue, and possessed of true understanding about his own position in the Universe and about God's goodness, wisdom, and power. That is his true nature, just as the nature of a lamb is to be gentle and of a horse is to be swift.)

If man is really "innocent, pure, true, free, inclined to right and virtue, and possessed of true understanding," then how can such a person forget his or her true nature? Just as "it is the nature of a lamb to be gentle and a horse to be swift," then it is "natural" for a human to do what is "pure and innocent" and not sin. It is impossible for a person to forget his or her true nature! (A person might completely disregard this claimed pure nature and indulge in sin because of outside influences, but it cannot be blamed on forgetfulness , because a person cannot forget his or her true nature!)

Would you please explain to me how a person can *forget* what he or she is by nature?

27. The Messenger Gabriel

Islam teaches that it was the angel Gabriel who revealed the contents of the *Qur'an* to Muhammad. However, Gabriel is never identified as the messenger in the *Qur'an*. At the outset, Muhammad was frightened, because he didn't know but what it might be a demon who had spoken to him. This makes it obvious that the angel Gabriel did not identify himself as the one who was speaking to Muhammad.

The Prophet-to-be hurried back to Mecca and expressed these fears to his wife Khadijah. She, who was a believer in just one God, assured him that this revelation was from God. She had a cousin Waraqa to whom she took Muhammad to consult, and they asked him about the strange episode in the cave. (At this time, Waraqa was quite blind and close to death. But he was a learned man, the first to translate parts of the Old and New Testaments into Arabic. There was a seed of restlessness in Waraqa, who had at different times embraced Judaism and Christianity, only to return to his ancient primitive faith.)

Waraqa was the one who assured Muhammad that it was the angel Gabriel who had appeared to him, the same spirit whom, he said, had appeared to Moses. (I don't know where he got this idea, because the Bible never says that Gabriel appeared to Moses.) The angel Gabriel is mentioned only twice in the whole Old Testament, and both occurrences are in the book of Daniel, which was not written till the late years of the Babylonian exile of the children of Israel. Muslim scholars can't allege that it was imperfectly rewritten because it obviously never was lost. Thus, the Word of God, as found in the book of Daniel, has to be a true revelation from God. Since Allah has promised to protect His revealed Word, then we know that the message found in the book of Daniel is true!

The first time Gabriel is mentioned is in Daniel 8:16, and he has "the appearance of a man." The second time Daniel sees him is mentioned in Daniel 9:21. Then in verses 24–27 of that chapter, the message that Gabriel gave to Daniel is recorded, and this message is very important. The message opens with the decree that the temple in Jerusalem, which had been destroyed by the Babylonians, would be rebuilt after a definite period of time. (This happened just as prophesied.) It also foretells the appearing of an Anointed One and clearly delineates when. Of course, this Anointed One is none other than the Messiah, the Lord Jesus Christ. (This prophecy was likewise accurately fulfilled.) But Gabriel also states that this Anointed One would be cut off, meaning that He would be executed. Thus, Gabriel said that the Messiah was coming and would violently die, so if you deny the death of Jesus Christ, then you are denying the revealed Word of God that was given through Gabriel.

Also, in this prophecy is mentioned the *second* destruction of Jerusalem, which occurred in the year AD 70. This is another prophecy that was accurately fulfilled.

Two later appearances of Gabriel are recorded in the New Testament, and what he proclaimed there is very important. In Luke 1:19, the angel Gabriel appeared to Zachariah, the father-to-be of John the Baptist, telling him about the upcoming birth of his son and the ministry that he would have. The testimony that John the Baptist gave concerning Jesus is significant.

Early in his ministry, John the Baptist said this concerning Jesus: "Behold, the Lamb of God, who takes away the sin of the world!" This great prophet proclaimed that Jesus Christ would die and be the sacrificial Lamb for the whole world, not just the Jewish nation. John also stated that the blood of the sacrificial Lamb would "take away the sin of the world." Obviously, Jesus was not just "another prophet." He was the eternal Son of God who came into this world and died willingly, and those who trust in the shed blood of Jesus Christ will have their sins completely forgiven and removed.

Again I emphasize, Jesus was not sent just to the Jewish race but came to die for the whole human race. This is the fulfillment of the prophecy given to Abraham, which is found in Genesis 12:1–3:

> Now the Lord said to Abram [Abraham], "Go from your country and your kindred and your father's house to the land that I will show you [the land of Palestine]. And I will make of you a great nation [the nation of Israel], and I will bless you and make your name great, so that you will be a blessing. I will bless those who bless you, and him who dishonors you I will curse [that is why it is so serious to despise the nation of Israel and try to destroy it], and *in you all the families of the earth shall be blessed.*"

In what way did the seed of Abraham, through Isaac and Jacob, become a blessing to the whole world? It was through the death and resurrection of Jesus Christ so that all who believe the good news may have their sins forgiven and be 100 percent sure of going to heaven the very moment they die. No, Jesus was not just a prophet and not just for Israel. He was the sacrificial Lamb who shed His blood for the sins of the whole world!

The final appearance of the angel Gabriel is found in God's Word, as recorded by Luke in 1:26–27, which reads, "In the sixth month the angel Gabriel was sent from God to a city of Galilee named Nazareth, to a virgin betrothed to a man whose name was Joseph, of the house of David. And the virgin's name was Mary."

And here are Gabriel's words:

> Do not be afraid, Mary, for you have found favor with God. And behold, you will conceive in your womb and bear a son, and you shall call his name Jesus. He will be great and will be called the Son of the Most High [how can you deny that God has a Son when the true messenger Gabriel proclaimed it?]. And the Lord God will give to him the throne of his father David, and he will reign over the house of Jacob forever, and of his kingdom there will be no end.

Why is it that Muslims will believe that Gabriel is a messenger sent from God—as is recorded in the revealed Word of God—and then reject the message that the angel Gabriel brought?

God then sent a message to Joseph, the foster father of Jesus, the act of which also is very important. Here is what was revealed to Joseph: "She [Mary] will bear a son, and you shall call his name Jesus, for *he will save his people from their sins*" (Matt. 1:21). Thus, the purpose for the Son of God coming into the world and becoming a tabernacle in flesh—in the human body that was provided through the virgin Mary—was to save people from their sins. There is no other religion that has a Savior who can save its followers from their sins!

In conclusion, I would like to ask you a very important question. Muslims believe the message of the *Qur'an* and claim that it was revealed to Muhammad. But in spite of the fact that the *Qur'an* never identifies the speaker, Muslims believe what is written in the *Qur'an*. In the Bible, in four places, Gabriel is clearly identified as the messenger, and then that message is accurately recorded. God has promised to protect His revealed Word from destruction or corruption. So why will Muslims not believe the message that was given by Gabriel and recorded accurately in the Bible?

28. Conversion: A Mistake or a Sin?

Here is a question that I would appreciate your answering for me.

Let's say an older Muslim realizes that he does not have many good deeds to his credit and comprehends that he does not have adequate time in this life to do enough good deeds to cancel out all his evil deeds. He feels utterly hopeless and downcast. He does not want to go to hell and suffer for all eternity but desires to go to Paradise to be with God but sees no hope.

At this point, he hears that there is hope for bad sinners in Christianity, because people do not get into heaven by their own good deeds but by the one good deed that Jesus did by shedding His blood on that Roman cross for the sins of all mankind, and thus, salvation comes as a gift from God, not something that can be earned. But before he can receive this gift, he must be willing to take the very difficult road of admitting that he is an ungodly sinner and repenting! So he opens his heart and becomes a true follower of Jesus Christ. He is given the Holy Spirit that will enable him to live a life of holiness. He is now a true child of God who has been given everlasting life; he is 100 percent sure of going to heaven the very moment he leaves this life and will be in the presence of God forever. Peace and joy flood his heart!

In Islam, would this be considered a mistake or a sin?

29. What Are a Muslim's Chances of Going to Paradise?

One *hadith* (taken from the website islamicworld.net, pages 36–39) states that 999 out of every thousand of the children of Adam will enter hell; thus, only one in a thousand will enter Paradise. Al-Bukhari narrates from Abu Sa'ed that the Prophet said the following:

> Allah will say, "O Adam!" Adam will reply, "I respond to Your call. I am obedient to Your commands, and all good is in Your hands." Then Allah will say to Adam, "Send forth the people of the Fire." Adam will say, "How many are the people of the Fire?" Allah will say, "Out of every thousand, take nine hundred and ninety-nine."
>
> When certain Muslims heard about this ratio (999 to 1), they were distressed and said, "O Messenger of Allah, who amongst us will be that man (one in a thousand)?"
>
> He said, "Be of good cheer: the thousand will be from Gog and Magog and the one will be from among you."
>
> Then Muhammad said, "By Him in whose hand is my soul, I hope that you will be one third of the people of Paradise."
>
> We praised and glorified Allah, and then he said, "By Him in whose hand is my soul, I hope that you will be half of the people of Paradise, as you are among the nations like a white hair on the hide of

a black bull or a round hairless spot on the foreleg of a donkey."

Another *hadith*, however, makes the ratio 99 to 1. In it, Allah said to Adam, "Send forth [into Hell] ninety-nine out of every hundred [of your descendants]."

Muslim commentators resolve the conflict by saying that these *hadiths* are referring to different groups. The *hadith* that mentions a ratio of 900 and 99 to 1 should be interpreted as referring to all the progeny of Adam, while the *hadith* that mentions a ratio of 99 to 1 should be understood as referring strictly to Muslims.

So at the most, a Muslim has only one chance in a hundred of going to Paradise. I don't think those are very good odds!

My question is, whatever the case, if only one out of one hundred Muslims is destined for Paradise, are these not likely men who have died in jihad? So what hope do you, my Muslim friend, have? And how can you call Allah compassionate? And yet you continue to dismiss the loving invitation given by Jesus the Messiah: "Whosoever will, may come." Why not trust Jesus and not your good works? They are puny, but He is mighty!

For more details, see appendix 8.

If you are interested in more questions for Muslims, you can go to my website: lovetoshareminstries.com.

14

---·※·---

Using the Qur'an to Witness

THERE ARE A number of *Qur'anic* passages that easily lend themselves to thoughtful questioning sessions with Muslims. Here are eight possible brief scenarios.

1. Commendable or Condemnded?

My friend, I have selected two verses from the *Qur'an* that mention both Jesus and His followers. Look them over please, and tell me what they should teach us:

> We caused Jesus, son of Mary, to follow, and gave him the Gospel, and placed compassion and mercy in the hearts of those who followed him. (Surah 57:27)

(*And remember*) when Allah said: "O Jesus! I am gathering you and causing you to ascend to Me, and am cleansing you from those who disbelieve, and am setting those who follow you above those who disbelieve until the Day of Resurrection." (Surah 3:55) [Note: The mission of Muhammad as a living man has ended, but this verse indicates that the mission of Jesus will not cease until the Day of Resurrection.]

To me, these verses say this: Allah allowed Jesus to have followers and has blessed those believers with hearts of compassion and mercy. Therefore, they are exalted above any people who disbelieve in Him, and this blessing will continue among them until the Day of Resurrection.

Q: I ask, should these faithful followers of Jesus be condemned or commended?

Q: If these blessed Christians were ever guilty of altering the Gospel and promoting falsehood, why does Allah not mention that fact and condemn them? Are they not at least guilty of *shirk*? (*Shirk* means ascribing a partner to Allah, which is blasphemy.) Yet Allah obviously commends them.

2. Muhammad Himself Had to Seek for the Right Path, Didn't He?

> Guide us to the Straight Path, the way of those whom You have favored. (Surah 1:5–6)

Q: Was this a prayer that Muhammad himself used or not?

Q: How can Muhammad show anyone the way if he himself needs to ask for guidance?

3. Muhammad Confessed He Did Not Know the Future

> Say to them: "I am no new thing among the Messengers. (*Just as all the former Prophets were mortals who had no share in Divine attributes and powers, so am I.*) I do not know what shall befall you tomorrow or what shall befall me. I only follow that which is revealed to me, and I am no more than a plain warner." (Surah 46:9)

Q: Can the blind lead the blind? The Prophet is not sure of his own fate, so how can he help you to be sure of yours?

Q: Jesus made many accurate predictions—that Judas would betray Him, Peter would deny Him, the Romans would crucify Him, that Jerusalem would be destroyed, etc. Is He not worthy of our trust, whatever our future may hold?

4. Was Jesus Sent as a Sign for All Peoples?

And (*remember that blessed woman*) [Mary] who guarded her chastity. Then We breathed into her of Our spirit, and We made her and her son a sign for all peoples. (Surah 21:91) [Muslims teach that each of the prophets was sent to a specific group of people, and that Jesus was for the Jewish people *only*. Only Muhammad was sent to *all* people, according to Islam.]

Q: Here, the *Qur'an* states that Jesus was "a sign for all peoples." Could you tell me in what ways Jesus was a sign for all peoples?

Q: Since the *Qur'an* states that Jesus was sent to all peoples, why does Islam resist this truth and teach that Jesus was sent to the Jews only?

5. The Obedient Son

We gave him [Abraham] tidings of a gentle son. And when (*his son*) was old enough to walk with him, (*Abraham*) said: "O my dear son, I have seen in a dream that I must sacrifice you, so look, what think you?" He said: "O my father! Do that which you are commanded. Allah willing, you shall find me of the steadfast." Then We ransomed him with a tremendous sacrifice. (Surah 37:101–102, 107) [All Muslims are familiar with this story. They say it involved Ishmael not Isaac, but the point is that an innocent animal was sacrificed in place of Abraham's son.]

Q: Please note that Abraham's son did not resist. Is this not a beautiful picture of Jesus who offered Himself as the innocent, perfect sacrifice to save us humans from our sins? Jesus Himself declared, "No one takes it [my life] from me, but I lay it down of my own accord" (John 10:18).

6. Who Is the Illustrious Messiah?

When the angels said: "O Mary! Allah gives the glad tidings of a word from Him, whose name is the Messiah, Jesus, son of Mary, illustrious in the world and the Hereafter, and one of those who shall be brought near (*to God*)." (Surah 3:45) [Jesus is here called the Messiah, which means the "anointed one." In the *Qur'an*, only Jesus is designated in this way.]

Q: What does it mean that Jesus was the Messiah?

Q: Could any prophet be more illustrious than Jesus was?

7. Jesus's Death: Past or Future?

> So peace be upon me [Jesus] the day I was born and the day that I die and the day that I shall be raised up to life (*again*). (Surah 19:33) [Muslims don't believe that Jesus died; rather, He went directly to heaven. They say He will come back in the future, live forty years on this earth, and then die. And He will be buried next to Muhammad. But this is not what the *Qur'an* states here.]

Q: Note that this verse states that Jesus was born, died, and was then raised up. This is the clear order of events. So why does Islam teach something contrary: that Jesus was born, was raised up to life, and sometime in the future will die? Is this not twisting the *Qur'an*?

8. How Was Jesus Allah's Messenger, Word, and Spirit?

> O People of the Scripture! Commit no excess in your religion, nor say nothing but the truth about Allah. The Messiah, Jesus son of Mary, was only a

messenger of Allah, and His word which He conveyed to Mary, and a spirit from Him.

Q: Though this verse somewhat diminishes Jesus, it also correctly elevates Him. What does it mean that Jesus was Allah's "word"?

Q: Do you know that the Bible also gives this title to Jesus: "In the beginning was the Word, and the Word was with God, and the Word was God" (John 1:1)? He was the perfect expression of the Father. The *Injil* teaches that Jesus was the Word Incarnate—the Word who became flesh, on our behalf.

Q: What does it mean that Jesus was a spirit sent from Allah? Does this not imply that Jesus existed before He came to earth as a human?

Another approach you might consider is this: sit down with your Muslim friend and read together a lengthy *Qur'anic* passage, scrutinizing it verse by verse. One excellent portion is Surah 3:42–55. Here is how I would do this:

What Surah 3:42–55 Teaches about Jesus
(Jesus is holy, all-powerful, and knows the way to heaven)

I. Facts about Mary: 42–44

> 42. And when the angels said: "O Mary! Allah has chosen you, and made you pure, and has preferred you above all the women of creation."

Q: Doesn't the *Qur'an* teach that Mary was made pure by *God*, not by or because of her deeds?

> 43. O Mary! Be obedient to your Lord, prostrate yourself, and bow with those who bow in worship.
>
> 44. This is of the tidings hidden, which We reveal to you (*O Muhammad*). You were not present with them when they cast lots to see which of them should be the guardian of Mary; nor were you present when they argued (*concerning this*). [Here is a comment found after this verse:] (According to the interpreters of the Holy *Qur'an*, the children of Israel threw their pens into the river to know which one would be the guardian of Mary. They decided that the guardian of Mary would be the man whose pen floated.)

Q: This is a tradition found among the Jews. How did a tradition of the Jews get into the *Qur'an*, which is supposed to be eternal?

Jesus is holy: 45–47

> 45. When the angels said: "O Mary! Allah gives the glad tidings of a word [a Word] from Him, whose name is the Messiah, Jesus, son of Mary, illustrious in this world and the Hereafter, and one of those who shall be brought near (*to God*)."

Q: Note that Jesus is the Word of God. What does this mean?

Q: Exactly what does the word *Messiah* mean? Is a definition of this term given anywhere in the *Qur'an*?

Q: Does the *Qur'an* ever identify anyone else as being a Messiah?

Q: An "anointed one," a Messiah, has been given this anointing for a special purpose. What was the special purpose that Jesus was anointed for?

Q: Doesn't being the Messiah set Jesus apart and place Him above all the other prophets?

Q: Jesus is one who is "near to Allah." Do we read this about any of the other prophets mentioned in the *Qur'an*?

> 46. He will speak to mankind in his cradle and in his manhood, and he is of the righteous.

Q: It says here that Jesus is "of the righteous." Does the *Qur'an* ever speak of any other prophet as being righteous?

Q: What made Jesus righteous and none of the other prophets?

> 47. She [Mary] said: "My Lord! How can I have a child, when no man has touched me?" He replied: "Such is the will of Allah. He creates what He will. When He decrees a thing He only says: Be! And it is."

Q: Doesn't this verse say that Jesus came directly from Allah and that he did not have a human father?

Q: Are there any other prophets who did not have a human father?

Q: Why did Allah plan to have Jesus born without a human father?

Jesus was taught by Allah: 48

> 48. And He will teach him the Scripture and wisdom, and the Torah and the Gospel. [This certainly proves that the Torah had not been corrupted prior to the days of Jesus—contradicting what Muslim scholars say happened during the Babylonian captivity!]

Q: Allah would not have taught Jesus a corrupted Torah, would He? If it had been corrupted, surely Allah would have intervened and corrected it! How can you maintain that we do not have exactly the same Torah that Jesus had?

Q: In order to know what Jesus told us to do, a person must read the Gospel—because not one word of what Jesus taught is found in the *Qur'an*! Have you ever read the Gospel of Jesus?

Jesus has power over death: 49

> 49. And will make him a Messenger to the Israelites. He will say: "I bring you a sign from your Lord. From clay I will make for you the likeness of a bird; I shall breathe into it and, by Allah's leave, it shall become a (*living*) bird. By Allah's leave I shall give sight to the blind, heal the leper, and raise the dead to life. I shall tell you what you eat and what you store up in your houses. Surely that will be a sign for you, if you are believers."

Q: All these three types of miracles are ascribed to Jesus in the Bible:

> "He gave sight to the blind" (Matt. 9:27–31, 11:4–5, 12:22, 15:30–31, 20:29–34, John 9:1–40).
>
> "He healed the leper" (Matt. 8:2–3, Luke 17:11–19).

"He raised the dead to life" (Matt. 9:18–26, Luke 7:11–15, John 11:1–44).

Doesn't this prove that the accounts found in the Bible describing these incidents are true and that major portions of the Bible were not changed or corrupted?

Q: One of people's greatest fears is death. Do you know of any prophet who had power over death like Jesus did? Jesus has other vital powers: 50–54

> 50. (*I come*) to confirm the Torah that has already been revealed, and to make lawful to you some of the things you were forbidden. I bring a sign to you from your Lord. So fear Him and obey me.

Q: Jesus was able to change some of the laws that had been given in the Torah. By what authority could Jesus do this?

Q: Our duty to God is to obey Jesus. What are some of the specific teachings of Jesus that you as a Muslim should be obeying?

Q: Since none of the teachings of Isa that you ought to obey are found in the *Qur'an*, then where should you go to discover what Jesus taught?

51. Allah is my Lord and your Lord, so worship Him. That is the straight path.

52. But when Jesus became aware of their disbelief he said: "Who will be my helpers in God?" The disciples said: "We will be Allah's helpers. We believe in Allah; and bear you witness that we have surrendered (*ourselves to Him*)!"

Q: Since God appointed the disciples (Matthew, John, and Peter) to help Jesus, then shouldn't we read and believe the carefully recorded accounts that these disciples wrote about the life and words of Jesus? They have been preserved to this day and are part of the New Testament.

53. Our Lord! We believe in that which You have revealed, and we follow him whom You have sent. Account us among those who witness (*the truth; i.e., the oneness of God and the truth of the prophets He has sent, including Jesus*).

Q: What are some of the recorded things that were revealed to Jesus that you are following? Remember, there is not one word of what was revealed to Jesus in the *Qur'an* so you have to find this outside of the *Qur'an*. Please be specific.

54. And they (*the disbelievers*) schemed, and Allah schemed (*against them*); and Allah is the best of schemers.

Jesus knows the way to heaven: 55

55. (*And remember*) when Allah said: "O Jesus! I am gathering you and causing you to ascend to Me, and am cleansing you of those who disbelieve, and am setting those who follow you above those who disbelieve until the Day of Resurrection. Then to Me you will all return, and I shall judge between you as to that in which you used to differ."

Q: Jesus has ascended to heaven. Can you suggest anyone who is better able to reveal the way?

Q: If you wanted to come to my house and you needed help in doing so, who would be best suited to help you? Naturally I would, because I know the way. So out of all of the prophets, which one do you think is the most capable of giving clear directions to heaven?

Q: Jesus said, "In my Father's house are many dwelling places...I go to prepare a place for you. And if I go and prepare a place for you, I will come again and will take you to myself, that where I am you may be also" (John 14:2–3). Here, Jesus is telling us that sometime in the future He will take all His true followers to heaven to be with Him. Is there any other religious leader who ever made such a claim?

Q: Jesus then continued by saying, "I [Jesus] am the way, and the truth, and the life. No one comes to the Father except through me" (v. 6). Jesus is claiming here to be the only way to heaven. But Jesus gave yet another thrilling and comforting promise. Here it is: "I [Jesus] give them eternal life, and they will never perish, and no one will snatch them out of my hand" (John 10:28). In order for Jesus to be able to offer the gift of eternal life, surely He has to possess eternal life Himself. Have you ever asked Him for this gift? I have. Would you like to?

Q: Allah said, "I am setting those who follow you [Jesus] above those who disbelieve." What might be the reason for His setting the Messiah's followers above those who believe in other religious leaders? Doesn't this show the superiority of Jesus?

Conclusion: Jesus is in Paradise, and He knows the way!

APPENDIX 1

The Formation of the Bible

WHATEVER YOUR RELIGIOUS background, it is helpful to understand something about the formation of the Bible.

The Old Testament (OT), which covers the period from Creation to about four hundred years before the coming of Christ, was written over a period of one thousand years by at least twenty-five different inspired authors. The first five books of the Bible, known as the Pentateuch or Torah, are from the pen of Moses, with the exception of the account of his death and burial in Deuteronomy 34. The last book of the Hebrew Scriptures was written by Malachi, in around 435 BC.

The Jews had professional scribes who made copies of the sacred scrolls. This was done with great care, for the scribes counted not only the words but also every letter, noting how many times each particular letter occurred, and they destroyed at once any sheet on which a mistake was detected. Outside of a few differences in numbers and the spelling of some names, there are very few questionable elements in the text of today's *Tanach* (the Jewish name for the OT). A Greek translation, known as the Septuagint, was made around 200 BC, so the Hebrew Old Testament documents had to be well established before that date.

Jesus, in Luke 24:27 and 44, set His approval on the Scriptures that were available to Him, which are the same as what we possess today. If there were any corruptions that had entered into the Bible before that time, Jesus would surely have corrected them. Thus, we can be confident that Jesus considered all of the Old Testament accurate.

In the New Testament, there are 295 Old Testament quotes made by Jesus and the authors, and all these citations can be found and compared. (There are a few places where the quotes in the New Testament differ slightly from the Hebrew Old Testament; the reason is a few of the quotes were taken from the Greek Septuagint instead of the Hebrew.)

There is one very important twentieth-century discovery that proves that the Bible in use in the days of Jesus was not corrupted later on. The Dead Sea scrolls were found between 1947 and 1956 in eleven caves at Qumran in Palestine. These 825 separate documents (fragmentary or complete) belonged to the Essene sect of the Jews; they had been hidden away, and many were well preserved by the dry atmosphere of that area. They were hidden around the time of the First Jewish Revolt (AD 66–70). Included among these scrolls are numerous copies of the Hebrew Scriptures, and these are the oldest Hebrew manuscripts in existence, yet no significant difference has been found between them and what we possess and use today.

Of great significance, two copies of the whole book of Isaiah were found among the Dead Sea scrolls. This is very important because Isaiah contains the greatest number of detailed prophecies, at least twenty-four, about the Messiah, Jesus Christ—more than of any other Old Testament book with the exception of the Psalms, which has at least thirty. Some of the prophecies found in Isaiah concerning Jesus contain the main tenets of biblical Christianity that the Muslims today deny.

Some of the key prophecies of the book of Isaiah about the birth, identification, nature, death, and resurrection of Jesus Christ are found in Isaiah 7:14, 9:6–7, 52:13–53:12. You, as a Christian, should be able to explain these passages to your Muslim friend.

It is interesting to note that the Jewish people apparently had a separate scroll composed of Messianic prophecies, and among them, in Jesus's day, Isaiah 53 was included. Knowing this helps us to understand Matthew 2:1–6. The wise men from the East came to Jerusalem, seeking the King of the Jews. Then in verses 3–6, we read,

> When Herod the king heard this, he was troubled, and all Jerusalem with him; and assembling all the chief priests and scribes of the people, he inquired of them where the Christ was to be born. They told him, "In Bethlehem of Judea, for so it is written by the prophet: 'And you, O Bethlehem, in the land of Judah, are by no means least among the rulers of Judah; for from you shall come a ruler who will shepherd my people Israel.'"

Since such a prophecy was in this Messianic scroll, it was very easy for the Jewish leaders to tell Herod where Jesus, the King of the Jews, was to be born. Thus, when Muslims deny the death and resurrection of Jesus Christ, they are denying the revealed and preserved Word of God.

I read one Muslim author who claimed that the books of the Old Testament written prior to the time of the Babylonian captivity (586 BC) were destroyed at that time and then later rewritten, thus intimating that when this was done they were corrupted.

Then I came across a comment after Surah 5:13 which stated the same thing:

And because of their breaking their covenant, We have cursed them and made hard their hearts. They change words from their context and forget a part of that wherewith they had been reminded. You will not cease to discover treachery among them, all save a few. But bear with them, and pardon them. Surely, Allah loves those who are kind. (During the time of Moses and his successors, only one copy of the Torah was made. When the Israelites fought with the Babylonians, and were taken captive by them, this copy was lost. When the Israelites regained their freedom, they tried to write it out again. Yet in the process, they began to distort the text, contriving to forget a good part of God's commandments to them. Today's Torah is a late, incomplete anthology of earlier material.)

Upon what grounds can the author of this comment "Only one copy of the Torah was made" assert? There is absolutely no evidence for such a claim. There are many facts to prove that such a theory is wrong. It is pure speculation. Here is some evidence that undercuts the allegation.

In Daniel 9:2, we read, "In the first year of his reign, I, Daniel, perceived in the books the number of years that, according to the word of the Lord to Jeremiah the prophet, must pass before the end of the desolations of Jerusalem, namely, seventy years." Most of the inspired writings by Jeremiah were written before the Babylonian captivity, and here, near the end of the exile, Daniel had a copy of Jeremiah, so it was not destroyed.

Most of the book of Ezekiel, which contains thirteen dated oracles or visions, was written during the captivity years.

The existence of these two books is solid evidence that during their seventy years of exile in Babylon the Jews possessed a number of their holy books, so to assume they had no access to copies of the Torah—Moses's writings—is beyond reason.

Another proof that the above claim is false is found in the book of Nehemiah, written in about 445 BC, which was after the return from Babylon. Nehemiah 9:3 states, "And they stood up in their place and read from the Book of the Law [Torah] of the Lord their God for a quarter of the day; for another quarter of it they made confession and worshiped the Lord their God." Thus, these people were clearly in possession of the Torah, and they revered it as authentic!

Of course, some of the Old Testament books—Daniel, Ezra, Nehemiah, Obadiah, Haggai, Zechariah, and Malachi—were written after the Babylonian captivity. I have never heard of any Muslims mentioning these books.

Since they were written after the Babylonian captivity, why do Muslims not accept these books as authentic?

An Answer to the Muslims' Objections

We know the claim by some Muslims that the Old Testament books written before the Babylonian captivity were consumed is not true. But let us now consider the crafty accusation about corruption in light of what Muslims believe about the *Hadith*. The *Hadith* was not written until about two hundred years after the death of Muhammad. Yet Muslims put a lot of confidence in the *Hadith*. It is said that the *Qur'an* could not be properly understood without the explanations of the *Hadith*. If the Torah or other parts of the Old Testament had perished during the Babylonian captivity, these books could have been reconstructed shortly after the return to Palestine.

That was an oral society, and many people knew lengthy portions of their Holy Scriptures by heart—so they would have been familiar with the original text. These returnees could have easily detected if there had of been any mistakes! Thus, in the light of what Islam teaches and Muslims believe, if parts of the Old Testament really had been lost and rewritten, it still would be far more accurate than what is found in the *Hadith*—because it would have been completed in a lesser span of years than the *Hadith* was.

It is hard for me to understand how and why Muslims make claims that have absolutely no support. In fact, there is much proof to the contrary.

I attended some talks by an imam at a mosque over a number of weeks. Several times he mentioned that Muslims should not tell lies, yet these types of falsehood continue to be written and spoken by Muslims. Why?

Previously, I quoted Surah 5:13 and noted the comment there about the Torah being lost. Following verse 14, there is a statement about the New Testament being corrupted:

> And with those who say: 'Surely, we are Christians, We [Allah] made a covenant, but they forgot a part of that whereof they were admonished. Therefore We have stirred up enmity and hatred among them till the day of Resurrection, when Allah will inform them of what they have done. (The early Christians suffered much persecution from the Romans and the Jews, and the Christians became widely scattered. The Christian Covenant which was given by Jesus to his apostles was lost in the process, and although a variety of gospels were written by various hands, they contained only an oblique reference to the fact that God's messages to man had not come to an end, and that the Comforter, Ahmad, would come to reestablish monotheism. See the Gospel of

John, xv.26, and xvi.7, where an echo has been preserved. True Christians are those who have accepted
not just Jesus, but all of Allah's prophets, and affirm
His absolute unity. The verse is also a reminder of
the enmity which Allah has set between Christians
and Jews, and which shall abide until the Last Day.)

When it comes to the New Testament, there is no evidence of the corruption that the Muslims are claiming! I
have heard it claimed quite a number of times by Muslims,
and have read it in their books, that the New Testament
was not actually written until several hundred years after
Christ's time on earth, inferring that it could not be accurate if it was written so much later.

This is a very strange argument coming from a Muslim,
because it is very well-known, as mentioned above,
that the first parts of the *Hadith* (sayings and actions of
Muhammad) were not written until about two hundred
years after his death, and other parts are dated hundreds of
years later. If delay doesn't affect the accuracy of the *Hadith*,
then why should it affect the Bible, if this false claim had
any validity? Jesus was upon this earth until about AD 33.
All the New Testament books—except for the writings of
the Apostle John (John 1, 2, and 3 John and Revelation,
which date from around AD 90–96)—were written and in
circulation before the fall of Jerusalem in AD 70.

This is very easy to prove. There are many writings by those who are known as the church fathers. These were Christian leaders in the early church. At least one personally knew the apostle John. These documents were written in the first couple of hundred years after the founding of Christianity, AD 100–200. In these writings, available today (one set contains thirty-one thick volumes), there are many sermons, church letters, and personal letters written by these early church fathers. In this material, there are thousands of quotes from the New Testament. In fact, if the whole New Testament were destroyed, there are enough quotes to be found in these postapostolic writings to almost completely reconstruct the entire New Testament. This clearly proves that the New Testament was written early in the history of the church, mostly before AD 70.

APPENDIX 2

Writings of the Early
Church Fathers

HERE IS SOME important information found in the writings of the early church fathers, as mentioned in appendix 1.

Clement of Rome (AD 30–100). The earliest citations of the Bible are found in his works. Clement apparently knew the apostle Paul personally and may have been with him in Philippi (see Philippians 4:3, where his name is mentioned). In his writing, he lays a lot of emphasis on the Old Testament, but he was familiar with several of the NT books at this early date. In referring to 1 Corinthians 1:11–15, he attributes inspiration to Paul's epistle, saying, "Take up the epistle of the blessed Apostle Paul...truly under inspiration of the Spirit he wrote concerning himself, and Cephas, and Apollos, because even then parties had been formed among you." He quotes 1 Corinthians 2:9 as "Scripture." He also quoted Hebrews 1:3–5 and alluded to 1 and 2 Timothy and Titus. His doctrine also reflects knowledge of Romans and Ephesians.

Polycarp (AD 69–155). He was a student of the apostle John. He wrote an epistle to the Philippians that has survived. He makes citations from NT writers in nearly every chapter, often in direct quotes, which include, Matthew 5:3 and 10, 7:1; Acts 2:24; 2 John 7; and 1 Peter 1:8. He often mentions the "blessed Apostle Paul." His quotes from Paul include 1 Corinthians 6:9; 2 Corinthians 5:10; Galatians 6:7; Ephesians 2:8–9, 4:26; and 1 Thessalonians 5:22.

Ignatius. He wrote seven letters in about AD 110 during his journey from Antioch to Rome for his martyrdom. He quotes from Matthew, 1 Peter, and 1 John and cites nine of Paul's epistles, and his letters bear the impress of the other three Gospels.

Papias (AD 70–155). He was a pupil of John. He wrote *An Explanation of the Lord's Discourses* in which he quotes from John, and records traditions about the origin of Matthew and Mark.

The Didache. This was written between AD 80 and 120. It makes twenty-two quotations from Matthew with references to Luke, John, Acts, Romans, Thessalonians, and 1 Peter, and it mentions the Gospel as a written document.

Tatian. About AD 160, he made a *Harmony of the Four Gospels* called the *Diatessaron*, which gave evidence for the Four Gospels—and only four—and that they were generally recognized among the churches.

Justin Martyr (born about the year the apostle John died). He wrote his *Apologies* about AD 140. He mentions Revelation and shows knowledge of Acts and eight of the epistles. He called the Gospels the *Memoirs of the Apostles* and says that they were read in Christian assemblies alternately with the *Prophets*.

Basilides. He was a Gnostic heretic who taught in Alexandria during the reign of Hadrian (AD 117–138). In his effort to distort accepted Christian teachings, he quotes from Matthew, Luke, John, Romans, 1 Corinthians, Ephesians, and Colossians.

Irenaeus (AD 130–200). He quotes most of the New Testament books as Scripture, which in his time had come to be known as the Gospel and the Apostles. The Old Testament books were called the Law and the Prophets.

Tertullian (AD 160–220). He was from Carthage and was living while the original manuscripts of the epistles were still in existence. He calls the Christian Scriptures the New Testament. (This title first appears in the writings of an unknown author in about AD 193.) In his writings, there are 1,800 quotes from the books of the New Testament.

In his work *Against Heretics*, he wrote the following:

> If you are willing to exercise your curiosity profitably in the business of your salvation, visit the Apostolic churches in which the very chairs of the Apostles still preside in their places; in which their very authentic Epistles are read, sounding forth the voice and representing the countenance of each of them. Is Achaia near you? You have Corinth. If you are not far from Macedonia, you have Philippi and Thessalonica. If you can go to Asia, you have Ephesus. If you are near Italy, you have Rome.

Origen (AD 185–254). He was a Christian scholar from Alexandria of great learning, and he did extensive traveling. He devoted his life to the study of the Scriptures. He wrote so extensively that at times he employed as many as twenty copyists. In his vast writings, two-thirds of the entire New Testament can be found in quotations. He accepted the twenty-seven books of the New Testament as we have them now.

Along with these abundant citations, there are many early biblical manuscripts available—about ten thousand— that prove the early existence of the New Testament. The earliest fragment of the New Testament, the John Rylands Fragment, is dated at around AD 117–138. The verses from John 18 that it preserves are identical to those found in later manuscripts and in today's New Testament. There are also the Bodmer Papyri, from the second-century AD; these twenty-two papyri preserve the whole books of Peter and Jude as we have them today, plus other biblical texts.

In short, there is solid evidence that the text of the New Testament as we have it today has not been corrupted.

APPENDIX 3

What about the Gospel of Barnabas?

IN RECENT YEARS, many Muslims have cited the book *The Gospel of Barnabas* (available on the web) in order to show that Jesus was a good Muslim. Jesus is portrayed in the book as a prophet who prays, speaks, and acts exactly like traditional Muslims.

The book was written in Spain sometime during the fourteenth to sixteenth centuries. A complete Italian manuscript of it exists, which seems to be a translation from the Spanish original, which exists only in part. It includes geographical and historical inaccuracies as well as errors about Christian and Islamic beliefs.

The Gospel of Barnabas manifests a garbled comprehension of Islamic doctrines. For instance, Muhammad is called the Messiah (which means the "anointed one"—Christ) while in normal Islamic belief Jesus is understood to be the Messiah. In fact, in several places, the *Qur'an* itself proclaims that Jesus is the Messiah. Yet in chapter 6 of this false gospel, Jesus is called the Christ. The author evidently did not realize that the word Christ is the Greek equivalent of the Hebrew word Messiah. This is a significant error!

Here are quotes from chapters 96 and 97:

> Jesus answered: "As God lives, in whose presence my soul stands, I am not the Messiah whom all the tribes of the earth expect, even as God promised to our father Abraham, saying: 'In your seed will I bless all the tribes of the earth.' But when God shall take me away from the world, Satan will raise again...making the impious believe that I am God and son of God, whence my words and my doctrine shall be contaminated...God will send his messenger...who shall come from the south with power, and shall destroy the idols with the idolaters...The name of the Messiah is admirable...Mohammad is his blessed name.

In short, *The Gospel of Barnabas* is a forgery.

PS: *The Gospel of Barnabas* should not be confused with *The Epistle of Barnabas*, a much-earlier noncanonical writing.

APPENDIX 4

The Sources of Islam

As Muhammad developed his Islamic beliefs, he borrowed from the various regional religions then present in the Mideast. Within Islam today can be found elements of Judaism, Christianity, Sabeanism, Zoroastrianism, and some practices and teachings reflecting the paganism of that area.

Judaism is the largest contributor to Islam. Muhammad borrowed from it many personalities like Adam and Eve, Seth, Enoch, Noah, Abraham, Lot, Ishmael, Isaac, Jacob, Joseph, Job, Jethro, Moses, Aaron, David, Solomon, Jonah, Isaiah, Jeremiah, etc. He also borrowed incidents found in the Torah and elsewhere in the Old Testament, sometimes accurately and in very minute detail. But many other incidents he greatly changed and perverted, seemingly quite deliberately.

So from my reading of Muslim sources and the *Qur'an*, I am convinced that Muhammad had an in-depth knowledge of the Old Testament, of the life of Jesus, and even of the book of Revelation. He also took material from the Talmud, the collection of Jewish laws and traditions that various rabbis later added to the Bible. (Jesus, while on earth, condemned similar traditions of the Jews a number of times.)

Also incorporated within Islam are a number of elements obviously derived from Christianity. However, much of this was taken not from biblical Christianity but from heretical sects such as the Gnostics and other groups. This helps to explain Muhammad's view that Jesus was not actually crucified but that someone else died in his stead, also the teaching that Allah rescued Jesus and took him to heaven alive.

APPENDIX 5

---·❊·---

Is Muhammad Mentioned in the Bible?

UPON ENTERING THIS subject, be careful lest the Muslim you are conversing with gets you into merely defending. What you need to do is ask thought-provoking questions. Muslims have a set mind on many issues, so it is very hard to reason with them. Often, they are familiar with the common arguments presented by Christians and have a ready answer, as many of our arguments are standardized. For this reason, I advise you to keep asking questions that are off the beaten path.

Muslims generally maintain that the Bible has been corrupted, changed, and parts of it deleted so that the original

Bible has been lost and our present Bible is vastly different from the original. Even so, they will utilize particular verses in an attempt to prove that Muhammad's coming was foretold in the Holy Scriptures.

As soon as a Muslim starts on this subject, you should say, "You are quoting from the Bible, yet at the same time you believe that the original Bible no longer exists. I've heard arguments that it was rewritten by men other than the original authors. Would you please tell me how you know the particular verses of the Bible you are quoting belong to the small portion of the original that was *not* corrupted?" I don't think you will receive a reasonable answer.

Ask your acquaintance if he has ever read the complete Bible. Point out that it is important to take all the verses of the Bible in context and to always "compare scripture with scripture." In many cases, the Muslim you are conversing with has never even seen a Bible, let alone read it. You can suggest that he read the Bible on his own before he starts quoting from the Bible.

Question him as to where he got the material that he is about to present as evidence that Muhammad is actually mentioned in the Bible. If he is truthful, he will have to admit that he obtained it from a book written by a fellow Muslim.

You might say, "Can we agree on this: If *you* can use Bible verses as being unaltered and trustworthy, will you allow me the same privilege concerning the verses that *I* present?" (If he or she does not agree, then say that you will just drop the whole subject.)

Here are some of the verses that Muslims frequently use to try to show that Allah's sending of Muhammad was predicted in the Bible:

1. Deuteronomy 18:17–18: "The Lord said to me [Moses]…'I will raise up for them a prophet like you from among their brothers. And I will put my words in his mouth, and he shall speak to them all that I command him.'" Muslims couple this with Surah 7:157, which reads, "Those who follow the messenger, the prophet who can neither read nor write, whom they will find described in the Torah and Gospel (*which are*) with them," claiming that the above verses of Deuteronomy refer to Muhammad. However, upon examination, it is very obvious that this declaration does not apply to him but to Jesus Christ.

   a. The Bible clearly refers these verses to Jesus. John 1:21 states, "And they [the priests and Levites from Jerusalem] asked him [John the Baptist], 'What then? Are you Elijah?' He said, 'I am not.' 'Are you *the Prophet?*' [mentioned in Deut. 18:18]. And he answered, 'No.'"

b. John 1:45 states, "Philip found Nathanael and said to him, 'We have found him of whom Moses in the Law [Deut. 18:18] and also the prophets wrote, Jesus of Nazareth, the son of Joseph.'" Here, Jesus is clearly identified as the prophet that Moses spoke about. It was Jesus, not Muhammad.

c. Acts 3:22 states, "Moses said, 'The Lord God will raise up for you a prophet like me from your brothers. You shall listen to him [Jesus] in whatever he tells you.'" This verse clearly identifies Deuteronomy 18:18 with Jesus.

d. Acts 7:37 states, "This is the Moses who said to the Israelites, 'God will raise up for you a prophet like me from your brothers."

e. Hebrews 1:1–2 shows that Jesus was the Prophet and the last Prophet: "Long ago, at many times and in many ways, God spoke to our fathers by the prophets, but in these last days he has spoken to us by his Son, whom he appointed the heir of all things, through whom also he created the world."

To show that this verse of the Torah does not apply to Muhammad, you can ask your friends a number of questions:

1. Ask them to turn with you to Deuteronomy 18:1–2. Verse 2 says that the Levites were told, "They shall

have no inheritance among their brothers." The Levites were Jews, and it is obvious that when, in verse 18, the Lord declares "I will raise up for them a prophet like you from among their brothers," it means this prophesied one would be of Jewish descent. Ask the Muslim you are speaking to if Muhammad was a Jew. Of course he was not, so this verse can't apply to him.

2. Ask if Muhammad was literate—knew how to read and write. If your acquaintance is honest, he will have to say Muhammad was not. Exodus 17:14 states that Moses could both read and write. This surely disqualifies Muhammad.

3. Ask him if Muhammad ever spoke directly to Allah and Allah himself ever spoke to Muhammad. (Muslims claim that it was the angel Gabriel who gave revelations to Muhammad.) Numbers 12:6–8, 13:1, and many other places state that God spoke directly, face-to-face, to Moses; therefore, Muhammad does not measure up.

4. Deuteronomy 17:15 reads, "You may indeed set a king over you whom the Lord your God will choose. One from among your *brothers* you shall set as king over you. *You may not put a foreigner over you, who is not your brother.*" Since God forbade the Jewish people from choosing a non-Jewish king, then why would He set up a non-Jewish prophet to rule over them?

5. Genesis 17:21 reads, "But I [God] will establish my covenant with Isaac." Genesis 21:12 states, "Through Isaac shall your off spring be named." Since God openly declared that this "prophet" would come through Isaac and not through Ishmael, of whom Muhammad came, then how can Muslims properly claim that this verse applies to Muhammad? Even the *Qur'an* agrees with this, for Surah 29:27 reads, "And We bestowed on him Isaac and Jacob, and We established the Priesthood and the Scripture among his [Isaac's] seed."

6. Moses did many signs and wonders. Ask your Muslim friend if Muhammad ever did any of the spectacular miracles that Moses did. Of course, Muhammad never did any.

7. Moses was known as the "meekest man upon the earth" (Numbers 12:3). Does the *Qur'an* ever claim that Muhammad was meek?

2. Psalm 45:3–5: "Gird your sword on your thigh, O mighty one, in your splendor and majesty! In your majesty ride out victoriously for the cause of truth and meekness and righteousness; let your right hand teach you awesome deeds! Your arrows are sharp in the heart of the king's enemies; the peoples fall under you."

BURNING QUESTIONS ABOUT ISLAM

Since these verses speak of one coming with the sword to subdue his enemies, Muslims sometimes cite it as a prediction of their prophet Muhammad, who was known as the prophet of the sword. Muslims insist it could not refer to Jesus since he never came with a sword as he himself admitted in Matthew 26:52. However, this does not apply to Muhammad for many reasons:

a. The very next verse, Psalm 45:6, reads, "Your throne, O God, is forever and ever. The scepter of your kingdom is a scepter of uprightness." This prophesy clearly refers to Jesus as found in Hebrews 1:8, which reads, "But of the Son [Jesus Christ] he [the Father] says, 'Your throne, O God, is forever and ever, the scepter of uprightness is the scepter of your kingdom.'" In no way could this verse possibly apply to Muhammad.

b. Jesus did not come the first time with the sword, but at his second coming (which even Muslims believe in), Jesus will lead "the armies of heaven." (See Revelation 19:11–16.) Yes, even the Muslims believe that when Jesus returns to the earth he will use the sword to kill all infidels.

3. Isaiah 9:6–7: Probably one of the most blasphemous slurs by Muslims is their misapplication of Isaiah 9:6–7—one

of the most wonderful and beautiful passages found in the Bible—to Muhammad. These verses read, "For to us a child is born, to us a son is given; and the government shall be upon his shoulder, and his name shall be called Wonderful, Counselor, Mighty God, Everlasting Father, Prince of Peace. Of the increase of his government and of peace there will be no end, on the throne of David and over his kingdom, to establish it and to uphold it with justice and with righteousness from this time forth and forevermore. The zeal of the Lord of hosts will do this."

Yes, not everything that was prophesied in these verses has been fulfilled, but Muslims and many other groups forget that the earthly ministry of Jesus is broken into two segments. The first time Jesus came, it was as the meek and humble servant, with the purpose of dying for the sins of all mankind. Then he rose from the dead and returned to heaven, and he will be coming back once again, this time as the mighty conquering King.

Here are a number of questions that you can ask to show how impossible it is to apply this passage to Muhammad (it can only apply to Jesus):

a. If you Muslims are going to use these verses, then you obviously must believe that they have been preserved accurately! But you must take them in their

BURNING QUESTIONS ABOUT ISLAM

context. Turn to Isaiah 7:14, which reads, "Therefore the Lord himself will give you a sign: Behold, the virgin shall conceive and bear a son, and shall call his name Immanuel [which according to Matthew 1:23 means 'God with us']." Muslims correctly believe in the virgin birth as it is prophesied here. This message was brought to Mary by the angel Gabriel, and all Muslims recognize him. My friend, do you believe the whole prophecy? If so, it declares that Jesus was more than just a prophet; he was actually "God with us"!

b. Since you Muslims believe "For to us a child is born," you must also believe "to us a son is given." Surely God needs to have a Son in order to be able to give him! You can't give something you don't have.

c. Where in the *Qur'an* is Muhammad ever called "Wonderful, Counselor"?

d. Where in the *Qur'an* is Muhammad ever called "Mighty God"? (Jesus is identified as the Almighty in Revelation 1:8: "I [Jesus] am the Alpha and the Omega,' says the Lord God, 'who is and who was and who is to come, the Almighty.")

e. "The everlasting Father." Since the Son was the Creator of everything, this phrase might better be rendered "father of eternity," because he created even the phenomenon we humans call time. In the book

Muhammad in the Bible, by Hadrat Mirza bashir-ud-Din Mahmud Ahmad, the author argues regarding this passage: "The fourth name is 'everlasting Father,' and this also does not apply to Jesus." This is quite interesting. The author states that it can't apply to Jesus but never shows how it could apply to Muhammad!

f. Here is another quote from the above-mentioned book: "The fifth name is 'Prince of Peace,' and even this cannot apply to Jesus. He never became king, so he never could bring peace to the world." But Jesus's work is not yet finished. Furthermore, Jesus truly *did* claim to be a king, as John 18:33–37 shows. This was one of the chief accusations made against Jesus. Matthew 27:37 says, "And over his head they put the charge against him, which read, 'This is Jesus, the King of the Jews.'" And while he was interrogated, what did the Roman soldiers do? "Kneeling before him [Jesus], they mocked him, saying, 'Hail, King of the Jews.'" Yes, Jesus did claim to be a king. We know that in the future he will become earth's king as stated in Revelation 19:16: "On his [Jesus's] robe and on his thigh he has a name written, 'King of kings and Lord of lords.'"

It is quite interesting that a Muslim would say such a thing about Jesus. If the title Prince of Peace does not apply to Jesus, it certainly does not apply to Muhammad! We just saw how some Muslims try to apply Psalm 45:3–5 to Muhammad because it talks about the "sword." Now they are saying just the opposite! Muhammad was certainly not known as a man of peace. He was known for his many battles—twenty-seven at least, not for peace!

g. "The throne of David." Clearly Jesus was from the line of David; see Matthew 1:1. Ask your Muslim friend to show you in the *Qur'an* where Muhammad came from the line of David. He cannot, because Muhammad was of the lineage of Ishmael and so had no right to David's throne. And of course, Muhammad was never declared a king.

h. "On the throne of David and over his kingdom, to establish it and to uphold it with justice and with righteousness from this time forth and forevermore." Muhammad was not an eternal king. He died, and that was the end of him. But this verse states that the kingdom Jesus will establish is to last "forevermore."

The coming of Muhammad is *never* prophesied in the Bible or any other place.

4. John 14:16–17: "And I [Jesus] will ask the Father, and he will give you another Helper [advocate or counselor; one who comes alongside], to be with you forever, even the Spirit of truth, whom the world cannot receive,

because it neither sees him nor knows him. You know him, for he dwells with you and will be in you." Desperate Muslim scholars see a prediction of Muhammad in this statement by Jesus about a coming "Helper" (Greek *paraclete*). They make this claim in Surah 61:6: "And remember Jesus, son of Mary, who said: 'O Children of Israel; I am the messenger of Allah to you, confirming that which was revealed before me in the Torah (*Books of Moses*) and bringing good tidings of a messenger who will come after me, whose name is Ahmad [one of the names of Muhammad].' Yet when he has come to them with clear proofs, they say: 'This is mere magic.'"

These Islamic scholars will even argue that the Greek word *paraclete* in verse 16 should really be *periclytos* ("blessed"), an equivalent to the Arabic word *Ahmad*, a shortened form of Muhammad. However, there is no basis for such a claim.

Another point: verse 16 states that the Helper will "be with you *forever*." Ask the Muslim if Muhammad is still alive. Of course he is not. And does he "dwell with you and *in* you"? Obviously not!

Conclusion: None of these four Bible passages have any connection with Muhammad. There is no prediction of Muhammad in the Bible.

APPENDIX 6

———— ✳ ————

What Muslims Fail to Believe about God

God is love.

—1 John 4:8

ISLAM DECLARES THAT Allah has "ninety-nine beautiful names." These names are "declarative emblems" of His nature; in other words, they reveal His eternal attributes. How thrilling this concept is! How uplifting should be the heartfelt recitation of these blessed names!

Unfortunately, though the God of Islam may possess ninety-nine worshipful "attribute-names," at this point, Islam is blatantly defective. It falls short! Even though love is one of them, it is not emphasized. There is no way under these circumstances for a Muslim to have a personal relationship with Allah in order to experience this love.

Faithful Muslims have a natural fear of Allah and continually try to appease Him. They hope that by saying their prayers five times a day, giving some of their money to the needy, observing Ramadan by fasting during the day for that month, and (if they have enough money) going on a pilgrimage to Mecca that these duties will somehow cancel out a few of their sins and cool the wrath of God against them. However, a Muslim can never know if he or she has done enough good to make up for the bad.

Divine love is one of the most exalted attributes of Yahweh, the God who reveals Himself in the Bible. And it is the sole ground for our responsive love.

"Beloved, let us love one another, for love is from God, and whoever loves has been born of God and knows God. Anyone who does not love does not know God, because God is love. In this the love of God was made manifest among us, that God sent his only Son into the world, so that we might live through him" (1 John 4:7–9).

By denying the death of Jesus Christ upon the cross, Muslims are shutting themselves out from ever knowing this wonderful love of God. John 15:13 reads, "Greater love has no one than this, than to lay down one's life for his friends." However, Jesus did not lay down His life for His friends, but for His enemies. Romans 5:8 says, "But God demonstrates His own love toward us, in that while we were still sinners, Christ died for us."

Of course, we Christians rejoice also because of John 3:16, that amazing verse that proclaims, "For God so loved the world that He gave His only begotten Son, that whoever believes in Him shall not perish but have everlasting life."

The verse in 1 John 4:10 says, "In this is love, not that we loved God, but that He loved us and sent His Son to be the propitiation for our sins." What good news! One cannot read the Bible without noticing the many places where the love of God is revealed. But the only way you or I can know the love of God experientially is by accepting Jesus Christ as personal Savior. What a glorious privilege!

APPENDIX 7

———— ✳ ————

How Can Islam Teach Four Different Ways of Salvation?

IF YOU WERE to ask a group of Muslims what Islam teaches about "salvation" you would likely get a wide variety of answers, for there is no consistency. The answer given would depend largely upon one's personal circumstances and what you, at the time, happened to be talking about.

Here is a pertinent quote from the *Hadith*:

> Paradise and Hell have already been created. They will never come to an end or cease to exist. Allah created Paradise and Hell before the rest of creation, and He created inhabitants for each of them. Whoever He wishes (will enter) Paradise by His

grace and mercy, and whoever He wishes (will enter Hell) as a result of His justice. Every person will behave according to that for which he was created, and his destiny will be that for which he was created; good deeds and evil deeds are foreordained for all men.

If Allah has determined the eternal destiny of every person before he or she was born, then why does Islam present four possible ways of a person going to Paradise?

The teachings of Islam are confusing as to how a Muslim might ultimately reach Paradise. It seems that there are at least four different conflicting ways, and none of these paths leaves a person with guaranteed certainty as to where he or she will spend eternity.

1. The one who sincerely repeats the *Shahadah*—"There is only one God, and Muhammad is his true prophet"—will enter paradise.

In the Muslim book *The Pillars of Islam & Iman* (Faith), written by Muhammad bin Jamil Zion, we read on page 17, "Whosoever says there is only one God, Allah, sincerely, will enter Paradise."

Then in page 20, we find, "[I] urge those of you who are on their deathbed to say the Shahadah; for verily, whoever's last words are *La ilaha illa-Allah* will eventually enter Paradise even if he has to go through (before that) whatever (punishment) he has to go through."

Then on page 21, it continues, "Whoever says *La ilaha illa-Allah*, it will be his salvation someday."

The *Qur'an*, in Surah 57:21, seems to confirm the statements made above.

This surah reads, "Hasten to forgiveness from your Lord and to a garden the extensiveness of which is as the extensiveness of the heaven and the earth; it is *prepared for those who believe in Allah and his apostle*" (M. H. Shakir).

The following *hadith* is in agreement:

> Hazrat Anas relates that the prophet of Islam was riding, followed by Maadh. When the prophet repeated thrice, "Anyone who honestly believes and repeats: 'There is but one God and Muhammad is his prophet,' shall never be doomed to the fi re of hell," Maadh said, "O prophet of God, shall I not proclaim these tidings?" The prophet answered, "In that case, they will believe in nothing else but this." (Mishkat)

Another *hadith* states the following:

> It is related from Abu Dharr that he said: "I came to the Prophet and he said: 'Any servant of God

who says, "There is no God but Allah," and afterwards dies relying on that, will enter heaven.' I said, 'Although he commit adultery or steal?'...He replied, 'Although he commit adultery and theft, and in spite of Abu Dharr.'" (Muslim and Bukhari)

Is this kind of statement really merciful and just? Here, a person who has spent his whole life doing evil will enter Paradise at death just because he repeated the *Shahadah*, while another who has spent his life in the fear of God, self-restraint, and good deeds will be cast into hell at death!

These statements seem to be in conflict with what Islam also teaches: that repentance, good works, and the free will of Allah will determine one's destiny on the Day of Judgment!

2. God is merciful and just, and if a person will repent, then he or she will be forgiven.

I received a letter from a young Muslim who made this claim. He stated,

> According to Islamic understanding, God Almighty forgives any sincerely repentant soul. Seeking forgiveness sincerely is one of the most important mechanisms in Islam. The door of forgiveness is

open to anyone until death. The going to heaven and hell is, of course, determined on the Day of Judgment. However, in Islam Paradise is given to the believer out of mercy and NOT earned by good deeds. Even though Muslim writers often describe the Day of Judgment as the weighing of good and bad deeds, the comprehensive and most accurate understanding is that Paradise is awarded to a believer out of the mercy of God Almighty and NOT earned by good deeds.

There is a Muslim tradition that would seem to indicate the same thing:

> Abu Huraira reported that the Prophet of Islam said: "No one of you will enter Paradise through his good works." They said: "Not even you, O Apostle of God?" "Not even I," he replied, "unless God cover me with His grace and mercy. Therefore be strong, and morning and evening, nay every moment, try to do good."

Here is another tradition along this line.

> Jabir reported that the Prophet of Islam said: "No good works of yours can ever secure heaven for

you, nor can they save you from hell—not even me, without the grace of God."

However, the *Qur'an* says the following:

> Repentance with Allah is only for those who do evil in ignorance, then turn (to Allah) soon, so these it is to whom Allah turns (mercifully), and Allah is ever Knowing, Wise. And repentance is not for those who go on doing evil deeds, until when death comes to one of them, he says: Surely now I repent; nor (for) those who die while they are unbelievers. These are they for whom We have prepared a painful chastisement. (Surah 4:17–18, M. H. Shakir)

So repentance is applicable only for those who do evil in ignorance and then forsake doing that particular evil.

But a further problem arises: If God is merciful, He is likewise just. If Allah should forgive by using His mercy only, would He not be evading the demands of His justice and righteousness? Such an evasion of His justice would show a defect in God. Certainly such an act would be unworthy of the glory of God.

3. At the end of the pilgrimage to Mecca, forgiveness of one's sins occurs.

The shaving of the head is a symbol of rebirth, signifying that the pilgrim's sins have been cleansed by completion of the *Hajj*.

Tradition has it that Muhammad said, "One who performs *Hajj* and does not speak obscenely, nor act corruptly, will return without his sins, like the day his mother gave birth to him." (To return to the day of birth obviously means that this person has a pure nature.)

If a person's sins are forgiven when he completes the *Hajj*, and were he then to immediately die, that would evidently make him eligible for Paradise. (Apparently, some Muslims believe this, because they pray that they might die as soon as they finish the pilgrimage.) But again, this is in obvious conflict with other teachings of Islam, among them that all must appear at the Day of Judgment. Also, this would hardly be a just way, because the *Hajj* is mainly for men, and among them the rich have an advantage and the poor lack an equal chance. Why should Allah be so partial to men, especially to the rich?

4. One's good deeds have to outweigh his bad deeds, but a Muslim cannot know the outcome until the Day of Judgment.

Surah 101:1–11 reads,

> The Calamity! What is the Calamity? Would that you knew what the Calamity is! It is a day on which men will become like scattered moths. And the mountains will become like carded wool. Then, as for him whose scales are heavy (*with good deeds*) he will be in a pleasing life. But as for him whose scales are light, the bottomless pit will be his home. What will convey to you what this is like! It is raging Fire. (Scales being heavy means good deeds; being light means lack of good deeds.)

First, let me remind you: Islam does not believe in original sin—the doctrine that the fallen nature of Adam and Eve was transmitted to their offspring so that humans are born with a sin nature and that, in turn, sinfulness is passed on to their children. In the book prepared by the Islamic Educational Services titled *Christian Muslim Dialogue* by Dr. Hasan M. Baagil, on page 28, it states, "All doctrines of modern Christianity are made by men," and he includes original sin.

In a letter from an imam, in answer to a letter I wrote to him asking about the concept of sin in the Muslim religion, he answered,

> First of all, we should know what is the definition of sin. And what are the kinds of sin. Sin means to be disobedient to God. Now there are two kinds of sins; one which is "committed intentionally" and the other is "committed unintentionally." They are called "great sins" and "small sins." We understand that sin is a poison and one cannot live after taking the poison…We [Muslims] do not believe that because Adam and Eve committed sin, the whole of mankind has inherited sin…We believe that every child is born with *A PURE NATURE* and that society and environment make him a sinner… We do not believe that sin is inherited. Everyone is responsible for his own sin.

In another place, I read that Muslims do not believe that children are responsible for their sins until the age of puberty; therefore, before that age, when children are disobedient and they sin, they are only lightly reprimanded, given a light tap on the hand.

Islam teaches that even though man was created and born with a pure nature, he sins because of ignorance and weakness. This is hard for me to comprehend because the *Qur'an* and the Bible both teach that Adam and Eve sinned knowingly (the "great sin"). Surah 7:22 reads,

> Thus did he [Satan] lead them by a deceit; and when they tasted of the tree their shame was manifest to them and they began to hide (*by heaping*) on themselves some of the leaves of the Garden. And their Lord called them (*saying*): "Did I not forbid you from that tree and tell you: 'assuredly Satan is an open enemy to you'?"

If man is not born with a sin nature and sinfulness is not transferred from parent to child, then there is but one conclusion I can come to: sin is something that must be taught! The ones who have the most influence on children are the parents. So I must believe that Muslim children are either taught how to sin by their parents or they see their parents sinning and follow their bad example. I do not see any other alternative.

But back to the question of salvation: What is the right path? Do good works play an important part? Yes, according to the above surah; a scale heavy with good deeds is necessary for a person to have any hope of receiving a favorable decision on the Day of Judgment. And the following verses agree:

They who turn (to Allah), who serve (Him), who praise (Him), who fast, who bow down, who prostrate themselves, who *enjoin what is good* and forbid what is evil, and *who keep the limits of Allah*; and give good news to the believers. (M. H. Shakir) (Surah 9:112)

Except him who repents and believes and *does a good deed*; so these are they of whom Allah changes the evil deeds to good ones; and Allah is Forgiving, Merciful. And whoever repents *and does good*, he surely turns to Allah a (goodly) turning. (M. H. Shakir) (Surah 25:70–71)

It seems quite clear from the *Qur'an* that a person needs a record of good deeds in order to enter into Paradise. Mere repentance, though helpful, is not enough.

Are there actually four ways of salvation? Will any of these possible paths prove to be effective? Or are they all dead ends?

Anyone who has read the *Qur'an* knows that it has much to say about the Day of Judgment (at least 375 references) and that all must appear there when their eternal destiny is to be decided, but it is impossible for any Muslim to be 100 percent sure of the outcome before the Day of Judgment. There is always that big *if.*

The average Muslim believes that if his good deeds (51 percent) outweigh the bad deeds (49 percent) that he will go to Paradise, but if it is the reverse, he will go to hell. (This is the general concept of most religions.)

But while the *Qur'an* talks often about good deeds, it never specifies what percentage one needs to have to make it to one of the seven heavens. Since the *Qur'an* leaves people in ignorance concerning this, what if on the Day of Judgment Muslims found out that Allah was more holy than they thought and required them to be 90 percent good? In that case, there would be very few, if any, who would make it to heaven.

But what happens if the words of Jesus are true when He declares, as recorded in Matthew 5:48, "You therefore must be perfect, as your heavenly Father is perfect"?

The Bible is very specific that it takes more than good works to outweigh one's evil works in order to get to heaven. God said in Revelation 21:27, "But nothing unclean will ever enter it, nor anyone who does what is detestable or false, but only those who are written in the Lamb's book of life."

In the final analysis, it doesn't matter how the Muslim measures up on the Day of Judgment. Since Allah is all-powerful, He can punish whom He will and forgive whom

He pleases. Surah 2:284 states, "He [Allah] will forgive whom He will and punish whom He pleases; He has power over all things."

So none of these four way is a guarantee that a Muslim will enter Paradise. Saying the *Shahadah*, repenting, going on the pilgrimage, doing good deeds—these have absolutely nothing to do with one's eternal destiny. How hopeless is anyone whose trust is in the teachings of the *Qur'an* and the *Hadith*!

O Muslim, pay attention to the words of the Prophet Jesus, God's Messiah:

> Enter by the narrow gate. For the gate is wide and the way is easy that leads to destruction, and those who enter by it are many. For the gate is narrow and the way is hard that leads to life, and those who find it are few. Beware of false prophets. (Matt. 7:13–15a)

> Truly, truly, I say to you, I am the door of the sheep. All who came before me are thieves and robbers, but the sheep did not listen to them. I am the door. If anyone enters by me, he will be saved. (John 10:7–9a)

APPENDIX 8

Islamic Sources State That Only One in a Hundred Muslims Will Go to Paradise

HERE IS MATERIAL taken from Muslim sources substantiating their astounding teaching that only one out of one hundred of all Muslims will be able to enter Paradise. Of course, all the rest will be condemned to hell. This material attempts to explain why in one place the *Hadith* states that "only 1 in 1,000" will enter Paradise and in another place it states that "1 in 100" go to Paradise. Moreover, the means by which Muslims try to resolve the contradiction contradicts another Muslim teaching. Islam confidently teaches that no one who is not a follower of Muhammad will enter Paradise. Yet in their attempt to solve the above problem, Muslim scholars state that the "1 in 100" refers to Muslims alone while the "1 in 1,000" refers to non-Muslims—so some non-Muslims apparently will get there!

You will notice in the following material that Muhammad taught that at least sevnety different sects would arise among the Muslims—and there are seventy-two Muslim sects today—and that only those people who adhere to the one group that will be selected by the return-ing Messiah will have the possibility of reaching Paradise. Furthermore, remember that the *Qur'an* teaches that those men who die in jihad will go directly to Paradise. So when you consider that only one out of one hundred Muslims have the possibility of making it to Paradise, surely most of those heavenly mansions have already been taken by the martyrs who were killed in the many battles that Muslims have fought and are still fighting. That doesn't leave many places for the average Muslim to squeeze into!

I am leaving this material the way I got it from the *Hadith* and other Muslim sources so that if you need to show it to your Muslim friend, it will be authentic. (Note: The *swt* and *saw* after Allah and Muhammad are abbrevia-tions meaning "Glorious and Exalted is He" or "Peace be upon him.")

Many texts indicate that nine hundred and ninety-nine out of every thousand of the children of Adam will enter Hell, and only one (in a thousand) will enter Paradise.

al-Bukhari narrates from Abu Sa'eed that the Prophet (saw) said: Allah will say, "O Adam!" Adam will reply, "I respond to Your call, I am obedient to Your commands, and all good is in Your hands." Then Allah (swt) will say to Adam, "Send forth the people of the Fire." Adam will say, "How many are the people of the Fire?" Allah (swt) will say, "Out of every thousand, take nine hundred and ninety-nine."

This speech distressed his [Muhammad's] Companions and they said, "O Messenger of Allah (saw), who amongst us will be that man (one in a thousand)?" He [Muhammad] said, "Be of good cheer: the thousand will be from Ya'juj and Ma'juj (Gog and Magog) and the one will be from among you." Then he said, "By Him in Whose hand is my soul, I hope that you will be one third of the people of Paradise." We praised and glorified Allah (swt) and then he said, "By Him in Whose hand is my soul, I hope that you will be half of the people of Paradise, as you are among the nations like a white hair on the hide of a black bull or a round hairless spot on the foreleg of a donkey." (al-Bukhari, Kitaab ar-Raqaaq, Baab Qawl Allaah Azza wa jalla, innaa zalzalat al-Saa'ah, Shay'un 'Adheem, Fath al-Baari, 11/388; see also Tafseer Ibn Katheer, 4/610, Musnad Ahmad 4/435)

It might be asked: how can we reconcile between these *hadiths* and the report from Abu Hurayrah in Sa'eeh al-Bukhari, in which the Prophet (saw) said that Allah (swt) said to Adam (*'alayhis-salaam*), "Send forth [into Hell] ninety-nine out of every hundred [of your descendants]"?

It is obvious that these reports do not contradict the other. Sa'eeh reports what we have quoted above, because these figures are referring to different groups. The *hadith* that mentions a ratio of nine hundred and ninety-nine may be interpreted as referring to all the progeny of Adam, while the *hadith* of al-Bukhari that mentions a ratio of ninety-nine may be interpreted as referring to the progeny of Adam excluding Ya'juj and Ma'juj.

This reconciliation is more likely to be correct—as Ibn Hajar suggests—because Ya'juj and Ma'juj are mentioned in the *hadith* of Abu Sa'eed whereas they are not mentioned in the *hadith* of Abu Hurayrah. It may be said that the first *hadith* refers to all of creation, so the ratio of people admitted to hell when all nations are taken into account is 999 in every thousand.

The latter *hadith* of al-Bukhari explains the ratio of people who will enter hell from this *ummah* [this is a word that applies to the Muslim community] alone. Ibn Hajar (said), "This interpretation is supported by the words of the Sahabah in the *hadith* of Abu Hurayrah (ra): "If ninety-nine out of every hundred are taken from us, what will be left of us?"

> This division of people could happen twice: once involving all the nations, when one in a thousand will enter Paradise, and a second time involving this *ummah* alone, when ten out of every thousand will enter Paradise. (Fath al-Baari, 11/390)

The Wisdom Behind There Being So Many People in Hell

The reason behind it is the fact that those who responded to the Messengers were few in number while those who disbelieved were great. Furthermore, many of those who responded were not pure and sincere in faith.

In his book, at-Takhweef min an-Naar, Ibn Rajab discussed the reason why so few people will enter Paradise and so many will enter hell:

> These *hadiths* and other similar reports prove that most of the children of Adam will enter Hell, and

that the followers of the Messengers are few in number when compared to the rest of mankind. Those who did not follow the Messengers will enter Hell, except for those whom the Message did not reach, or who could not understand it because of the garbled form in which they heard it. Many of those who claim to be followers of the Messengers are in fact adhering to a distorted religion and an altered book, and they too will be among the people of Hell.

As for those who claim to follow the Book and Law of Allah (swt), the true religion, many of them will also enter Hell. These are the *Munaafi qoon* (the hypocrites) who will be in the lowest level of the Fire. Many of those who claim to follow it openly and in secret will be tested by ambiguities and doubts— these are the misguided inventors and followers of *bid'ah* (reprehensible innovations, heresies). Several *hadiths* have been narrated which state that the *ummah* will split into seventy-odd sects, all of which will be in Hell except for one. Many people will also be tested with forbidden desires for which the promised punishment is Hellfi re, although in this case it is not necessarily an eternal punishment. No one from this *ummah* will be saved from the Fire, or deserve the absolute promise of Paradise, apart from the one sect or group, who follow the example and practice of the Prophet (saw) and his Companions openly and in secret, and are saved from the temptation and trials of desires and doubts. Such are very few indeed, especially in latter times." (at-Takhweef min an-Naar, Ibn Rajab, p. 214)

At-Tirmidhi, Abu Dawud, and an-Nasaa'ee report from Abu Hurayrah (ra) that the messenger of Allah (saw) [Muhammad] said, "When Allah (swt) created Hell, He told Jibreel [Gabriel], "Go and look at it." Jibreel went and looked at it, and when he came back he said, "By Your Glory, I fear that no-one who hears of it will enter it." So He surrounded it with desires, and said, "Go and look at it." Jibreel went and looked at it, and when he came back, he said, "By Your Glory, I fear that there will be no-one left who does not enter it." (The version narrated by an-Nasaa'ee adds the words, "and at what I have prepared for its inhabitants in it") [Jaami al-Usool, 10/250, # 8068. at-Tirmidhi described it as sahih hasan].

This material was taken from the website Islamworld. net, pages 36–39.

BIBLIOGRAPHY

Abdullah, F. and Zakiuddin Sharif. *Did the Prophet Muhammad Predict the Second Coming of Jesus and World War III?*. Bloomington: 1983.

Adams, Moody. *The Religion that is Raping America*. Baton Rouge: Moody Adams Evangelistic Association, 1996.

Ahmad, Hadhrat Mirza Tahir. *An Elementary Study of Islam*. Islam International Publications Ltd., Surrey, UK, 1997.

Ahmad, Mirza Bashiruddin Mahmud. *Life of Muhammad*. Islam International Publications Ltd., Surrey, UK, 1990.

Ahmad, Mirza Ghulam. *The Philosophy of the Teachings of Islam*. Islam International Publications Ltd., Surrey, UK, 1996.

Ahmad, Dr. Israr. *Rise and Decline of the Muslim Ummah*. Markazi Anjuman Khuddam-Ul-Quran, Lahore, Pakistan, 1993.

Asiddiqi, Shamim. *The Commitment.* The Forum for Islamic Work, Flushing, NY. (No date given.)

Ataur-Rahim, Muhammad. *Jesus, Prophet of Islam.* Tahrike Tarsile Qur'an, Inc. 1991.

Al-Araby, Abdullah. *ISLAM Unveiled.* Los Angeles: The Pen vs. The Sword, 2004.

Aygei, Ahmad. *Sharing the Love of Christ with your Muslim Neighbour* and *ISHMAEL Shall be Blessed.* Your Helper in Muslim Evangelism, Kumasi, Ghana, West Africa. 2002.

Baagil, Hasan. *Christian Muslim Dialogue.* Islamic Educational Services, Mt. Holly, NJ. 1984.

Barrett, Paul M. *American Islam. The Struggle for the Soul of a Religion.* New York: Farrar, Straus and Giroux, 2007.

Caner, Ergun Mehmet and Emir Gethi. *Unveiling Islam.* Grand Rapids: Kregel, 2002.

Emerson, Steven. *American Jihad. The Terrorists Living Among Us.* New York: The Free Press, 2002.

Esposito, John L. *UNHOLY WAR. Terror in the Name of Islam.* New York: Oxford, 2002.

Gabriel, Mark A. *Islam and Terrorism.* Bartlesville: The Voice of the Martyrs, Inc., 2002.

Geisler, Norman L. and Abdul Saleeb. *Answering Islam.* Baker Books: 1993.

Guillaume, Alfred. *Islam.* New York: Penguin Books, 1954.

Gurganus, Gene. *PERIL of ISLAM. Telling the Truth!* Truth Publishers: 2004.

Haines, John. *Good News for Muslims. Tools for Proclaiming Jesus to Your Neighbor.* Philadelphia: Middle East Resources, 1998.

Hoskins, Edward J. *A Muslim's Heart. What Every Christian Needs to Know to Share Christ with Muslims.* Colorado Springs: NavPress, 2003.

Huntington, Samuel P. *The Clash of Civilization and the Remaking of World Order.* Touchstone Books, New York, NY. 1996.

Ibn Naasir as-Sa'dee, Shaikh Abdur-Rahmaan. *The Characteristic of The Slaves of the Merciful.* Birmingham, UK: Salafi Publications, 2007.

Ibrahim, I.A. *A Brief Illustrated Guide to Understanding Islam.* Darussalam, Houston, TX. 1997.

Jabbour, Nabeel T. *The Crescent Through the Eyes of the Cross—Insight from an Arab Christian.* NavPress, Colorado Springs, CO. 2008.

Jomier, Jacques. *The Bible and the Qur'an.* San Francisco: Ignatius Press, 1964.

Hamza Mustafa Njozi. *The Sources of the Qur'an*, Riyadh, Saudi Arabia: World Assembly of Muslim Youth, 1991.

Ibn Kathir. Translated by Wa'il Abdul Mut all Shihab. *The Battles of The Prophet* Pub. Dar Al-Manarah, El-Mansoura, Egypt. 2000.

Khan, Muhammad Muhsin. *Road to Paradise.* Houston: Dar-us-Salam, 2002.

LeBlanc, Abdul Malik. *The Bible Led Me to Islam.* Toronto: Al-Attique Publisher, Inc., 2000.

Lewis, Bernard. *What Went Wrong? Western Impact and Middle Eastern Response.* New York, Oxford Press, 2002.

Madany, Bassam M. *The Bible and Islam. Sharing God's Word with a Muslim.* Palos Heights: The Back to God Hour, 1992.

Madany, Bassam and Shirley W. *An Introduction to Islam.* Middle East Resources, Upper Darby, 2006.

Manji, Irshad. *The Trouble with Islam Today.* New York: St. Martin's Griffin, 2003.

Masood, Steven. *The Bible and the Qur'an.* OM Publishing: 2001.

Mawdudi, Abul A'la. *Towards Understanding Islam.*

McCurry, Don. *Healing the Broken Family of Abraham: New Life for Muslims.* Colorado Springs: Self-published, 2001.

McDowell, Bruce A. and Anees Zaka. *Muslims and Christians at the Table: Promoting Biblical Understanding Among North American Muslims.* Phillipsburg: P&R Publishing, , (C) 1999.

Medearis, Carl. *Muslims, Christians, and Jesus—Gaining Understanding and Building Relationships.* Minneapolis: Bethany House, 2008.

Mehar, Iftikhar Ahmed. *Al-Islam.* West Paterson: Self-published, (2003.

Menezes, J. L *The Life and Religion of Mohammed, the Prophet of Arabia.* Harrison: Roman Catholic Books, 1911.

Miller, William M. *A Christian's Response to Islam.* Phillipsburg: Presbyterian and Reformed Publishing Co. (C) 1976.

Nasr, Seyyed Hossein. *ISLAM. Religion, History, and Civilization.* San Francisco: HarperSanFrancisco, 2003.

Palmer, Bernard. *Understanding the Islamic Exposion.* Christ for the World.

Payne, Robert. *The History of Islam.* New York: Barnes and Noble Books, 1959.

Rauf, Feisal Abdul. *What's Right With Islam?* Harper San Francisco, 2004.

Richardson, Don. *Secrets of the Koran.* Ventura: Regal, 1999.

Saal, William J. *Reaching Muslims for Christ.* Chicago: Moody Press, 1991.

Schlorff, Sam. *Missiological Models in Ministry to Muslims.* Upper Darby: Middle East Resources, 2006.

Segev, Tom. *One Palestine, Complete.* New York: Henry Holt and Co., 1949.

Sheikh Mohammmed 'Aal-'Uthaymeen. *Rights Basic to the Natural Human Constitution, and Affirmed by Divine Law.* Miami, FL: the Daar of Islamic Heritage, 1994.

Shay, Shaul. *The Endless Jihad.* Herzliya, Israel: International Policy Institute for Counter-Terrorism, 2002.

Shoebat, Walid with Joel Richardson. *God's War on Terror— Islam, Prophecy and the Bible*. 2011.

Spencer, Robert. *The Politically Incorrect Guide to Islam (And the Crusades)*. Washington, DC: Regnery Publishing, Inc., 2005.

Spencer, Robert. *Stealth Jihad: How Radical Islam is Subverting America without Guns or Bombs*. Washington, DC: Regnery Publishing, Inc., 2008.

Spencer, Robert. *The Truth About Muhammad, Founder of the World's Most Intolerant Religion*. Washington, DC: Regnery Publishing, Inc., 2006.

Taylor, John B. *The World of Islam*. Friendship Press, 1979.

Tisdall, W. St. Clair. *Christian Reply to Muslim Objections*. London: Society for Promoting Christian Knowledge, 1904.

Trodusdale, Jerry. *MIRACULOUS MOVEMENTS* Nashville: Thomas Nelson, 2012.

Understanding Islam and the Muslims. Washington, DC: the Embassy of Saudi Arabia.

Warraq, Ibn, editor. *The Origins of the Koran*. Amherst, NY: Prometheus Books, (S) 1998.

Yahya, Harun. *Death Resurrection Hell*. New Delhi, India: Goodword Books, 2002.

Zaka, Anees. *Ten Steps in Witnessing to Muslims*. Philadelphia, PA: Church Without Walls, 1998.

Zaka, Anees and Diane Coleman. (C) 2004. Phillipsburg, NJ: *The Truth About Islam*. P&R Publishing, 2004.

Zino, Muhammad bin Jamil. *The Pillars of Islam and Iman and What Every Muslim Must Know about the Religion.* Houston, TX: Darussalam, (M) 2000.

Websites

www.alrisala.org.

www.cpsglobal.org.

www.alquranmission.org.

www.islamicity.org

www.searchislam.org

www.islamreligion.com

www.islamworld.net.

www.islamhouse.com

http://www.answering-islam.org.

www.islamfinder.com

http://en.wikipedia.org./wiki/History_of_islam

CPSIA information can be obtained
at www.ICGtesting.com
Printed in the USA
LVOW12s0004160916
504815LV00013B/51/P